The Assassination of John F. Kennedy

Political Trauma and American Memory

Alice L. George

Routledge
Taylor & Francis Group

NEW YORK AND LONDON

First published 2013
by Routledge
711 Third Avenue, New York, NY 10017

Simultaneously published in the UK
by Routledge
2 Park Square, Milton Park, Abingdon, Oxon OX14 4RN

Routledge is an imprint of the Taylor & Francis Group, an informa business

Library of Congress Cataloging in Publication Data
George, Alice L., 1952–
    The assassination of John F. Kennedy: political trauma and
    American memory/Alice George.
    p. cm.
    Includes bibliographical references and index.
    1. Kennedy, John F. (John Fitzgerald), 1917–1963—Assassination.
    2. Kennedy, John F. (John Fitzgerald), 1917–1963—Influence.
    3. United States—History—1961–1969. 4. United States—
    Politics and government—1963–1969. 5. United States—Social
    conditions--1960–1980. I. Title.
    E842.9.G46 2012
    973.922092—dc23

ISBN: 978-0-415-89556-9 (hbk)
ISBN: 978-0-415-89557-6 (pbk)
ISBN: 978-0-203-12078-1 (ebk)

Typeset in Bembo and Helvetica Neue
by Florence Production Ltd, Stoodleigh, Devon

Printed and bound in the United States of America
by Edwards Brothers, Inc.

The Assassination of John F. Kennedy

On November 22nd, 1963, the assassination of President John F. Kennedy set into motion a series of events that irrevocably changed American politics and culture. The media frenzy spawned by the controversy surrounding the death of JFK has since given way to a powerful public memory that continues to shape the way we understand politics, the 1960s, and the nation.

In *The Assassination of John F. Kennedy: Political Trauma and American Memory*, Alice George traces the events of Kennedy's assassination and Lyndon B. Johnson's subsequent ascension to the presidency. Covering both the political shifts of the time and the cultural fallout of the national tragedy, this book introduces students of the twenty-first century to both an iconic event and to the context in which that event was heralded as iconic. Drawing on newspaper articles, political speeches, letters, and diaries, George critically re-examines the event of JFK's death and its persistent political and cultural legacy.

For additional documents, images, and resources please visit *The Assassination of John F. Kennedy* companion website at www.routledge.com/cw/criticalmoments

Alice L. George is an independent scholar and the author of five books on twentieth century American history.

Critical Moments in American History
Edited by William Thomas Allison

The Battle of the Greasy Grass/Little Bighorn
Custer's Last Stand in Memory, History, and Popular Culture
Debra Buchholtz

The Assassination of John F. Kennedy
Political Trauma and American Memory
Alice L. George

Freedom to Serve
Truman, Civil Rights, and Executive Order 9981
Jon E. Taylor

**To Clois Williams,
who has always been
on my side**

Contents

Series Introduction   ix
List of Figures   x
Acknowledgments   xi
Timeline   xii

1   Unforgettable   1

2   Texas Tragedy   35

3   Mourning in the Shadows   68

4   Life After Death   104

5   Culture of Conspiracy   136

Documents   173
Notes   201
Bibliography   224
Index   229

Series Introduction

Welcome to the Routledge *Critical Moments in American History* series. The purpose of this new series is to give students a window into the historian's craft through concise, readable books by leading scholars, who bring together the best scholarship and engaging primary sources to explore a critical moment in the American past. In discovering the principal points of the story in these books, gaining a sense of historiography, following a fresh trail of primary documents, and exploring suggested readings, students can then set out on their own journey, to debate the ideas presented, interpret primary sources, and reach their own conclusions — just like the historian.

A critical moment in history can be a range of things — a pivotal year, the pinnacle of a movement or trend, or an important event such as the passage of a piece of legislation, an election, a court decision, a battle. It can be social, cultural, political, or economic. It can be heroic or tragic. Whatever they are, such moments are by definition "game changers," momentous changes in the pattern of the American fabric, paradigm shifts in the American experience. Many of the critical moments explored in this series are familiar; some less so.

There is no ultimate list of critical moments in American history — any group of students, historians, or other scholars may come up with a different catalog of topics. These differences of view, however, are what makes history itself and the study of history so important and so fascinating. Therein can be found the utility of historical inquiry — to explore, to challenge, to understand, and to realize the legacy of the past through its influence of the present. It is the hope of this series to help students realize this intrinsic value of our past and of studying our past.

William Thomas Allison
Georgia Southern University

Figures

1.1. John F. Kennedy delivers his inaugural address
January 20, 1961   9
2.1. Lyndon B. Johnson takes the presidential oath on
Air Force One with Jacqueline Kennedy at his side   45
3.1. Kennedy's body lies in state in the White House   73
4.1. With his wife, Lady Bird, at his side, the new president,
Lyndon B. Johnson, speaks upon arrival at Andrews
Air Force Base   107
5.1. Marine photo of Lee Harvey Oswald   148

Acknowledgments

Both the Harvard University Archives and Heyden White Rostow provided permission for me to quote from Theodore H. White's papers, which are not in the public domain.

I also received permissions from private individuals I interviewed—Margaret Glose, Robert Cromey, Janet Fishburn, Karel Ramsey, Adrianne Carr, Frank Schwiegert, Patricia C. "Kathy" Connally Lux, Michael Ensley, Richard McGowan, and Dennis Hatchell.

No other text permissions were necessary. All material was taken from archival sources that are in the public domain, from published works, or from interviews with public figures.

I would like to thank James W. Hilty for sharing his expertise, and I also want to express my gratitude to the staffs of the John F. Kennedy Library archives, the Lyndon B. Johnson Library archives, and Archives II. I am grateful to those individuals who shared their recollections with me in interviews. Furthermore, I am indebted to Rebecca Novack and Bill Allison for their feedback in the editing process and to Elliot Blake for his many errands on my behalf. Finally, I offer heartfelt thanks to Lou Oschmann, my life partner, sounding board, and proofreader.

Timeline

Friday, November 22, 1963

11:55 a.m. Central Standard Time
        Motorcade leaves Love Field.

12:30 p.m.   John F. Kennedy is shot twice, once in the upper back and once in the head; Governor John Connally is also wounded by rifle fire.

12:38 p.m.   Television networks begin reporting the shooting.

12:58 p.m.   Priests arrive at Parkland Hospital to perform last rites for president.

1:00 p.m.   Doctors at the hospital declare JFK dead.

1:12 p.m.   Dallas police officer J.D. Tippit is shot and killed.

1:33 p.m.   Malcolm Kilduff announces Kennedy's death to nation.

1:39 p.m.   Lyndon and Lady Bird Johnson reach Air Force One.

1:50 p.m.   Police arrest Lee Harvey Oswald.

2:04 p.m.   Coffin leaves Parkland Hospital.

2:14 p.m.   Coffin reaches Air Force One at Love Field.

2:38 p.m.   Judge Sarah Hughes administers oath of office, officially making Lyndon Johnson the thirty-sixth president of the United States.

2:47 p.m.   Air Force One leaves Dallas.

5:58 p.m. Eastern Standard Time
        Air Force One reaches Andrews Air Force Base.

6:26 p.m.   Helicopter carrying Johnsons, McGeorge Bundy, and Robert McNamara lands at White House.

6:55 p.m.   President Kennedy's body reaches Bethesda Naval Hospital.

7:35 p.m.   Autopsy begins.

Saturday, November 23, 1963

Midnight, Eastern Standard Time
        Pathologists near end of autopsy; embalmers ready to begin their work.

3:56 a.m.   Kennedy party leaves hospital with coffin en route to White House.

10:00 a.m.   Kennedy family and friends attend Mass in White House's East Room; more than seven hours of visitation follow.

3:51 p.m.   President Lyndon Johnson declares Monday, November 25, a national day of mourning.

Sunday, November 24, 1963

11:45 a.m.	Caisson leaves White House for Capitol.
12:21 p.m. (11:21 p.m. Central Standard Time)	
	Jack Ruby shoots Lee Harvey Oswald during transfer to county jail; police capture Ruby.
2:02 p.m.	Eulogies begin in Capitol rotunda.
2:16 p.m. (1:16 p.m. Central Standard Time)	
	Oswald dies, almost exactly two days after Kennedy's death.

Monday, November 25, 1963

8:25 a.m. Eastern Standard Time	
	Police cut off line of people waiting to view coffin in Capitol rotunda.
9:00 a.m.	Lying in state ends as bronze doors of Capitol close.
10:39 a.m.	Jacqueline, Robert, and Edward Kennedy arrive at Capitol, kneel beside coffin.
10:43 a.m.	Military pallbearers raise coffin from catafalque, carry it to caisson, where it is placed five minutes later.
10:50 a.m.	Cortege leaves Capitol Plaza, joining military units on Constitution Avenue for procession and moving toward White House at 11:00 a.m.
11:00 a.m.	Ruby is transferred to county jail without incident.
11:35 a.m.	Cortege reaches White House.
11:40 a.m.	Walking procession led by Jacqueline Kennedy and brothers-in-law Robert and Edward gets under way for St. Matthew's Cathedral; participants include world and national dignitaries.
12:13 p.m.	Cathedral doors close as Mass begins.
1:15 p.m.	Mass ends; cathedral doors open.
1:30 p.m.	Caisson resumes procession to Arlington National Cemetery.
2:43 p.m.	Caisson reaches cemetery.
3:08 a.m.	Army bugler sounds taps at Arlington Cemetery.
3:15 p.m.	Mrs. Kennedy lights eternal flame and receives flag previously covering coffin.
3:34 p.m.	Coffin is lowered into grave.

1964

March 14	Jack Ruby is convicted of murdering Lee Harvey Oswald, sentenced to electric chair.
July 2	Civil Rights Act becomes law.
August 7	Congress passes Gulf of Tonkin Resolution.
November 3	Lyndon B. Johnson is re-elected president in landslide over Barry Goldwater; Robert F. Kennedy is elected to U.S. Senate representing the state of New York.

1965

February 22	Johnson OKs sending two battalions of U.S. Marines as fighting men, not advisers, to Vietnam.
March 2	Operation Rolling Thunder, major bombing campaign against North Vietnam, begins.
April 28	Johnson sends U.S. troops to Dominican Republic.

1966

July 4	Johnson signs Freedom of Information Act, opening door to document-by-document declassification of assassination records.
August 16	New York Times reviews Mark Lane's Rush to Judgment, which will become the year's top-selling hardback book.
October 5	Appellate court orders new trial for Jack Ruby.

1967

January 3	Ruby dies of cancer.

1968

March 12	Johnson narrowly defeats Eugene McCarthy in New Hampshire primary.
March 16	Robert F. Kennedy enters race for Democratic presidential nomination.
March 31	Johnson announces he will not seek re-election.
April 4	Martin Luther King Jr. is assassinated in Memphis; race riots break out in cities all over the nation.
June 5	Robert F. Kennedy is shot after winning California primary; dies the next day.
August 26–29	Police, protesters clash in Chicago outside Democratic National Convention.
November 5	Richard Nixon defeats Hubert Humphrey and George Wallace to win presidency.

1974

August 9	Richard Nixon resigns in disgrace after evidence shows he participated in a criminal cover-up of information related to the Watergate break-in; Gerald Ford becomes president.

1975

January 4	In wake of Watergate revelations about CIA activities, Gerald Ford names Commission on CIA Activities within the United States, later known as the Rockefeller Commission.
January 27	The so-called Church Committee begins a Senate investigation of intelligence activity, eventually uncovering CIA plots to kill foreign leaders, including Cuba's Fidel Castro.
June 6	Rockefeller Commission issues report, dismisses possibility of CIA involvement in assassination.

1976

April 14	Church Committee issues the Investigation of the Assassination of John F. Kennedy: Performances of the Intelligence Agencies.

1977

March 27	House Select Committee on Assassinations begins investigation.

1979

March 29	Based on erroneous acoustical evidence, the House Select Committee on Assassinations concludes that probably more than one gunman shot at JFK and that his murder probably was a conspiracy.

1982

October 8	The National Academy of Science's Committee on Ballistic Acoustics reports that acoustical data given to House Select Committee was erroneous.

1991

December 20	Oliver Stone's *JFK* debuts.

1992

October 26	President George Herbert Walker Bush signs President John F. Kennedy Assassination Records Collection Act, establishing the Assassination Records Review Board.

1993

August 21	Gerald Posner's *Case Closed* is published.

1998

September 30	Assassination Records Review Board finishes its work and submits its final report.

2004

June 18	A Fox News poll shows that 74 percent of Americans believe in an ongoing government cover-up about JFK's assassination.

CHAPTER 1

Unforgettable

> *"From Dallas, the flash apparently official,*
> *President Kennedy died at one o'clock*
> *Central Standard Time—two o'clock*
> *Eastern Standard Time—some thirty-eight*
> *minutes ago."*
> Walter Cronkite, November 22, 1963[1]

John F. Kennedy's assassination is probably the most thoroughly investigated murder in human history. Classicists may still ponder the death of Julius Caesar, but two millennia of study cannot match the intense scrutiny and the technological tools applied to the study of Kennedy's murder. If curiosity about events in Dallas had died with the 1960s, Kennedy's death might have faded into the past like James Garfield's or William McKinley's; however, the unending quest to know more about JFK's passing and the development of new investigative weapons have made it an unending story, one in which the accumulation of evidence and evolving methods of analysis may actually make it more difficult to see the truth.

Why so much sustained interest in Kennedy's death? Neither a savior nor a saint, he was a son who fulfilled his father's dreams; a man who made mistakes and learned from them; a leader who gravitated toward crisis management rather than long-term solutions; a president who was popular with the public but largely ineffectual in his dealings with Congress; a husband and father who flouted traditional morals. Neither his strengths nor his shortcomings seem to have affected the public fascination with his death; instead, it remains a vivid moment in American cultural history because it ripped through the fabric of America's self-image. By showing the lie inherent in Americans' belief that they could accomplish anything with ingenuity and a can-do attitude, the assassination bred distrust and, over time, it became impossible for Americans to believe any simple solution to such a momentous event. Not all Americans were sorry to see Kennedy go, but most were startled by his murder more than sixty years after the most recent presidential assassination. Since McKinley died in 1901, Americans had learned to fly, eradicated polio, developed radio and television, launched men into space, and created bombs that could kill millions, and yet human nature stayed the same. The capacity of petty men to slay leaders remained unchanged.

When shots sounded within Dealey Plaza on November 22, 1963, no one could have guessed that the truth about Kennedy's assassination would remain contested territory almost five decades later. Continuing debate about possible conspiracies reveals Americans' unwillingness to let go of their questions and accept the simplest explanation of all—that one political rebel bought a mail-order gun and changed history. In the years since his death, JFK has held on to a corner of America's center stage. Fifty-six percent of Americans initially believed the Warren Commission's 1964 findings that the accused assassin, Lee Harvey Oswald, had acted alone in slaying the president;[2] nevertheless, by 1967, 64 percent of Americans, including President Lyndon Johnson, were open to the idea that Oswald, a one-time defector to the Soviet Union, was part of a conspiracy.[3] By 1983, about 70 percent gave credence to the idea of a conspiracy, and after Oliver Stone's 1991 conspiracy-theory film, JFK, a poll showed 77 percent of Americans thought a conspiracy was possible.[4] A Gallup Poll in 2003 found that only 19 percent of Americans believed the assassination was the work of one man,[5] and a Fox News Poll in 2004 revealed that 74 percent of respondents thought that a government cover-up continued to hide the facts about JFK's death.[6] And interest in this topic is not restricted to those old enough to remember the assassination. A thirtysomething woman told this author, "When I get to heaven, my first question for St. Peter will be: 'Who killed JFK?'"

Continuing and sometimes obsessive interest in Kennedy's death suggests that the assassination remains an open wound in the American psyche. When the injury occurred, there was no readily available cure. After surprise attacks on Pearl Harbor in 1941 and on the East Coast on September 11, 2001, military action provided an outlet for overflowing emotions, but in the wake of an assassination with no surviving assassin, there was no satisfying recourse. Even today, mention of Dallas conjures up dark images of a motorcade, a mad rush to Parkland Hospital, the oath of office administered aboard Air Force One, Jacqueline Kennedy's blood-stained clothes—slow-motion memories cast in black and white.

Many Americans maintain a strong emotional connection to Kennedy. In the year prior to his death, one million people visited Arlington National Cemetery, but during the first six months after his slaying, nine million traveled to the cemetery.[7] The current number of visitors is about four million per year.[8] The John F. Kennedy Library and Museum in Boston attracts about 225,000 visitors each year,[9] and the Sixth Floor Museum, set up in Oswald's Dallas sniper's nest, draws 325,000 visitors annually.[10]

In *The Making of the President 1964*, Theodore H. White described initial news of the assassination as "an episode to be remembered, a clap of alarm as sharp and startling as Pearl Harbor, so that forever they would ask one another—*Where were you when you heard the news?*"[11] And indeed, that question became an eerily universal and often-repeated topic of conversation among Baby Boomers and their parents, even decades later. Testifying to one's position on that day at that time seems to be a way of situating one's self within the larger event—an event with such a wide impact that each individual pinpointed his own position on the broader canvas. In this way, the assassination drama encompassed every workplace, every classroom, every supermarket, and every automobile. It became *our* story, one that touched every facet of American life on that November day in 1963, and, because of its breadth, the event became a rare cultural phenomenon. Letters of condolence to the Kennedy family, now stockpiled at the John F. Kennedy Library, demonstrate this well. While voicing their sympathy to Mrs. Kennedy, many letter writers felt compelled to tell the former first lady where they had been when they heard the news, as if hearing their stories would mean something to the woman who cradled the dying president's head in her lap.

Twentieth-century technological advances contributed to the stunning nature of the day's events. Kennedy was shot, treated, declared dead, loaded into a casket, and returned to Washington in less than six hours. The gunman was able to fire accurately from a sixth-floor window because of the scope on his rifle. Radio and television spread news of the assassination at unprecedented speed. A jet carried the coffin from Dallas to Washington in a little more than two hours. And, perhaps most disorienting of all, Americans could sit in their living rooms and see JFK alive and well, joking with Texans just hours earlier.

Two days later, Jack Ruby deepened the feeling of unreality that rattled the nation by gunning down Oswald on live TV. Then came the ritual and pageantry of a state funeral unlike any other and filled with memorable scenes that would flutter at the edges of American consciousness for decades to come. That weekend almost half a century ago remains an all-too-familiar blur viewed through the numbness of shock and the cascade of tears. The martial drumbeat, the riderless horse, the eternal flame—all have become icons of an event we cannot forget, a weekend when Americans learned that, while flames might be eternal, even a charmed life is fragile and transient. So much of John F. Kennedy's rhetoric had been crafted to envision a better tomorrow, achieving the "High Hopes" of his 1960 campaign theme song. On that day, the promising tomorrow seemed to vanish. In the words of TV anchorman David Brinkley, "the events of those days don't fit, you can't place them anywhere, they don't go in the intellectual luggage of our time. It was too big, too sudden, too over-whelming, and it meant too much. It has to be separate and apart."[12]

The assassination represented a disconnect in the flow of history during the 1960s—and it jolted Americans' expectations. The event was so unexpected, so unsettling, that it resulted in a collective trauma that, like all cultural traumas, raised questions about beliefs in society. The trauma itself reverberated with disbelief about the violent death of a young and vital national leader. Incredulous, many Americans commented that this was not the type of event that happened in America. Violence against a leader was something that happened in other nations that were less developed, less democratic, or less civilized than the prosperous and powerful United States of the postwar era. Ruby's actions reinforced nagging questions about what kind of nation the United States really was. Generally, the experience of a cultural trauma involves some acceptance of responsibility for shocking events. Although many Americans openly accepted shame for being part of the violent culture that spawned the president's murder, others rejected any responsibility. Part of America's sadness sprang from a loss that went far beyond the death of one man. Arthur G. Neal has argued that "the conditions surrounding a trauma are played and replayed in the national consciousness in an attempt to extract some sense of coherence from a meaningless experience. When the event is dismissed from consciousness, it resurfaces in feelings of anxiety and despair."[13] Certainly, anxiety and despair stalked the land for much of the mid- to late 1960s as new traumas piled atop this most disquieting event. While JFK's assassination seemed unthinkable in 1963, the subsequent assassinations of Martin Luther King Jr. and Robert Kennedy felt almost inevitable in the tumult of 1968.

Many view JFK's assassination as a detonator, setting into motion the upheaval and disorder of the 1960s. Twenty years after Kennedy's death, *Time* noted that his assassination had two obvious effects: It provided an impetus for passage of his long-stalled legislative program, and it "let loose monsters, to unhinge the nation in some deep way that sent it reeling down a road toward riots and war and assassinations and Watergate."[14]

In his 2008 book *Boom! Talking about the Sixties*, Tom Brokaw contended that November 22, 1963 was really the first day of "what we now call the Sixties," that ragged time of discord and distrust.[15] Frederic Jameson wrote in 1985 that the assassination "played a significant role in delegitimizing the state itself and in discrediting the parliamentary process." Jameson was politically skeptical about Kennedy, but he saw JFK's lasting impact in "the rhetoric of youth and of the 'generation gap'" later in the 1960s.[16]

A collective trauma threatens to topple the building blocks that give meaning to a society. Initial responses to Franklin D. Roosevelt's death were, in many ways, similar to those noted after the assassination: incredulity, anxiety, and grief.[17] After more than twelve years with FDR as president, the idea of change was disconcerting, but the natural death of a man does not generate the same kind of nervous collapse as an assassination. The slaying of a leader creates a growing sense of vulnerability among the population. Some may have thought: If someone murdered the president, are any of us safe? Others feared the assassination was one step in an attack on the nation as a whole. Some thought it might be a prelude to nuclear war. Johnson promised continuity, but he was very different from Kennedy. Those differences created a briefly held but memorable feeling of discontinuity, which was minimized within a few days as Johnson grappled with his new role and won voter confidence.

Twenty years later, *Ladies Home Journal* tried to explain the nation's emotional response to Kennedy's assassination: "His office conferred on him the status of national patriarch, but his full head of hair, impish small children and glamorous young wife made him also seem a brother, a son, a contemporary. If he was so vulnerable, who and what could the rest of us take for granted? If his time was so savagely cut short, what use should we be making of ours?"[18] In a 1965 article in the *New York Times Magazine*, James Reston provided this vision of America's loss: "What was killed in Dallas was not only the president, but the promise. The death of youth and the hope of youth, the beauty and grace and the touch of magic."[19] One man wrote to his sister on November 22, 1963, "His death is disquieting to me beyond reason, perhaps, but the death of an ideal is profoundly worse."[20] The *New York Times'* Tom Wicker later wrote about America after JFK's death, calling it a "dark and malignant place" and declaring that "the chill of the unknown shivered across the nation."[21]

Trauma does not always imply large societal change. Kennedy's death did not precipitate sharp changes in policy during Johnson's presidency. If anything, the shock may have made it more difficult for Johnson to see and adopt policy options that Kennedy might have chosen if he had lived to be re-elected. Because Johnson followed the well-liked, martyred JFK, he felt locked in to policies as Kennedy left them. Though Kennedy later might have veered away from some earlier choices, LBJ seemed riveted into pre-set directions. Continuity was his primary theme in 1964 and to a degree, it colored his administration until the end.

As Johnson knew well, Kennedy was not just a president of the United States; he was the most popular president since political polling began during Franklin Roosevelt's administration. He was well regarded outside the United States, as well. When he visited Mexico City in 1962, people wept at the sight of him, ogled his wife, and cheered his words—and he generated similar reactions in other places like West Berlin and Ireland. Immediately after the assassination, *U.S. News & World Report* reported stunned disbelief in London, Paris, Bonn, Geneva, Rome, Caracas, Ottawa, Mexico City, and Tokyo.[22] Decades later, writer Pete Hamill got a flat tire as he was driving through rural Mexico, and when a man stepped outside to welcome Hamill into his modest home, the American journalist was surprised to see two pictures on the wall: one of the Virgin of Guadalupe and one of John F. Kennedy.[23]

Politicians as diverse as Bill Clinton, Gary Hart, and Ronald Reagan have tied themselves to American memories of Kennedy. Twenty years after the assassination, historian William Leuchtenburg wrote that Kennedy had become part of myth more than part of history. "Like the fair youth on Keats's Grecian urn, Kennedy will be forever in pursuit, forever unfulfilled, but also 'forever young,' beyond the power of time and the words of historians."[24] Revisionist historians began pummeling Kennedy's record in the 1970s, but by the early years of the twenty-first century, Kennedy's stock was rising among historians. A C-SPAN survey of sixty-five historians in 2009 showed JFK ranked sixth among all presidents in leadership. He finished just ahead of Thomas Jefferson and was the only president in the Top 10 who had not served more than one term.[25] He had ranked eighth in a similar C-SPAN survey in 2000.[26] (Abraham Lincoln topped both surveys.) These ratings indicate a marked rebound in Kennedy's standing among historians. His handling of the Cuban Missile Crisis, which some had labeled as reckless, gained new praise as evidence showed that his approach had been far more cautious than revisionists had believed. Some historians have questioned Kennedy's claim to the "liberal" label, given his hesitancy to act on civil rights and his weak performance in pushing social legislation through Congress. Even his most supportive biographers have made it clear that early in his presidency, he did not understand African Americans' sense of urgency about obtaining equal rights. And yet, his decision in 1963 to take a moral stand on the issue garnered praise that would cling to his lasting image. In *Gunfighter Nation*,

Richard Slotkin argues that Kennedy portrayed the president as a hero, and this contributed to the myth that fully blossomed after his death.[27]

Perhaps, he is most memorable for an attribute that came naturally to him: The camera loved him. Print media and television exploited that quality and profited from it. Thousands of magazines were sold by designing a cover that featured JFK with or without his equally photogenic wife and children. Television, likewise, took advantage of this asset. In life, Kennedy had an unusually good relationship with journalists, counting a few as intimate friends and bantering with others at his televised news conferences. In death, he became the unbeatable story in many journalistic careers.

To Kennedy's supporters, his growth as a leader seemed to parallel America's own ascendancy to world leadership as it struggled to fulfill its own promise. Though a cynical man, he came to represent American optimism. Later, when it became clear that instead of soaring in triumph, the United States would wallow in the failures of Vietnam, Watergate, repeated energy crises, and continuing racial friction, many saw that day in Dallas as a stumbling block to American prospects. By throwing everything out of kilter, the assassination seized the nation's imagination, projecting a long series of "what ifs" into the future: How would JFK have handled Vietnam? Would his leadership have affected racial tensions later in the decade? Would his extramarital affairs have become public knowledge and tarnished his image? Would one or more of his brothers have followed him into the White House? If he had been allowed to grow old, would a paunchy, wrinkled JFK have lost his magic? Did the assassination give him more glory than he deserved? Americans found themselves tantalized by these questions, in part because of their unanswerable nature. President Kennedy's potential seemed unlimited because it would forever be untested. And his memory came wrapped in the myth of Camelot, a hallowed time in American history never to be found again.

Looking back at the assassination, Walter Cronkite concluded,

> There's no question the assassination was a serious blow to our national psyche—to have a president killed, and in particular one who had inspired a following among youth to the degree he had. The trauma was very deep. But to suggest as some do that everything that has gone wrong since then somehow stemmed from that event—that life would have been better somehow if Kennedy had lived—I think is kind of reaching for Camelot really, instead of appreciating the reality. I don't think it does much good.

Uncertain that Kennedy would have avoided the morass of the Vietnam war, he said,

> I don't know that you can say that the Kennedy years, had they continued, would have matched the sense of Camelot, returning us to some marvelous, mythical kingdom in the sky. But I think that Kennedy did bring to the White House something that is unfortunately rare, and that is a sweeping, all-encompassing view of the historical moment—a feeling for where America was in the world and where it should be.[28]

Americans could never experience what might have been. One way of filling that gap was to memorialize Kennedy. His face appeared on stamps and coins. Cape Canaveral was briefly renamed Cape Kennedy, and when historical tradition won out over contemporary sentiments, the cape regained its old name, but the National Aeronautics and Space Administration facility there became the Kennedy Space Center. The City of New York renamed Idlewild Airport, calling it John F. Kennedy International Airport. Washington's national center for the performing arts took his name, as did innumerable man-made constructs, such as schools, libraries, highways, streets, and bridges. Even outside the United States, the Kennedy name garnered new honors. Canada designated a peak as Mount Kennedy, and Britain set aside land at Runnymede, where the Magna Carta was signed, to honor Kennedy's memory. The Kennedy administration was not much like the myth of Camelot immortalized in song, but Americans and admirers around the world gave the slain president more than the "fleeting wisp of glory" described in Alan Jay Lerner's wistful lyrics.

As a president, Kennedy attracted a great deal of interest, but as an assassination victim, he found a place at the center of a grand mystery that remains unsolved in the minds of most Americans. This is probably not the way he would have wanted to be remembered. Later generations— those born after the assassination—do not recall his eloquence, wit, and cautious leadership, but they do know some of the details of his death. As to whether his death set off a chain reaction that clattered through the confounding 1960s, Kennedy's assassination clearly affected the nation's equilibrium, making Americans less trustful, and the attack's success may have offered encouragement to other would-be assassins in the 1960s. It is safe to say that JFK's death placed Lyndon Johnson at a disadvantage in confronting the decade's problems. Still, he toiled, feeling that he lived within the darkness cast by Kennedy's looming shadow. A president functioning in the light of day with his own leadership team might have seen his way around some of the problems that hobbled the nation by the

Figure 1.1 John F. Kennedy delivers his inaugural address January 20, 1961. U.S. Army Signal Corps photograph, John F. Kennedy Presidential Library and Museum.

decade's end, but it is unlikely that any president could have averted all of the period's turmoil.

JFK AND THE PUBLIC

John F. Kennedy was elected president by a hairsbreadth, and yet he was astoundingly popular. In retrospect, many people assume that public fascination with Kennedy is strictly a result of his violent death, but when he was alive, he outdid every president from Franklin Roosevelt through Barack Obama. Over the course of his presidency, Gallup Polls show that an average of 70.1 percent of Americans approved of his work. When his rating hit its all-time low of 56 percent in 1963, the drop represented an emotional response to his introduction of historic civil rights legislation. His all-time high rating of 83 percent occurred after his biggest mistake, limited support for a failed Cuban invasion at the Bay of Pigs by refugees.[29]

Despite his popularity, Kennedy attracted seething hatred from arch-conservatives in both parties. Passionate hostility toward Kennedy was as fervent as the adulation of his greatest fans. Some distrusted him because they believed that his father had become rich from bootlegging. Others opposed his Catholicism, viewed him as a spoiled rich kid, thought his wife was a snob, or were outraged that Kennedy had named his own brother, Robert or "Bobby," to be attorney general. For many, the problem was "the Kennedys," not simply JFK. The close-knit Kennedy family was an anachronism at a time when increased mobility was weakening family ties all over the United States. The Kennedys achieved political goals by working together with the efficiency and shared purpose of a twenty-first-century computer network. Many foes feared that Joseph P. Kennedy planned to put three sons in the White House. During his presidency, JFK's ties to the civil rights struggle angered some voters, although civil rights leaders thought he had been too cautious about taking a stand. Others asserted that he was "soft on Communism." In short, the anti-Kennedy crowd, a clear but noisy minority, had no shortage of complaints.

> Often labeled a liberal, John F. Kennedy described himself as "an idealist without illusions."

While this opposition was intense, many Americans actually moved toward JFK during his presidency. Although he won only 49.7 percent of the vote in 1960, 59 percent of the voting public claimed to have voted for him by the middle of 1963, and after his death, 65 percent stated that they had chosen him over Richard Nixon.[30] Immediately following his death, 52 percent considered him "one of the best" presidents; 25 percent, "above average;" 13 percent, "about average;" 3 percent "below average;" and 1 percent, "one of the worst."[31]

Newsweek commissioned a Gallup Poll for the twentieth anniversary of JFK's death and found that Kennedy was the former president Americans would most like to see back in the White House. Thirty percent said that he would be their first choice to be president in 1983. FDR ranked second, with 10 percent. Most Americans tied Kennedy's name to civil rights, activism, working people, the poor, glamor, style, youth, and a hard line toward the Soviet Union.[32] A similar 1996 poll still showed Kennedy as the top choice to fill the White House, with the support of 28 percent of respondents. By that point, Reagan had outstripped FDR, but his backing was just half of Kennedy's.[33] In a September 1988 poll, 34 percent of Americans identified Kennedy as the most effective president since World War II.[34] When a *60 Minutes/Vanity Fair* poll asked Americans in November 2009 what president's face they would add to Mount

John F. Kennedy's Life

Born May 29, 1917, John F. Kennedy grew up in the boisterous and wealthy family of Joseph P. Kennedy and Rose Fitzgerald Kennedy. The second of nine children, JFK was a sickly child, and his physical frailty continued throughout his lifetime. Severe back trouble and Addison's disease became his most troublesome health problems. Kennedy's family traveled widely. His father served as U.S. ambassador to Great Britain from 1937 until 1940, but the elder Kennedy's stubborn support for U.S. neutrality in World War II eventually led to his resignation. Known to his friends and family as Jack, Kennedy attended prep school at the elite Choate and graduated from Harvard in 1940. Although the United States had not yet entered the war, Kennedy enlisted in the U.S. Navy in September 1941. About two years later, a Japanese destroyer rammed *PT-109*, which he commanded. He was able to save all of his crew, except two men who died in the collision. Kennedy hauled one injured man to shore by clinching a life preserver strap in his teeth as he swam. He was later cited for "extremely heroic conduct."

Over the years, Joseph P. Kennedy had groomed JFK's older brother Joseph P. Kennedy Jr. to enter politics; however, Joe Jr. died during a dangerous military mission in 1944. Consequently, his father's political ambitions landed on Jack's shoulders. After a brief sojourn as a journalist, he ran for a U.S. House seat in 1946. He was victorious and represented a Boston district in the House until 1952, when he was elected to be one of Massachusetts' two U.S. senators. Often considered a playboy, JFK married Jacqueline Bouvier in 1953. During the mid-1950s, he underwent surgery on his back and hovered near death for a while. In 1956, Democratic presidential nominee Adlai Stevenson allowed the Democratic National Convention to choose his running mate. Kennedy finished second, but the contest gave him valuable national exposure.

Kennedy's first child, Caroline, was born in 1957, and in that year he received the Pulitzer Prize for *Profiles in Courage*. Some historians credit Kennedy speechwriter Ted Sorensen and others with doing the lion's share of the work on the book, although Sorensen always asserted that Kennedy was the foremost contributor to the project, which tells the stories of U.S. senators who showed political courage by taking controversial stands. According to Jacqueline Kennedy, JFK insisted that Sorensen collect all royalties from the book.[35]

JFK was re-elected to the Senate by a landslide in 1958 and began devoting a significant portion of his time to the race for the presidency in 1960. By winning every primary he entered, Kennedy was able to capture the Democratic nomination, and during the campaign he made history by participating with Republican nominee Richard Nixon in television's first series of presidential debates. These debates helped the lesser-known Kennedy to triumph in one of the closest elections in the nation's history. Just weeks after his victory, JFK welcomed a second child, John F. Kennedy Jr.

On January 20, 1961, he became the first Catholic president of the United States and delivered one of the most acclaimed inaugural speeches in U.S. history. The new president's most controversial early decision was successful nomination of his brother, Robert, to be attorney general. In 1963, another son, Patrick, was born, but he died after living less than forty-eight hours. A little more than 1,000 days after taking office, John F. Kennedy was slain during a motorcade in Dallas. Two days later, his accused assassin, Lee Harvey Oswald, was shot on live television. The following day, the nation and the world watched an august and memorable televised funeral, which attracted many world leaders as well as ordinary Americans.

Rushmore, Kennedy again came in first.[36] Fifty years after his 1960 election, a *USA Today*/Gallup Poll showed that one third of Americans rated JFK as a "great president."[37] A December 2010 Gallup Poll showed that Kennedy received the highest approval rating of any president since 1960. Eighty-five percent approved of Kennedy's handling of his job, and that was actually a one-percentage point increase over a similar 2006 poll.[38] Starting in 1975, Kennedy began to rack up high scores in polls asking voters to name the nation's greatest president. In that first poll, he garnered 52 percent of the votes. He held onto first place until 1991 when he dropped to second, with 39 percent, one percentage point less than the winner, Abraham Lincoln.[39] Lincoln and Kennedy remained alone at the top of annual President's Day polls until 2001, when Ronald Reagan ranked alongside them.[40] In 2009's Gallup Poll, the three were in a virtual tie, with Reagan two percentage points ahead of Lincoln and Kennedy, both of whom received support from 22 percent. Reagan's support is heavily weighted by the responses of middle-aged and older Americans, but both Kennedy and Lincoln enjoy fairly even distribution of support among all age groups.[41]

During his life, JFK anticipated the important role that a former president could play in the nation's future life. "For each president," he wrote in January 1962, "we must remember, is the president not only of all who live, but, in a very real sense, of all who have yet to live. His responsibility is not only to those who elected him, but also to those who will elect his successors for decades to come. (This fact is a useful reminder to those who urge, in a moment of frustration or impatience, the kind of dramatic action that in one brief moment could alter the lives—or even the chance of life—of generations yet unborn.)"[42]

Beginning in the 1970s, Kennedy's marital infidelities received significant public attention. When the Senate Select Committee on

Intelligence headed by Frank Church of Idaho was investigating government activities in the aftermath of Watergate, the panel revealed the relationship between Kennedy and Judith Campbell Exner, an associate of mobsters Sam Giancano and John Roselli, both of whom had taken part in CIA plots to kill Fidel Castro. The *Washington Post* broke this news on November 16, 1975. Exner subsequently described herself as being close to Kennedy during his presidency, but did not reveal more. Some expected this news to sully Kennedy's golden reputation, but they were wrong. In a 2003 poll of Americans over forty, 73 percent said revelations about Kennedy's sex life had no effect on their judgment of his presidency.[43] Many felt that the topic only deserved discussion if there was proof that his extramarital activities affected his performance as president. Although mainstream newspapers and magazines initially shied away from exploiting the sexual side of JFK's life, they eventually faced the inevitable push to reveal the dirt, particularly as the nation became less enamored with heroes in the post-Vietnam, post-Watergate years. Promiscuity and even sexual addiction are now tied to the John F. Kennedy of popular culture, but to many average Americans and historians this is a side issue that does not affect his standing as president. If we are to believe all of the reports of Kennedy's indiscretions, his infidelities may have outnumbered those of any of his predecessors, but we know today that more than a few presidents have been guilty of sexual misconduct.

Both Kennedy and his assassination remain hot topics for the media. Newspaper and magazine articles, television specials, documentaries, and movies have cashed in on Kennedy's name or his story. *The Readers' Guide to Periodical Literature* shows that, from 1975 through 2008, Kennedy was the topic of almost five times as many articles as his immediate predecessor, Dwight D. Eisenhower, and more than three times as many as his successor, Johnson. (That count does not include coverage of congressional investigations of the assassination in the mid-1970s.)[44] Since Johnson was president almost twice as long as Kennedy, and Eisenhower served even longer, these figures are noteworthy. Similarly, the *New York Times Index* figures for Kennedy in 1975 are bloated by congressional investigation coverage, but even if you look at coverage for 1980, 1985, 1990, 1995, 2000, and 2005, Kennedy articles total 111; Johnson, eighty-six; and Eisenhower, fifty. LexisNexis searches of broadcast transcripts for 2000–2010 show 4,692 citations of Kennedy, only 667 mentions of Johnson, and 327 of Eisenhower.[45] These raw counts offer some empirical data to back up the conclusion that Kennedy's life and his assassination have deepened his imprint on American culture.

What Kennedy magic survived the assassination? The answer is clear in surveys. Almost 65 percent of those Americans interviewed by *Newsweek* in 1983 believed that "American society would have been much different" if Kennedy had not been slain. Sixty-six percent contended that more work and money would have been invested in helping the poor, and 32 percent thought "the great social unrest and alienation among young people in the Sixties" would not have occurred. More than half of those with an opinion doubted he would have involved the United States in a full-scale war in Southeast Asia.[46]

We will never know what might have been.

LIVING IN AMERICAN MEMORY

The average age of the men leading Great Britain, West Germany, France, the Soviet Union, Nationalist China, Communist China, and the United States was 72 in 1960; in that year, 43-year-old JFK became the youngest man ever elected president of the United States.

For many Americans who remember those eerie days in 1963, JFK remains a vibrant figure. His death is a tragedy not to be forgotten, a puzzle that defies assembly, and a trauma that colors memories of their younger selves. Because Kennedy's murder and its aftermath became a shared experience of virtually all Americans, he holds a prominent place in the nation's collective memory of the twentieth century, an indelible image enlarged by frequent media coverage. In a way, modern media have extended his stardom and allowed him to conquer the finality of death. Bill Clinton's 1992 presidential campaign, recognizing the power of a single image, adopted footage of JFK shaking the teenaged Clinton's hand in a biographical documentary. In the moment when the scene was shown at the 1992 Democratic National Convention, the crowd erupted in cheers. Cynicism about Kennedy's motives and his ideals is lost on those for whom he is frozen in time—forever young and forever hopeful, full of potential, smiling and waving to a boisterous crowd in Dallas. This is especially true within the Democratic Party, which held the White House for only twenty of the forty-eight years from January 1964 through 2011.

Because of his assassination and because his photogenic visage remains pleasing to many Americans, Kennedy has defied common expectations about collective memory. Defining the limits of this special form of memory in 1915, French sociologist Emile Durkheim wrote: "Though very strong as long as men are together and influence each other reciprocally, [sentiments] exist only in the form of recollections after the assembly has ended, and when left to themselves, these become feebler and feebler; for since the group is now no longer present and active, individual temperaments easily regain the upper hand." Durkheim wrote before radio had become a prevalent medium and in no way could have foreseen an event in which an entire nation mourned together through the medium of television. However, he thought that "if the movements by which these sentiments are expressed are connected to something that endures, the sentiments themselves become more durable."[47] Writing almost ninety years later, Amy Adamczyk argued that "collective memory reconstructs the past rather than preserving it whole."[48] The media's pervasive coverage of his assassination and its continuing attention to JFK have helped to preserve and enhance memories of him.

The current meaning of the term "collective memory" can be traced to sociologist Maurice Halbwachs' 1925 work *Social Frameworks of Memory*. In it, he contended that society frames all memories and that historical memories allow groups to define their identity.[49] Thus, it seems possible that Americans needed to remember Kennedy's life and death in a certain way to confirm their identity as members of a moral society—not a nation of gun-wielding killers. Since Kennedy, in the minds of many, embodied what was good about the United States in the 1960s, maintaining a belief in him as an honorable and heroic figure is logical. Some remember the Kennedy years as a more innocent time and see that innocence as something precious that has been lost but not irretrievably. Of course, remembering an unsullied Kennedy era requires an individual to minimize the Cold War's inherent dangers of a nuclear holocaust, the brutal confrontations of the civil rights struggle, and revelations about CIA operations to assassinate foreign leaders. This is a case, it seems, in which selective amnesia about the past can generate faith in the future. Literary theorist Svetlana Boym contends that "the fantasies of the past, determined by the needs of the present, have a direct impact on the realities of the future."[50] Instinctively reflexive fantasies about the Kennedy era have received societal endorsement in the many and often-government-sponsored commemorations of his death.

Textbooks provide a gateway into understanding how a collective memory is passed from one generation to the next. A multi-volume U.S. history textbook series from the Oxford University Press published in the first decade of the twenty-first century allocates only one paragraph to James Garfield's life and his assassination, while it allots somewhat more space to William McKinley's presidency and about one and a half paragraphs to his death. In contrast, author Joy Hakim devotes a four-page chapter to Kennedy's assassination, exactly the same amount of space she fills with an account of Lincoln's death.[51] Her entire consideration of Oswald, Ruby, and conspiracy theories is confined to a single extended caption. A 1985 study of 111 American history texts published since 1963 showed that 40 percent described the assassination by stating "almost unequivocally" that Oswald alone killed Kennedy.[52]

Children's books, too, show how memories are perpetuated and shaped. There are a surprisingly large number of children's books about JFK's assassination, and many of them devote attention to the crime's destruction of American innocence. This theme is missing from similar books about the other assassinated presidents—Lincoln, Garfield, and McKinley. It is easy to imagine that Americans in the prosperous early 1960s might be more easily shocked than their counterparts at the close of the bloody Civil War. Furthermore, the era of Garfield and McKinley is often characterized as an age of extremes when societal conflict was common. Nevertheless, the Kennedy era was neither placid nor devoid of ugly moments. Less than twenty years removed from Adolf Hitler, the Holocaust, and Hiroshima, 1963 was a period of dramatic confrontations over civil rights and Cold War policy. Peering backward in search of a time of innocence, Americans demonstrate a need to recapture the moment just before the trauma of Kennedy's assassination and an equally strong compulsion to see that instant as better than everything that followed.

Divergent ideas about Kennedy's death and suspicions about conspiracies reflect a loss of confidence in government explanations. If official rationales lack credibility, citizens often try to construct a narrative that makes more sense to them.[53] From the moment of the shooting, there have been gaps and conflicts in the assassination narrative. Shaken journalists, scrambling to get news as quickly as possible, unknowingly reported rumors and half-truths, and Dallas authorities, eager to put themselves in a good light, made erroneous statements in the first hours and days after the assassination. At the same time, the FBI and the CIA had secrets to protect. Confusion began in the chaos of the moment and received reinforcement from government secrecy. After decades of reading new facts and speculation about the assassination, many Americans believe that the hurried Warren Commission report stands on a house of cards. Although the report contained credible, well-researched conclusions on many issues, Americans became increasingly unwilling to believe it because some facets of its narrative were shattered. Americans' distrust of government explanations became almost as crucial as the need to believe that the loss of JFK had been the single event that set the nation into a downward spiral.

Psychologist, philosopher, and sociologist George Herbert Mead suggested that collective memory enables people to use the past to make sense of the future.[54] Additionally, Claude Lévi-Strauss argued that "hot moments" help a culture evaluate its significance.[55] In the case of JFK's assassination, the hot moment is obvious, but its only positive reflection on American culture is the fact that there was a peaceful change of leadership from Kennedy to Johnson. Since the minutes after Kennedy's death, many Americans have struggled to find added meaning in that hot moment; sadly, in the final analysis, JFK's demise seems both important and meaningless. If Kennedy had been slain by a Chinese spy or a white supremacist, it would be easy to say that he died protecting his nation's values. Lincoln's assassination is a coherent event because it was the work of angry supporters of the fallen Confederacy. James Garfield was slain by an office seeker who did not get the job he wanted, and an advocate of anarchism took the life of William McKinley, often considered the first representative of the more powerful, modern presidency. When John Hinckley shot Ronald Reagan in 1981, he had a motive that was both clear and demented: He wanted to impress actress Jodie Foster. Only in Kennedy's case does the motive remain unclear and unavailable for analysis and understanding, partly because the apparent assassin died without shedding any light on his actions.

The strongest collective memories typically are developed in adolescence or early adulthood, but a sociological study shows that even those who were 8 to 12 when JFK was slain carry strong recollections of that time. The huge Baby Boom generation thus was primed to carry this memory into the future. A study of 1,410 Americans who were 18 or older in 1985 showed that, when asked to name the two most important events of the previous fifty years, the highest number of respondents mentioned World War II. This is true despite the fact that many survey participants were too young to recall the war; obviously, many imbibed memories of the war from their parents and other sources. Coming in second, third, and fourth in the survey results were three big events of the Baby Boomers' youth—the Vietnam war, space exploration, and JFK's assassination. The civil rights movement, which remade significant parts of American culture, finished fifth. Those born between 1950 and 1960 were most likely to cite the assassination as one of the two most significant moments.[56] Similar polls in later years asked Americans in an open-ended question to name the most memorable historical event of their lifetimes. In 1994, 30 percent rated JFK's assassination as number one, far exceeding mentions of World War II, and, in 1998, 24 percent gave it their highest rating.[57]

Greater understanding of American historical memory can be found in the work of Americanist Michael Frisch. He conducted studies to show that "the relationship between history and memory is peculiarly and perhaps uniquely fractured in contemporary America."[58] He concluded that selective amnesia and artificial distancing from past events have disjointed American history and American memory, making it difficult to learn from the past. On several occasions, Frisch asked classes of college students to list ten important Americans in the history of the United States through the end of the Civil War, and he asked them to exclude presidents, soldiers, and statesmen. What he found was that his students almost always named Betsy Ross near the top, although the story of Betsy Ross and the American flag is total fiction, injected into the Revolutionary War saga more than a century after its conclusion by an ambitious Ross descendant. Other legitimate historical figures whom popular culture has largely mythologized, like Pocahontas and Daniel Boone, ranked high on the students' lists, too. It seems apparent that college students' best memories of non-governmental figures in American history come from popular culture.[59] If the apocryphal Betsy Ross narrative could become so powerful without one shred of evidence or even one reliable likeness of her, it is easy to see how it could become difficult to separate fact from fiction in the myths surrounding JFK's life and death. Deciding where to draw the line between fact and myth is difficult once a leader has died. Instead of clarifying the historical JFK, the many handsome images of Kennedy when he was alive and the meticulously dissected frames in Abraham Zapruder's assassination film make it more difficult to sever the connection between myth and truth.

Most Americans who were alive in 1963 recall how they learned about Kennedy's assassination in great detail. For example, John A. DeFrancisco remembered being in school when "a voice over the PA system solemnly announced that President John F. Kennedy had been shot . . . The next few moments seemed to be moving in slow motion. I looked throughout my classroom from face to face. The sights and sounds of the room just blended together into one overlapping emotion: disbelief. Was this some kind of sick joke? This kind of thing just didn't happen in the United States."[60] Memories of this kind are called "flashbulb memories" because they retain an unusually high number of specific details. Some flashbulb memories may be attached to personal shocks, but when the phenomenon was first identified by psychologists Roger Brown and James Kulik in 1977, JFK's assassination became the prime example. Average Americans recalled tiny details of the moments when they heard about the attack on the president, and over the years they continued construction of these memories by reciting them repeatedly. Flashbulb memories are exceptional because they often preserve trivial elements and because they remain vivid decades after the event that prompted them. Kulik and Brown studied eighty Americans more than twelve years after the assassination and found that seventy-nine out of eighty had a flashbulb memory of that day; only forty-three, most of whom were black, had similar memories about when they learned that Martin Luther King Jr. had been slain in April 1968.[61] According to a 1999 study, 90 percent of Americans old enough to remember the assassination reported that they still recalled what they were doing when they first heard about gunshots in Dallas.[62]

Although he did not use the term "flashbulb memories," F.W. Colegrove reported this kind of remembering in 1899 after examining a group of Americans' recollections of the instant when they heard about Abraham Lincoln's murder. In his study, 127 out of 179 were able to provide sharp details of that moment in their lives.[63] Psychologist Ulric Neisser has argued that these memories are not locked into place at the moment they occur but assigned there perhaps hours, days, or years later, when the event's significance becomes clear.[64]

The September 11, 2001 terrorist attacks on the World Trade Center and the Pentagon have been compared to the assassination in shock value, but there has been little corresponding proliferation of flashbulb memories that people revisit over and over again, locating themselves within the larger narrative. While diffusion of information about Kennedy's assassination was breathtakingly fast by the standards of the mid-twentieth century, dispersion of details about the September 11 attacks was so rapid that many Americans experienced five or six potential flashbulb memories over the course of a few hours, and during that time individuals may have moved from place to place while still following the news via cell phones, internet sources, car radios, and TVs in workplaces, bars, and restaurants. The mind may have had difficulty identifying a single evocative moment when both the national memory and the autobiographical memory coalesced into a single overpowering memory. Images of an airliner hitting the World Trade Center competed for brain space with views of tower occupants leaping to their deaths and with the sound and the fury of the towers' eventual collapse.

As powerful as flashbulb memories are, the collective memory of JFK's assassination contains more than recollections of the disorientation Americans felt when they heard the news. For some, the weekend of Kennedy's assassination was filled with memorable sights that remain freeze-frame images in their minds. Mary Augusta Rodgers recalled "the dreamlike horror of the weekend," and the shock of seeing General Charles de Gaulle and Emperor Haile Selassie taking part in the funeral march from the White House to St. Matthew's Cathedral. "It would have seemed no more fantastic if the announcer had mentioned the presence of Charlemagne and the Black Prince."[65] Many people recall one scene best of all: John F. Kennedy Jr. on his third birthday saluting his father's flag-draped coffin. Jérôme Bourdon argued that media coverage of a leader's funeral can "redress or repair" the damage caused by the initial trauma of his death.[66] Kennedy's funeral may have helped the nation ease its trauma, but its elaborate nature enhanced the number of intense, emotionally charged images recalled from that weekend.

Among those born too late to recall the assassination, some may have drawn from their parents' and grandparents' memories to develop an interest in Kennedy, but for many, his life and his assassination are viewed through the lens of popular culture. In this context, he becomes a handsome lady's man whose head was blown apart repeatedly in Oliver Stone's 1991 film, *JFK*. The blood and the gore are now a part of the elegant man's remembered wardrobe.

TELEVISION'S COMING OF AGE

Television's non-stop coverage of the assassination and its aftermath enabled many Americans to feel, for the first time, that they were taking part in events that carried huge national significance. The weekend revealed the medium's previously untapped power to unite Americans under a big tent created by airwaves. Together, they watched the president's funeral, and many saw his apparent assassin become the first man slain on live TV. William Manchester called it "the greatest simultaneous experience this people or anyone else ever had."[67] Elmer W. Lower, then president of news, special events, and public affairs for ABC, concluded that "television held this nation together for four days, keeping people informed by a steady flow of news, and showing them vividly that President Johnson had taken command of the situation and that the transfer of power had taken place smoothly."[68]

Just months before the assassination, the three major television networks had confined their evening news broadcasts to fifteen minutes and, although CBS and NBC expanded to thirty minutes in the fall of 1963, ABC retained the fifteen-minute format until 1967. Satellite footage debuted in 1962 alongside wider usage of videotaped reports. When Kennedy was shot, a medium just emerging from its infancy struggled to shoulder the vast responsibility of providing constant communication for Americans on what was unquestionably the biggest news story since World War II. Television rose to the occasion journalistically and realized how thinly stretched its resources were. The absence of live news cameras on Dealey Plaza and the nation's dependence on amateur film footage to reconstruct the scene may have pointed the way to a future in which cameras are ubiquitous in American life.

Television had played a significant role in Kennedy's rise to power and in his relationship with the American people. More than presidents

The New Frontier

After campaigning for president as an agent of change on America's New Frontier, John F. Kennedy entered the White House at a time of great tension in the Cold War and in race relations within the United States. From the beginning, it was clear that Kennedy was more keenly focused on foreign affairs. Just months after taking office, he committed a huge blunder by giving his support to an invasion of Cuba by CIA-trained refugees of the island at the Bay of Pigs. The invaders were overwhelmed by Cuban forces and were either killed or captured after Kennedy refused to expand U.S. support for the operation. Kennedy took full responsibility for the failure, although he had received bad advice from military and intelligence leaders, who had hatched the plan during Dwight Eisenhower's administration. In the summer of 1961, there was a clash of giants in Germany, where Soviet forces threatened to swallow up West Berlin, a small patch of capitalist democracy within the Soviet bloc. Kennedy feared the crisis might escalate into nuclear war, but it ended in a Soviet decision to divide the city by building a wall.

The biggest international crisis of his presidency was the Cuban Missile Crisis of October 1962. When the United States discovered Soviet nuclear missile sites under construction in Cuba, just ninety miles off the American coast, both the United States and the Soviet Union felt the closeness of nuclear war. Kennedy established a naval blockade to block the shipment of missile parts to Cuba and to create time to find a peaceful resolution of the crisis as the U.S. military prepared for war. Soviet Premier Nikita Khrushchev contended that the Cuban missiles were no more provocative than U.S. missiles just outside the Soviet Union in Turkey. Ultimately, Khrushchev ordered ships carrying military equipment to turn back. The crisis ended with Khrushchev's promise to remove the missiles. Kennedy made two concessions to end the crisis peacefully: He publicly guaranteed that he would not invade Cuba, and privately promised to withdraw U.S. missiles from Turkey. In June 1963, Kennedy spoke at American University in Washington and declared that, contrary to Cold War rhetoric, peaceful coexistence with the Soviet Union was possible. Later that year, he successfully completed a treaty ending atmospheric nuclear tests by the United States, the Soviet Union, and the United Kingdom. During his presidency, Kennedy expanded Eisenhower's commitment to South Vietnam, increasing the number of military advisers from 692 to 16,700, but his last action on Vietnam was to order withdrawal of 1,000 troops.

On the domestic front, Kennedy began by treating civil rights conflicts in the south on a case-by-case basis rather than taking a strong stand on African American rights. As non-violent African American civil rights forces challenged white supremacy on various fronts, the Kennedy administration found itself drawn into the confrontations over and over again. In 1961, JFK sent four hundred federal marshals to protect Freedom Riders who traveled through the south on Trailways buses in violation of laws requiring segregation in public transportation. In the fall of 1962, he sent first federal marshals and later National Guardsmen and federal troops to make it possible for African American veteran James Meredith to enroll in the University of Mississippi. After watching police violence against peaceful black demonstrators in Birmingham, Alabama, in 1963, Kennedy decided that the time had arrived for a major civil rights initiative. During that year, he federalized the National Guard to integrate the University of Alabama, proposed the most significant civil rights legislation since Reconstruction, and met with black leaders of the March on Washington, where Martin Luther King Jr. delivered his famous "I Have a Dream" speech. Over the course of Kennedy's presidency, his administration initiated voting rights challenges in 145 southern counties.[69] "He was, at his death, undergoing a transformation from a hesitant leader with unsure goals to a strong figure with deeply appealing objectives," according to King.[70]

Kennedy, who tended to view life as a series of challenges, is remembered for starting the Peace Corps, a volunteer organization that sent Americans to provide assistance in developing nations, and he is generally credited with bolstering American activism by encouraging young people and adults to get involved in their society's work. He set the goal of sending an American to the moon by the end of the 1960s, an achievement completed in 1969 during the presidency of his 1960 rival, Richard Nixon.

in the radio age, he had been a part of Americans' daily lives for almost three years. They had watched him accept blame for the agonizing defeat at the Bay of Pigs, and they had taken pride in his peaceful resolution of the Cuban Missile Crisis. They had admired his stylish, young wife, and chortled over memorable images of young Caroline and John Jr. In the nation's increasingly mobile society, many Americans probably knew JFK better than they knew neighbors down the block. He was a frequent visitor in their living rooms.

Kennedy was the first television president. He demonstrated how a national leader could use television to reach out to his constituents. His polished performances in televised debates with Republican opponent Richard Nixon increased his credibility among voters and helped him to claim a tight election victory. He was the first president to conduct live, televised news conferences. In those sessions, he verbally tussled with reporters, often displaying a quick wit and detailed knowledge of the issues. In times of crisis, he used television to address the nation, and on a lighter note, his wife hosted a televised view of the finished product in her White

A 1960 CBS poll reported that four million Americans decided which presidential candidate they were going to back after the four televised Kennedy–Nixon debates, and 78 percent of those voters chose JFK.

House redecoration project. Twenty-five years after the assassination, Don Hewitt, longtime executive producer of the Columbia Broadcasting System's *60 Minutes*, told an interviewer, "I keep hearing about how Jack Kennedy was the first president who knew how to use television. That's like someone saying [esteemed twentieth-century Shakespearean actor] Sir Laurence Olivier knows how to use a stage." Newton Minow, chairman of the Federal Communications Commission in the Kennedy administration, said, "In many ways, he was better on television than he was in person—the reverse of a lot of political people . . . He was at ease with it." Minow said Kennedy knew that he "never could have been elected without television."[71] And his death induced television's coming of age as a news medium.

When Kennedy was shot, it fell into the hands of broadcast journalists to deliver the unthinkable news of his death to the American people. Five minutes after the announcement in Dallas that Kennedy had died, a weary Cronkite removed his glasses and looked at the clock as he told his audience that the nation had lost its president. In an uncharacteristic display of emotion, Cronkite's voice cracked during these emotional moments. Later, he reflected, "We knew it was coming, but still it was hard to say."[72] On NBC, newsman Frank McGee experienced a similar loss of control. The concept of journalistic objectivity faced a new challenge. Hammering a story into a typewriter is much easier than looking into a camera and telling millions of Americans that their leader is dead.

Over the course of four days, TV journalists narrated America's nightmare, sometimes speaking to the audience and at other times, speaking for them. From 1:40 p.m. Eastern Standard Time on Friday until Tuesday morning, no regular programming aired. All commercials were canceled as well. "In respect for the feelings of a shocked nation, the CBS Television Network and the CBS Radio Network will carry no commercial announcements and no entertainment programs until after the president's funeral," CBS president Frank Stanton announced hours after the assassination.[73] NBC offered its assassination coverage to stations not affiliated with a network and to stations in Mexico and Canada. Highlights were supplied to TV outlets in twelve additional foreign nations, and live coverage of the funeral was beamed via satellite to twenty-five European nations.[74] CBS, NBC, and ABC provided a total of about 200 hours of coverage.[75] The *New York Times* estimated television's losses from this special advertisement-free period at $100 million. Combined, the three networks usually brought in about $14 million during prime time hours each evening. On top of that, individual stations lost income from commercials, and the cost of producing uninterrupted coverage was estimated to be more than $2 million.[76]

During the weekend of the assassination, the Nielsen organization, which tracks TV viewership, estimated that the average American home had a television tuned to coverage of the event for 31.6 hours, approximately eight hours each day. Moreover, Nielsen figures indicate that at a time when the U.S. population, including children, totaled less than 190 million, roughly 166 million Americans in more than 51 million homes watched part of the coverage and occupants of one sixth of the homes spent more than eleven hours per day in front of their televisions.[77] At some times, more than half of all Americans were watching the same events unfold on their TV screens.[78] At least 95 percent of Americans watched or heard some coverage on all four days. (In contrast, after the death of FDR, only 88 percent of Americans listened to radio coverage of FDR's death and funeral *at any time*.) Even JFK's political adversaries spent six to seven hours each day following the news.[79] New York audience measurements showed that more than 90 percent of the city's television sets were tuned to the funeral procession at the same time.[80] A Boulder, Colorado, study found that at least three-quarters of respondents spent more than two hours watching coverage on each of the three days after the assassination: 87 percent on November 23, when the Kennedy family received mourners privately at the White House; 75 percent on November 24, when Oswald was slain; and 80 percent on the day of the funeral, November 25.[81] In the city where the crimes occurred, the average Dallas resident watched for 34.8 hours over four days.[82]

Anchorman Chet Huntley was having lunch with advertisers in New York when he heard that Kennedy had been shot. He ran to NBC's emergency studio, where another newsman was already on the air. Huntley, who had covered FDR's death, knew the terrain. At first, he did not absorb the fact that Kennedy had died. "I guess I'm enough of a professional and there is enough cynicism in me—it's a professional disease, we constantly see our heroes turn bad, sour, we see our great figures develop feet of clay time and time again, so I was enough of a pro not to get carried away by the assassination," he later told an interviewer. Nevertheless, he worried about the possibility that anxiety-driven journalists might agitate the public, causing panic. "There's a great tendency to speculate when the president is shot, you can create pandemonium. I was thinking who's in charge of the A-bomb at this point . . . I was concerned that this could have been a plot on the part of our adversaries. I didn't expect it, but the notion was in my mind."[83] (In fact, to avoid exacerbating fears, NBC News chose not to report that the Strategic Air Command, which controls the nation's nuclear arsenal, had received a special notification of the assassination.)[84] Huntley said he was unable to reminisce about Kennedy on that first day. "You just can't have a breathing president Friday morning, have an obituary and have him buried Friday night. It's just too fast."[85]

Huntley's co-anchor in Washington, David Brinkley, was in his office when the news broke. Because it was lunchtime, no one with the authority to cancel local programming was available. "Two, three, four, five minutes after the news broke, they were still running some silly women's program out of here, so I called the local manager's office. He was out, and I screamed at his secretary to find him, to get that junk off the air, and put the news on the air . . . She tried to find him, but the phone system had collapsed." When Brinkley did get on the air, he recalled, "In the first hours, neither I nor anyone else made any points. There was no time for analysis . . . It's your job to get the facts distributed. There really isn't any time to think about anything else." Three weeks after the assassination, Brinkley did not recall any concern about the possibility of a national panic, although he feared violence in Dallas until a suspect had been taken into custody. Brinkley said that he attempted to avoid showing any emotion, but admitted that one sentiment naturally emerged: "that it was sad, shocking, hideous."[86] He added, "I was quite impressed by Mrs. Kennedy's behavior . . . her dignity. I pointed that out two or three times. On Friday night, the great rapidity with which it all happened made it almost impossible to absorb—got me to thinking about the fact that at 1:15 p.m. [Eastern Standard Time], Kennedy was in Dallas alive and well, and at 6:30, he was back here dead. In previous cases, like Lincoln and FDR, they had been transported by train across the land. I didn't go on the air with this because it seemed tasteless. It was so fast that his wife hadn't even had time to change her dress."[87]

When the weekend was over, ABC's Howard K. Smith admitted that he collapsed under the weight of his emotions once he was off camera. Covering the funeral, he was struck by the behavior of John F. Kennedy Jr. "When the kids appeared, the fidgety little boy John-John, he saw it as a tremendous pageant, and so did I."[88]

Broadcast journalists took pride in television's growth over these days as it emerged from its youth as almost exclusively an entertainment medium to its maturity as a news medium and a unifying force in American culture. For almost forty years, coverage of Kennedy's assassination and its aftermath stood as television's bright and shining moment. Only round-the-clock coverage of terrorist attacks on the World Trade Center in 2001 could compare in thoroughness and in audience interest, although commercials did not cease during that coverage. NBC reporter Sander Vanocur saw the president's assassination as a unique event. "Nothing like this had ever happened in the age of television and you had a lot of very talented people who were set loose to do as best they could . . ." Television, he said, "happened—not by design—to bind the nation together."[89] CBS News' Robert Pierpoint agreed: "Television came into its own during that period."[90] Recalling the funeral, United Press International correspondent Wilborn Hampton noted, "Words couldn't quite convey the emotion that seeing it did."[91]

"There is no question that this changed the world as far as the media goes," Time's Hugh Sidey said. "The advent of the television world was suddenly kind of expanded so that everybody realized it was on us— television [now] being the principal news purveyor and not only giving us the breaking news but the emotions around it. The legend of Kennedy was born. Four days of continuous television, I think, is really the foundation of the Kennedy mystique. What this did was focus the world's attention on the White House, on the presidency, like never before, and [led to] the realization that [the president of the United States] was not only the most powerful man but probably the most interesting man in the world."[92]

"More than a hundred million Americans watched the late president's funeral," Newsweek reported, "but the funeral did not take place in Arlington Cemetery alone. It took place in a living room in Los Angeles, in Grand Central Terminal in New York, in kitchens and offices across the U.S. John F. Kennedy's casket did not ride down Pennsylvania Avenue only. It rode down Main Street."[93] To make this miracle happen, the networks relied on shared broadcast images so that no single operation had to provide enough cameras to follow the coffin's extended travels through the streets of Washington and into Arlington.

Not everyone was happy with television's round-the-clock coverage. Pop artist Andy Warhol objected to the tone of the coverage, saying, "What bothered me was the way the television and radio were programming everybody to feel sad."[94] Some viewers objected to persistent replays of Oswald's murder.[95] A young mother from Shreveport, Louisiana, called the White House to complain about the constant reporting, which she called "disturbing." Kennedy Press Secretary Pierre Salinger suggested that she turn her TV off.[96] Although about a third of viewers wished for a break from television's assassination news, most continued to watch because they feared "being in the dark" or "not knowing what was going on." Researchers found that among forty-eight Minneapolis viewers, none felt free at any time to detach themselves from the flow of news.[97] Radio proved its ongoing value as a mobile source of information for Americans who had to leave home but wanted to remain tied to events in Dallas and Washington in an era when cell phones and the internet were beyond imagination.

In retrospect, it is obvious that the networks practiced a degree of political correctness over the weekend and framed events perhaps too neatly. For instance, reporters avoided talking about the nature of Kennedy's wounds, and when panning a crowd of mourners, cameramen avoided scenes of people who were laughing or behaving in a manner that seemed inappropriate. The networks steered clear of partisan politics whenever possible. Beyond that, obsessive focus on the president's death was enforced by choosing not to report unrelated events, such as the death of author Aldous Huxley, who had written the great science fiction novel *Brave New World* in 1932.[98] And always, correspondents were reminded to maintain cool objectivity. When Oswald was gunned down, Smith, who was anchoring television coverage for ABC News, could not stifle an angry outburst, questioning how this could happen and why the United States had lost four presidents to gunshots. The network, according to Smith, applauded the rightness of what he said, but urged him to avoid further emotional displays.[99]

This long weekend helped to set the agenda for television news' future. Its limited ability to provide live coverage in Dallas during the hours immediately following the assassination left anchormen like Cronkite, Huntley, Brinkley, Smith, and others in the position of having to describe the scene based on telephone reports from correspondents in Dallas. To fulfill its role as the most vital source of news, television needed to expand its capacity for live coverage, and that meant allocating money to provide greater deployment of resources as well as maximum use of new technology. The networks' hunger for additional footage of the scene in Dallas created demand for more thorough coverage of the president—just in case. Twenty-four-hour news channels would have been unthinkable in 1963, but those four days revealed a potential appetite for more news on television.

VICE PRESIDENT JOHNSON

Riding two cars behind Kennedy in the Dallas motorcade was a miserable man. As a person accustomed to wielding the power of Senate majority leader, Lyndon Johnson found the vice presidency's limitations frustrating and demoralizing. In the Senate, Johnson had been a powerful man who saw Kennedy as a lightweight. After the election, Kennedy was in charge, and Johnson was dependent on his goodwill. Their new relationship was not an easy one, but Kennedy worked hard to establish an arrangement that made use of Johnson's abilities while generally positioning him just outside the spotlight's glow. The president and vice president meticulously exhibited respectful behavior toward one another in public as well as in private. Without becoming best friends, they found enjoyment in each other's company, and, without fanfare, Kennedy invited Johnson to participate in resolving some of the era's most important issues, thus preparing the way for Johnson's transition to the presidency.

This partnership had begun unsteadily at the 1960 Democratic National Convention, where Robert Kennedy and Johnson cemented mutual mistrust and became enemies for life. JFK had spent most of that election year traveling around the country and competing in Democratic primaries; Johnson, on the other hand, had remained at work in the Senate. Johnson mistakenly believed that his power in Congress would make it possible to claim the presidential nomination. He was disappointed when Kennedy entered the National Democratic Convention in Los Angeles with virtually all of the votes he needed to capture the nomination. Johnson's associates made somewhat desperate attacks on Kennedy, such as revealing that JFK had Addison's disease, an accusation that the Kennedy campaign dishonestly denied. Robert Kennedy and others in the campaign were appalled by the allegation and hated Johnson because of it. While Robert nurtured grievances, Jack Kennedy could easily put past conflicts behind him. After winning the presidential nomination, JFK decided to offer Johnson the vice presidential nomination. Johnson accepted, but news of a Kennedy–Johnson ticket caused upheaval in Kennedy's campaign, where liberals exhibited horror and predicted that the choice would hurt JFK's candidacy. Jack Kennedy believed that Johnson could help draw votes in the South, where he knew he was weak. Nevertheless, facing strong opposition within his brother's own camp, Robert Kennedy made two or three visits to Johnson's suite in hopes of nudging Johnson to withdraw his name from consideration. Robert, who was furious about Johnson's aides' efforts to draw attention to JFK's medical condition, was determined to oust Johnson from the ticket. He had several unsatisfactory conversations with Johnson's associates, who argued that JFK should talk to Johnson directly if he had doubts. Meanwhile, Jack Kennedy remained above the fray without talking to Johnson or telling his brother to cease his crusade. During the hours when RFK was making enemies in the Johnson camp, JFK became more convinced that Johnson was the right choice. Unfortunately, the presidential nominee did not contact his brother in time to avert an emotional confrontation between RFK and LBJ.[100] The end result of the day's events was that both Robert Kennedy and Lyndon Johnson felt humiliated—Kennedy because he had taken a strong stand and his brother had overruled him, Johnson because he had been offered something and then almost lost it. And from that humiliation, a strong animus grew and festered.

When JFK and LBJ eked out their victory in 1960, Kennedy knew that one of his most demanding jobs would be keeping his vice president busy and making sure that he was treated with respect. Johnson played a subdued but active role in Cabinet and National Security Council meetings as well as in meetings with congressional leaders. Kennedy named him to head the President's Space Council and the National Advisory Council of the Peace Corps. And, during the Cuban Missile Crisis, Johnson served on the Ex Comm, Kennedy's elite decision-making body.

Furthermore, LBJ traveled the globe as Kennedy's emissary. Some missions dispatched him to diplomatic backwaters, where little of importance was likely to happen. However, one of Johnson's first trips was to the increasingly troublesome nation of South Vietnam, where he gathered first impressions that would affect his thinking over the coming years. Kennedy also sent Johnson to the Cold War's hottest spot—Berlin—in the summer of 1961, when the threat of nuclear war seemed frighteningly real. The Soviet Union had announced plans to sign a peace treaty with East Germany that would end West Berlin's unique, post-World War II status as an oasis of democracy within the apparent desolation of Soviet-dominated eastern Europe. The United States threatened to respond militarily if West Berlin was threatened. Ultimately, the Communist bloc solved its real problem—the flood of Germans from East Germany into West Berlin—by building a wall that divided the city. Less than a week after the wall's construction, Kennedy asked Johnson to go to the divided city as his representative. The president believed construction of the wall was in some ways a gift because it confirmed West Berlin's boundaries and guaranteed its continued existence. Nonetheless, U.S.–Soviet tensions remained high. Johnson could not be sure that his journey would be safe, but he went to Berlin, where he was greeted by tearful, cheering crowds. He stayed to see the equally uproarious reception for new American troops who had traveled on the Autobahn through East Germany to reach West Berlin.[101]

Moreover, Johnson stood shoulder-to-shoulder with Kennedy as he confronted the most volatile domestic issue of the 1960s—civil rights for African Americans. Although he often was not deeply involved in resolving individual crises, Johnson was a significant player in the development and promotion of the administration's civil rights policy. Beginning in 1961, he led the Equal Opportunity Committee, which was responsible for making sure that African Americans had equal opportunities for jobs in companies with government contracts. Although the Kennedy administration never canceled a contract because of a company's employment practices, the committee made small steps forward, convincing companies to set internal policies for increased minority hiring. This became another field of conflict for Johnson and Robert Kennedy, who expected the committee to produce more impressive results. Although the NAACP had voiced cynicism about the committee's work, the organization's leader, Roy Wilkins, later commented that "Mr. Johnson began to emerge during the Kennedy administration wholly unexpectedly and to the delight of the civil rights forces in areas that we didn't expect him to be active as a vice president."[102]

While Johnson focused on employment, the Kennedy administration established a pattern of careening from crisis to crisis on civil rights issues until JFK decided in the spring of 1963 to propose civil rights legislation. Johnson supported Kennedy's proposal, but he feared that Kennedy had moved prematurely by proposing the bill before starting the work of winning over Congress. Johnson worked alongside Kennedy to persuade lawmakers. A master of the Congress, Johnson at times had commented that Kennedy had "all of the minnows and none of the whales" in the Capitol,[103] and on this issue the vice president did what he could to overcome that weakness. In an effort to sway public opinion, President Kennedy, Robert Kennedy, and Johnson held White House meetings with influential Americans—businessmen, labor leaders, educators, lawyers, civil rights advocates, state and local officials, and clergymen. Morris Abram, a Georgia civil rights lawyer, recalled attending a White House meeting for attorneys on June 21, 1963. Both Kennedys had spoken, but "there was no passion in any of it until LBJ took the podium. And he gave an impassioned speech about what kind of country is this that a man can go die in a foxhole and can't get a hamburger in a public restaurant."[104]

By inconspicuously positioning Johnson in the middle of the action, Kennedy readied him for the presidency. In the process, Johnson became much more thoroughly prepared than Harry S. Truman had been in April 1945, when Franklin Roosevelt died after a long illness. The vice presidency did not carry as much power as Johnson had wanted, but being vice president and enjoying Kennedy's show of confidence simplified his ascendance to the presidency.

Lyndon Johnson had long-held beliefs about the presidency, and those ideas provide an important window into understanding the nuances in his performance as vice president and president. Throughout his political career, an underlying theme had been a strong belief that the presidency warranted almost unquestioning devotion. He maintained this philosophy from his arrival in Washington as a young man during Franklin D. Roosevelt's presidency until his death in 1973. From this perspective, the vice presidency was a cog in the wheel of government powered by the presidency. This conception explains much of Johnson's behavior: his quiet support for Kennedy during his vice presidency; his expectation of total,

unquestioning loyalty during his own presidency; and his heartbroken
bewilderment when he did not receive it.

Obviously, betraying JFK would have been unforgivable under
Johnson's own ethos. As vice president, he surprised friends and foes alike
by swallowing his gargantuan ego. He could not hide his dejection, but
he seldom complained. As the Kennedy administration began, Johnson
tried to expand the vice president's power in Congress and in the executive
branch, but both efforts evaporated. Still, Kennedy made Johnson the first
vice president to have an office in the Executive Office Building.[105]

Kennedy urged aides and Cabinet members to show deference to
Johnson.[106] Walt Rostow, chairman of the State Department's Policy
Planning Council, recalled Kennedy actively seeking Johnson's advice.
Rostow recalled one meeting in which LBJ was absent. Kennedy asked
where Johnson was and learned that his plane was circling Washington.
Kennedy responded, "We will take some other item up, but I want him
here when we discuss Laos."[107] Many observers in the White House's inner
sanctum witnessed genuine affection between Kennedy and Johnson.
"The president and vice president, to the astonishment of many and
somewhat to the surprise of them both, got along famously," according
to Sorensen. "The president never doubted his vice president's loyalty, as
so many presidents have, took pains to have him present at all the major
meetings . . . and publicly praised him as 'invaluable.'"[108] Johnson's friend
and future Supreme Court Justice Abe Fortas shared Sorensen's perspective.
Kennedy "was very warm toward Vice President Johnson," Fortas said.[109]
As a veteran of Washington's bureaucracy, Secretary of State Dean Rusk
said, "I had long been used to the favorite indoor sport around Washington
—making fun of vice presidents. But I never saw the slightest trace of
that in John F. Kennedy."[110] Kennedy's congressional liaison, Lawrence
O'Brien, concurred: "In a professional sense, Jack Kennedy was extremely
appreciative of Johnson's support, which was evidenced in every way."
O'Brien's history with Kennedy went back to JFK's days in the House of
Representatives, and he said, "I never heard Kennedy say a bad word about
Lyndon Johnson."[111]

However, a common joke in Washington at the time was: "Where's
Lyndon?" Members of Kennedy's Irish Mafia referred to him as the
"Judge Crater" of the vice presidency. *Time* reported that "although
Johnson is often seen, he is not really heard . . . He is free to speak up,
but nobody, really, has to heed him anymore . . ." An article in the *Reporter*
called Johnson a man "who chases around continents in search of the duties
of his office."[112]

Johnson's daughter, Lynda Bird Johnson Robb, was a teenager when
her father became vice president, and she has only fond memories about

the relationship between her parents and the Kennedys: "I never heard anything but good things said by my parents about the Kennedys, and I would believe that the President and Mrs. Kennedy felt the same way from what I personally witnessed and heard." She rejected stories about conflict between the president and vice president.[113] Robb learned about politics as the daughter of one politician and the wife of another, Charles Robb, a Virginia lieutenant governor, governor, and United States senator.

Speaking of the vice presidency years later, Johnson told CBS's Walter Cronkite, "I was disappointed at times . . . I missed the active role I played. I think anyone who becomes vice president is disappointed, particularly if he's been an active man in public life as they often are like President Nixon, or the [1968] Democratic nominee for president, Mr. [Hubert] Humphrey."[114] Over the course of Kennedy's presidency, Johnson agreed with most of JFK's decisions, but he was squeamish about the Kennedys' use of Justice Department powers as a means of pressuring steel companies to abandon a proposed price hike in 1962. And he opposed Kennedy's acquiescence to the coup that toppled Ngo Dinh Diem in South Vietnam.

Despite a congenial relationship between JFK and LBJ, rancor was all too obvious between their inner circles. Robert Kennedy probably was the most vehement Johnson antagonist, but he was not alone. Some Ivy Leaguers looked down on Johnson because he worked as a janitor to pay his tuition to Southwest Texas State Teachers College. Calling Johnson "Uncle Cornpone," many insiders made jokes about his crudeness. Kennedy aide Harris Wofford called it "a certain snootiness of class."[115] John Siegenthaler, an aide to Robert Kennedy, said, "I just have a sense that Bob was on Lyndon's mind too much . . . And maybe Bob's mind was on Lyndon too little."[116]

Johnson was resentful. "The men of ideas think little of me; they despise me," he told Doris Kearns Goodwin. "My daddy always told me that if I brushed up against the grindstone of life, I'd come away with far more polish than I could ever get at Harvard or Yale. I wanted to believe him, but somehow, I never could."[117] Vicious jokes about him were one ingredient in the party mix at Robert Kennedy's Hickory Hill home, journalist Hugh Sidey recalled. "Bob Kennedy and Ethel—oh, they used to . . . some of the jokes in that were just awful."[118] Of course, RFK and his associates vented most of their hostility behind Johnson's back. Assistant and later Deputy Attorney General Nicholas Katzenbach described face-to-face exchanges between LBJ and RFK as "polite and stiff."[119] Johnson, in his darkest days as vice president, believed that the Kennedys were seeking to replace him on the ticket for 1964, but in November 1963, at the first strategy session for the election, Johnson's spot on the ticket was a foregone conclusion. Johnson's staff compiled a list of each occasion in which he came into contact with Kennedy during his vice presidency. The two men had 544 contacts over 1,036 days, if we begin our count on January 21, 1961, the first full day of the Kennedy administration. When weekend days, holidays, and vacation days are subtracted along with Johnson's almost ten weeks abroad and Kennedy's own frequent trips away from Washington,[120] it becomes clear that the two men interacted almost every day when both were in Washington—a far cry from Truman's two non-Cabinet meetings with FDR during the eight weeks he served as vice president before Roosevelt's death. Because of this, LBJ was adequately prepared for the big job, although he had no expectation of ever getting it.

A SUNNY DAY IN DALLAS

In the late morning of November 22, Air Force One and the unofficially pegged "Air Force Two" raced down the runways at Dallas's Love Field. Already, JFK had delivered two speeches in Fort Worth before making the short hop to Dallas. From here, his schedule included a ten-mile, 45-minute motorcade through the city followed by a luncheon at the Trade Mart as well as a reception and a fund-raiser in Austin. His three-day trip to Texas had two goals: lessening political tensions between liberal Senator Ralph Yarborough and conservative Governor John Connally and laying the groundwork for the 1964 election in a heavily contested, must-win state. Though crowds had been friendly so far, Kennedy knew the Lone Star State was home to many right-wing extremists, who saw the 46-year-old president as Public Enemy no. 1. On the day he reached Dallas, 5,000 handbills had popped up on the city's streets displaying "mugshots" of the president under a headline that read: "WANTED FOR TREASON." That morning's *Dallas Morning News* carried a full-page ad by the American Fact-Finding Committee that accused Kennedy of being soft on Communism and of persecuting loyal Americans. About a month earlier, a violent Dallas mob had attacked UN Ambassador Adlai Stevenson, hitting him on the head with a sign and chanting that "Stevenson's going to die—his heart will stop, stop, stop, and he will burn, burn, burn."[121] Into this cauldron of extremism, the president entered, just hours after talking with old friend and aide Kenneth O'Donnell about how easy it would be to assassinate a president—a familiar topic for the fatalistic JFK.[122]

Traveling with the president was first lady Jacqueline Kennedy in her first major step out of the seclusion that had circumscribed her life since the August death of their infant son, Patrick Bouvier Kennedy, when he was less than two days old. This loss, along with the stillbirth of a child years earlier, left her feeling vulnerable, but observers believed they saw a new closeness between the president and his wife, an intimacy born of shared pain. Though campaigning was not her favorite activity, Texas crowds had been welcoming, especially to her. They had hooted in response to her chic wardrobe, including today's pink suit with a matching pillbox hat. The first lady, who always looked immaculate, had worried for days about the planned motorcade through Dallas. If the bubble top was not up on the limo, she was sure that her hair would become windblown as she melted beneath the Texas sun.[123]

On Air Force Two, Lyndon Johnson had his own set of anxieties. In addition to articles about the ruptured state of the Democratic Party in his home state, today's *Dallas Morning News* presented a story under the headline "Nixon Predicts JFK May Drop Johnson." Although the vice presidency offered Johnson an annoyingly limited range of power, he wanted to keep the job. He feared that Robert Kennedy was campaigning to remove him from the ticket. LBJ suspected that the attorney general was attempting to damage his reputation by accentuating LBJ's ties to Bobby Baker, Johnson's ex-aide who had recently been forced to resign as secretary to the Senate following charges that he had accepted kickbacks from defense contractors. Johnson was apprehensive, too, about the possibility that extremist anti-Kennedy activity in his home state might damage his reputation.

With all of these thoughts in mind, President Kennedy, Mrs. Kennedy, and Vice President Johnson began a Dallas visit that would alter the nation's future and its self-image. Chapter 2 will provide the generally agreed-upon facts about what took place in Dallas and Washington; Chapter 3 will examine the assassination's immediate effects on Americans; Chapter 4 will consider how the Kennedy legacy affected the Johnson administration and the rest of the 1960s; and Chapter 5 will take a look at conspiracy theories and why they arose, while also examining how the assassination and suspicions of conspiracy have entered popular culture.

CHAPTER 2

Texas Tragedy

"At his best, man is the noblest of all animals; separated from law and justice he is the worst."

Aristotle

A ir Force One, perhaps the most majestic representation of the modern American presidency, glides down the runway at Dallas's Love Field, and an eager crowd erupts in cheers. Alongside it, the almost identical Air Force Two delivers Vice President Lyndon Johnson and his party. A gaggle of government and party officials stand ready to greet the John F. Kennedys, and thousands of citizens jostle for position behind a fence. The plane's door opens and stands empty as the crowd thrums with anticipation. After a few moments, a figure fills the void—an astonishingly beautiful woman wearing a striking pink outfit. Ignoring protocol, the president has sent his wife ahead of him. Onlookers shriek with surprise and excitement. Jacqueline Kennedy looks as she always does at public appearances: precisely perfect. The president, with his thick brown hair and impeccable clothes, quickly follows his wife, making his way vigorously down the steps. As they disembark, one TV reporter comments that the president's tan is visible from yards away. Robert Donovan, the *Los Angeles Times'* Washington bureau chief, later describes them as "two beautiful people that day, glamorous [and generating] a screaming reception."[1]

> JFK's constant tan, which added to his handsomeness, was not the result of outdoor activity; it was a symptom of his Addison's disease.

As he leaves the plane on this Friday morning, Kennedy brings with him almost three years of experience in the White House. In his first two years, he experienced defeat at the Bay of Pigs, stalemate in divided Berlin, and a peaceful resolution of the Cuban Missile Crisis. But, in 1963, he has come into his own. Finally accepting the political risks, he has taken a tough moral stand on civil rights; defying Cold War rhetoric, he has acknowledged that the United States and the Soviet Union can survive side by side without conflict; making his way through Europe, he has wrung tearful cheers from Berliners and uproarious welcomes from the Irish in his ancestral home; and easing one of the globe's toughest problems, he has skillfully concluded a treaty with the Soviet Union banning atmospheric nuclear tests. His always-high approval ratings have slipped a bit, which is not surprising: When a leader drives change into the lives of reluctant constituents, as Kennedy has done by taking a strong position on civil rights, a slide in approval ratings is likely. Now, he stands on the tarmac in Dallas, where he hopes to start building support for his 1964 re-election campaign.

Kennedy takes in the scene and, like a moth to a flame, he feels an irresistible pull and charges toward the boisterous multitude. Ignoring carefully assembled schedules and special security precautions, he extends his arms into the buzzing mass of humanity behind the fence. Kennedy knows that potential danger lies there, but he feeds off the throng's energy. Seventeen years earlier, he was a shy and somewhat stiff, first-time candidate for the House of Representatives. Now, he plunges into crowds, knowing that even a glancing touch of his hand could easily make the day of a potential supporter. The First Lady, Johnson, and his wife Lady Bird join Kennedy in the bustling hive. As crowd members jockey for better views, reporters struggle to follow the presidential party, using Mrs. Kennedy's pink hat as a presidential locator. Just a glimpse of this scene makes Secret Service agents wary.

Agents assigned to protect the president have been working with the Dallas police force for weeks to ensure JFK's safety. They have reviewed the motorcade route, developed special precautions for today's luncheon venue, and taken steps to make sure the president's food supply is untainted. Dallas Police Chief Jesse E. Curry has placed 350 extra uniformed police officers on the president's security detail. To provide maximum protection, Curry has called up reserve officers, eliminated all leaves, and added state police, firemen, and sheriffs to the security force. "Nothing must occur that is disrespectful or degrading to the president of the United States," Curry has warned his forces.[2]

FOUR HOURS IN DALLAS

After spending about ten minutes immersed in the tumultuous sea of constituents, journalists, and guards, the Kennedys slide into the back seat of their limousine, with Texas Governor John Connally and his wife Nellie in the jump seat in front of them. A Secret Service agent drives with another beside him. The clouds have parted to reveal bright sunlight as the temperature climbs toward 80 degrees. Kennedy's aides decide to forgo the car's plastic bubbletop so that the waiting Texans will have a chance to get a clear view of the president and his wife, just as the motorcade crowds did in San Antonio and Houston yesterday. (The bubbletop was not bulletproof, but might have made the assassination more difficult.) The lead car driven by Curry is several car-lengths ahead of the 1961 Lincoln convertible that carries the presidential party. Behind the president's car is a black Cadillac known as the Queen Mary. The specially converted Secret Service vehicle carries two Secret Service agents in the front seat, two in the back, and four on the running boards. Among their armaments is an AR–15 .223-caliber automatic rifle powerful enough to disconnect an assailant's head from his body. Sitting in the jump seat are two of JFK's closest friends and aides, Kenneth O'Donnell and Dave Powers. Behind that car is a light blue Lincoln convertible carrying two Secret Service agents, Vice President Johnson, Lady Bird, and Texas Senator Ralph Yarborough. Next in the caravan is another Secret Service car, followed by the national press "pool" car, a blue-grey Chevrolet sedan, holding four journalists and Assistant Press Secretary Malcolm Kilduff. Farther back, two buses carry the rest of the press corps.

Thick, lively throngs line the streets. Dallas police estimate 150,000 have turned out to see the Kennedys. Staring into the glare of the hot Texas sun, Jacqueline Kennedy instinctively reaches a gloved hand to grab her sunglasses, but her husband stops her: He wants the crowd to have an unobstructed view of his wife. He reminds her to look to the left and wave because he will be looking to the right. Twice, the president halts the motorcade. First, he responds to a group of small children holding a sign that says, "Mr. President, Please Stop and Shake Our Hands." With the motorcade stopped, he steps out of the car, greets the children, and wraps his flawlessly manicured and tanned hands around theirs. Later, the nation's first Roman Catholic president interrupts the procession's flow so that he can speak to a nun surrounded by youngsters.

As the motorcade makes the turn from Houston Street onto Elm, the Secret Service sends word to Dallas's new Trade Mart that JFK will arrive in five minutes for today's luncheon with business leaders. Relishing the friendly welcome, Nellie Connally turns and smiles at Kennedy.

"You sure can't say Dallas doesn't love you, Mr. President," she declares, and he replies, "That is very obvious."[3]

Within seconds, a loud, staccato boom cuts through the raucous roar of the crowd. Then another and another—all in less than nine seconds. The first bullet apparently is a clear miss. The second strikes the president. Speechless, his body contorts after the bullet travels into his upper back and out of his throat. Then comes the death blow. The third shot causes a mortal wound, striking his head, shattering his skull and scattering parts of his brain. Connally is struck, too, probably by the same bullet that struck Kennedy's back. Both men topple into the laps of their wives. Connally screams, "They're going to kill us all!"[4] A Boy Scout watching the motorcade sees Kennedy's face go blank just before he collapses.[5] Standing along the parade route, amateur photographer Abraham Zapruder watches the president's head explode as he stares through the lens of his camera. "They've killed him! They've killed him!" he cries out.[6] As Kennedy pitches to the left, one of his feet dangles over the side of the convertible. It is 12:30 p.m. Central Standard Time.

Smeared with her husband's blood and brains, 34-year-old Jacqueline Kennedy finds herself in a situation in which no rules of etiquette apply. Apparently seeing part of her husband's brain on the car's trunk, she crawls out of the back seat and onto the back of the car as Secret Service agent Clint Hill runs toward the rear fender. (Mrs. Kennedy later will have no recollection of this part of her shocking day.) Secret Service agent Roy Kellerman, who is riding in the front seat of Kennedy's car, speaks into his radio: "We're hit!" The Secret Service notifies Curry in the lead car to get the motorcade to the nearest hospital immediately. As the car speeds up, Hill struggles to hang on. After great effort, he manages to vault into the car, pushing both Kennedys to the floor. Having witnessed the last shot, he knows already that he is too late to save the president. In frustration, he slams his fist into the back of the Lincoln. (For years, Hill will struggle with substance abuse and ponder what might have happened if his reaction time had been one half-second faster.[7]) "They've killed my husband! They've shot his head off!" says Jacqueline Kennedy. "I have his brains in my hand."[8] Secret Service agents in the follow-up car leap out with their weapons. They look for a target, while O'Donnell and Powers helplessly watch in horror, realizing that one of their oldest friends is dying. Agent Emory Roberts recognizes that the nation has lost its president. He uses the radio to tell Rufus Youngblood in the Johnson car: "Rufus, cover your man."[9] Youngblood is already sitting on top of Johnson after hurdling from the front seat and pushing Johnson down. Mrs. Johnson and Senator Yarborough crouch on the floor. Within the crowd at Dealey Plaza, there is sudden bedlam. Some people are not sure what has happened, but others respond by throwing their children on the ground and falling on top of them.

The first group of cars in the motorcade sets off for Parkland Hospital, barreling down the Stemmons Expressway at a speed that may have exceeded eighty miles per hour.[10] As the cars accelerate within view of the Trade Mart, Secret Service agent Dave Grant sees them and dashes inside to call the White House and ask what is happening. Soon afterward, word of the shooting reaches the luncheon crowd waiting at the Trade Mart, first in the form of a fast-moving rumor visibly rumbling through the crowd and later as an official announcement.

Four cars behind the presidential limousine, United Press International reporter Merriman Smith, one of the pool reporters, witnesses the shooting and, after hesitating in momentary shock, he grabs a radio telephone to file his report. Just four minutes after the shooting, UPI sends a news flash around the world, spreading the message that three shots have been fired at the presidential motorcade. As the front of the motorcade speeds away, journalists on the press buses realize something dramatic has happened. Many jump off, landing near the spot where Kennedy was shot.

As the presidential party races toward the hospital, the news spreads rapidly. Just outside Washington at his McLean, Virginia, home, Attorney General Robert Kennedy receives a call from FBI Director J. Edgar Hoover, who reports that the president has been shot. Senator Edward Kennedy is presiding over the Senate when he learns what has happened. He rushes from the chamber.

When the motorcade's lead cars reach Parkland, the emergency room is unprepared for the scope of the catastrophe. Governor Connally is drenched in blood and, behind him, the First Lady whispers to her husband in the back seat. The desperate rush to the hospital delivers a president who is technically alive but essentially dead. As people pile out of the cars arriving at the hospital, the pool reporters end a wrestling match over their car's radio-phone and rush ahead on foot to gather information. Smith asks Hill how the president is, and Hill replies, "He's dead, Smitty."[11] Mrs. Kennedy tells Dave Powers the same thing.[12] A minute later, UPI reports that the president has been wounded, "perhaps fatally." Outside the ER, Kellerman yells for two stretchers on wheels as other Secret Service agents hustle Johnson inside. Because Connally is sitting in front of the president, he is removed first and wheeled inside the ER. Mrs. Kennedy remains in the back seat clutching her husband. Though Secret Service agents believe he is dead, Hill appeals to the First Lady to move so that doctors can help the president. The agents themselves, along with a sobbing Dave Powers, lift his body onto a gurney. Kennedy is taken to Trauma Room 1; doctors work on Connally in Trauma Room 2.

Although the president appears to be dying or dead, conscientious doctors pour into the emergency room in hopes of reviving him. Dr. Charles Carrico, only 28, is the first to analyze Kennedy's condition. What he sees is an ashen man whose respiration is undergoing death throes. The body is spasmodic with no voluntary movement. The eyes are open, pupils dilated, no evident pulse. Carrico orders other doctors to open a vein in his right leg and another in his left arm for IVs, and in his examination, Carrico detects only a faint heartbeat. Dr. Malcolm O. Perry performs a tracheotomy at the site of a neck wound without rolling Kennedy over to determine whether the gaping hole represents an entry or exit wound. (When asked why no one checked the president's back, Carrico later will testify that "I suppose nobody really had the heart to do it.")[13] Dr. William Kemp Clark, Parkland's senior neurosurgeon, joins the growing crowd of physicians. Dr. Paul C. Peters makes an incision in the right side of the chest to drain blood, while another doctor inserts a chest tube on the left side.[14] Kennedy's personal physician, Dr. George Burkley, joins the roomful of medical personnel in their hopeless battle.

Jacqueline Kennedy sits outside Trauma Room 1 in a straight-back chair. (At one point, Lady Bird Johnson approaches her to offer her support. "You always think of her—or somebody like her—as being insulated, protected . . . She was quite alone. I don't ever think I saw anybody so much alone in my life," she later will recall.)[15] After waiting quietly for a while, Mrs. Kennedy makes an attempt to enter the trauma room. Her way is blocked, but she tells Burkley that she wants to be with JFK when he dies. After trying to convince her to take a sedative, Burkley leads her inside and guides her to a corner of the room. Within a few minutes, the president's heart monitor registers no rhythm. Dr. Clark declares John F. Kennedy dead. Out of deference to Mrs. Kennedy, he sets the time of death at 1:00 p.m. to minimize the span between his official time of death and the time when a priest will perform last rites. As the battle ends in Trauma Room 1, John Connally is on his way to surgery.

> A computer in the Government Accounting Office in Washington cut Kennedy's pay at the moment he was declared dead. He earned 14/24 of a day's work.

Gradually, more journalists arrive at the hospital, where distraught White House photographer Cecil Stoughton issues an edict and a plea: "No pictures, no pictures."[16] He does not want the public to see the bloody presidential limousine where the First Lady's roses lie intermingled with pools of blood and Kennedy's brain matter. Minutes after Kennedy's death, two priests—the Rev. Oscar Huber and the Rev. James Thompson—

arrive from Dallas's Holy Trinity Church. Huber, the senior priest, is a small man of 70. When police usher him into the room where the thirty-fifth president of the United States has just been declared dead, he greets the widow, expresses his sympathies, and then sets to work. First, he lifts the sheet covering Kennedy's face. Then he chants: "*Si vivis, ego te absolvo a peccatis tuis. In nomine Patris et Filii et Spiritus Sancti, amen.*" ("If you are living, I absolve you from your sins. In the name of the Father and of the Son and of the Holy Ghost, amen.") He takes a small vial of holy oil from his pocket and marks a cross on the late president's forehead. Mrs. Kennedy joins him in his prayers—her voice unwavering, her eyes dry. Before he leaves, Huber tells her, "I am shocked." She thanks him, and he reassures her, "I am convinced that his soul had not left his body. This was a valid last sacrament." She again expresses her gratitude, and he departs.[17]

When Secretary of Defense Robert McNamara receives news of the shooting, he meets with the Joint Chiefs of Staff. They dispatch a flash warning to all U.S. military bases. The message reports the attack in Dallas and orders all military personnel to assume alert status. At this moment of crisis, six members of Kennedy's Cabinet are flying high above the Pacific on their way to trade talks in Tokyo. The pilot of their plane receives a brief flash after the shooting, and Secretary of State Dean Rusk orders the plane back to Washington.

At the White House, national security adviser McGeorge Bundy is busy changing the locks on JFK's files just in case he does not survive. At 1:05 pm., the president's naval aide, Captain Taz Shepherd, calls Robert Kennedy with word of JFK's death. Overwhelmed by his own anguish, the devoted brother and chief lieutenant grapples for words, eventually telling his wife Ethel, "He had the most wonderful life."[18] In the White House's family living quarters, a Secret Service agent enters with an unhappy Caroline Kennedy in tow. The almost-6-year-old girl is unhappy: She does not understand why she is being denied a sleepover at a friend's house. On Capitol Hill, Speaker of the House John McCormack, 71, hears a report that Johnson, too, may have been injured in the attack. Next in line for the presidency, McCormack finds the news overwhelming and soon learns that Secret Service agents are on their way to protect him.

Upon leaving the hospital, Father Huber becomes the first eyewitness to confirm the president's death. "He's dead all right," the parish priest tells reporters.[19] Journalists update their editors, but none of the TV networks accepts his statement as proof that Kennedy has died. They await an official announcement.

Washington Star reporter David S. Broder's notebook capsulizes the rapidly changing tenor of the day. He begins by filling the pages with the routine details of a presidential appearance less than a year before the next election. He scribbles down a summary of a *Houston Chronicle* article reporting that JFK would lose the state by 100,000 votes if his re-election went before the voters today.

Turn the page.

At first, he spots only friendly signs at the Dallas airport, proclaiming, "Hooray JFK" and "Forward Jack." Later, he sees a few big signs in the crowd. One declares: "Because of my high regard 4 the presidency, I hold you and your blind socialism in complete contempt."

Turn the page.

He notes that the crowds in Dallas are big—as big as they were during the 1960 campaign. "EM [Elm?] & Houston—12:29 p.m."

Turn the page.

"Police Chief M.W. Stevenson.[20] Parkland Hospital."

Turn the page.

"Gov & Pres hit—both carried in—3 shots. Believe seriously hit. She's safe."

Turn the page.

Broder identifies the source of the shots as the Texas School Book Depository.

"Negro man pulled his daughter and ran and police chased him."

Turn the page.

"Prez motionless. Mrs. K. leaning over him. Carried in stretcher. Connally leaning back in front seat—holding chest & stomach."

Turn the page.

"Father Oscar Huber, Holy Trinity—Is he dead? 'He's dead, all right!'—1 p.m., 2 EST. Gunshots."[21]

As the world changes around him, the new president, Lyndon Johnson, is virtually a prisoner of Secret Service agents in a secure area of the hospital's emergency room. Ten to fifteen minutes after doctors acknowledge that Kennedy is dead, Secret Service shift leader Emory Roberts makes time to deliver the news to Johnson. O'Donnell, who has acted as emissary between the Kennedy and Johnson camps at the hospital, tells Johnson that Mrs. Kennedy will not leave without her husband's body. O'Donnell plans to stay at the hospital with her. Assistant Press Secretary Kilduff asks Johnson whether he should make an immediate announcement about Kennedy's death. Fearing a conspiratorial attack on the nation's leadership, Johnson decides that he should leave the hospital before Kilduff issues his statement. Already, it is clear that the rapid transition from one president to the next is fraught with unfortunate possibilities. For example, during his time at the hospital, Johnson has been surrounded by men who woke up this morning as the vice-presidential Secret Service team: They know Johnson and his associates but have no idea who Warrant Officer

Ira Gearhart is. This is a problem, because Gearhart is the man carrying the briefcase that holds the codes to launch U.S. nuclear missiles, and he needs to be close to the new chief executive, not barred from his side and forced to stand alone in a treatment enclosure. At 1:26 p.m., Lyndon and Lady Bird Johnson leave the hospital in separate unmarked cars under heavy guard. Gearhart forces his way into one of the getaway cars and ends up sitting on a policeman's lap. Curry drives the car carrying the new president.

In the media, chaos crackles through the air. Frantic for information—any information—reporters release unsubstantiated and often erroneous reports from witnesses and Dallas police officers: A Secret Service man is shot and killed instantly during his attempt to save the president; a gun-wielding man and woman shoot Kennedy from an overpass; the assassin fires from the second floor of the Texas School Book Depository; Vice President Johnson enters the hospital holding his arm, indication of a possible gunshot wound or heart attack; a hearse carrying Kennedy's body is headed toward a Dallas funeral home.

At 1:33 p.m., a visibly shaken, sweat-soaked Malcolm Kilduff faces the press. He begins by saying, "Excuse me, let me catch my breath." Then, looking like a man existing within a fog, he pauses for about a minute before announcing the death of the president.[22] The *New York Times'* Tom Wicker starts to ask about when LBJ will take the oath of office, but he is overwhelmed by his emotions.

On the streets of Dallas, the Johnsons experience a harrowing ten-minute ride to Love Field, with the tall Texan crouching down in the back seat so that his head never rises above the bottom of the windows. At one point, a delivery truck unexpectedly blocks the cars' path, and Secret Service agents pull their guns, ready for a surprise attack. After that encounter ends innocently, Curry turns on the siren and speeds up. Both Johnson and Secret Service agents tell him to silence the noise: They are trying *not* to attract attention. Before they reach the airport, Lady Bird Johnson notices a flag already flying at half-staff, and the shock of the last hour's events becomes heightened. At the airport, Secret Service agents fear snipers, so the fiftysomething Johnsons must run up the steps and onto Air Force One. Under Secret Service orders, local police and airport personnel have evacuated all buildings, hangars, and warehouses near Air Force One and Air Force Two.

Once he is settled aboard the plane, Johnson calls Robert Kennedy. While expressing his condolences, Johnson really wants to find out the details of being sworn in as president. Shocked by the swiftness of the afternoon's happenings, the attorney general promises to see what he can find out. Later, he calls back and tells Johnson that the oath, which is part of the Constitution, can be administered by any sworn federal official. Johnson reaches Federal District Court Judge Sarah Hughes, a Kennedy nominee chosen on Johnson's recommendation, and asks her to come to the airport quickly.

At this time, Johnson seems clearly concerned about behaving in such a way that the Kennedy family could take no offense. He is aboard Air Force One and not Air Force Two because the presidential plane has superior communications equipment. Furthermore, that is exactly where the Secret Service wants him to be. In fact, the Secret Service wants him in that plane and in the air, but Johnson insists on waiting. He wants to take the oath of office, and he intends to wait for Mrs. Kennedy and the late president's coffin.

In a final moment alone with her husband, Jacqueline Kennedy impulsively removes the wedding ring from her finger and places it on his. (Later, she will regret her decision, and O'Donnell and Burkley will retrieve the ring.) Sheltered in a coffin, JFK leaves Trauma Room 1. His widow emerges alongside the casket. Her suit and stockings tainted with blood, she rests one hand on the wooden box holding her dead husband. The Kennedy entourage faces one final battle before escaping from Parkland Hospital: Medical examiner Dr. Earl F. Rose insists that an autopsy must be performed in Dallas. Both Dr. Clark and Dallas District Attorney Henry Wade tell Rose to let the body go, but he refuses to budge. A justice of the peace, Theron Ward, supports Rose's position and goes so far as to say that "it's just another homicide, as far as I'm concerned."[23] Secret Service agents and Kennedy aides must use force to push the casket out of the hospital and place it in a hearse. After a brief conversation with Wade, Ward comes outside and gives his approval to take the body to the airport; nevertheless, Kennedy's Air Force Aide Godfrey McHugh fears that Dallas officials may trail them to Love Field and try to reclaim the body. No one has thought ahead about how the coffin will be lifted onto Air Force One, so no forklift is on hand to perform that task. Consequently, when they reach the airport, Secret Service agents and Kennedy aides precariously heft it up the steep stairs to the plane.

When the coffin and Mrs. Kennedy are aboard, the Kennedy party is eager for a quick takeoff; most Kennedy aides are unaware that Johnson is present and that he wants to delay takeoff until he takes the oath of office. Some assume that he is taking Air Force Two back to Washington. The pilot, Colonel James Swindal, has been urged to prepare for a quick takeoff. As a result, although the plane has been broiling on the tarmac for hours, he has disconnected it from the ground source that supplies power for the air-conditioning system and lights. Conditions aboard Air

Force One are stifling. McHugh orders Swindal to take off, and the pilot refuses, citing Johnson's orders. McHugh responds by telling Swindal: "I have only one president, and he's lying back in that cabin."[24] In an oral history years later, McHugh describes finding Johnson in a state of panic-driven mental collapse in an airplane lavatory;[25] all other sources report that Johnson's calm helps to salve the ragged nerves all around him.

When Mrs. Kennedy gets to the plane's private presidential suite, she walks in and freezes as she sees Johnson lying across the bed talking on the telephone. Johnson bolts off the bed and out the door. This incident embarrasses Johnson, who had not been told that Mrs. Kennedy had arrived. Johnson has told his Secret Service detail that he wants her to be able to take advantage of the suite's amenities on the flight home. After that awkward encounter, Johnson asks his wife to join him in visiting the widow and expressing their condolences. Mrs. Johnson tearfully gives voice to their sadness over Kennedy's death, and adds, "You know we never even wanted to be vice president and now, dear God, it's come to this."

Figure 2.1 Lyndon B. Johnson takes the presidential oath on Air Force One with Jacqueline Kennedy at his side. Lyndon B. Johnson Library photo by Cecil Stoughton.

Mrs. Kennedy tells them that she is happy she was with her husband today. Mrs. Johnson encourages Mrs. Kennedy to change out of her bloody clothes, but Jacqueline Kennedy displays a new ferocity that will propel her through the coming days. "I want them to see what they have done to Jack," she says defiantly.[26] The sight of the typically immaculate fashion plate in blood-soiled clothes becomes one of the memorable images associated with this tragic weekend.

At 2:30 p.m., Judge Hughes arrives, and Johnson gathers people in a small stateroom. The room is sweltering, and Hughes is ready to begin immediately. Johnson hesitates. He wants Mrs. Kennedy standing beside him when Stoughton captures this historic moment on film. He asks O'Donnell to see whether she will participate. O'Donnell resists the suggestion, saying, "You can't do that! The poor little kid has had enough for one day, to sit here and hear that oath that she heard a few years ago! You just can't do that, Mr. President!" Despite his misgivings, O'Donnell asks Mrs. Kennedy. "Yes, I think I ought to," she replies. "At least I owe that much to the country."[27] She takes her place on one side of Johnson, while his wife is mostly hidden on the other side. In all, twenty-eight people share the room's stale air. Westinghouse reporter Sid Davis is stunned to see the widow's disheveled appearance. "I had never seen her with a hair out of place," he recalled later.[28] With his hand resting on what is believed to be a Bible but is actually a Catholic missal, Johnson takes the oath of office at 2:38 p.m. and allows no opportunity for congratulations once the ceremony is ended. The photograph of this scene carries a clear message: The business of the United States will continue as usual; the change of power is peaceful; there is no reason to fear. With that message sent, the 55-year-old new president gives the order to leave Dallas behind: "Let 'er roll," he commands.[29]

At 2:47 p.m., Air Force One's wheels lift off the runway in an especially steep takeoff. Swindal drives the plane upward 12,000 feet beyond its cleared altitude of 29,000 feet. During the climb, he burns a gallon of fuel each second.[30] The high altitude spares the plane from troubling weather conditions below and offers a sense of safety from the earthbound violence that has fueled a national nightmare.

A TIME TO MOURN

Air Force One reaches Andrews Air Force Base at 5:58 p.m. Eastern Standard Time, less than four and a half hours after Kennedy last waved to the Dallas crowd. Now, his coffin lies at the rear door of the plane. Standing at the door are McHugh and Secret Service agents, who will hoist the coffin onto a lift, which will deliver it to the ground. Behind these ad hoc pallbearers stands Jacqueline Kennedy in her blood-spattered suit. Holding her hand is Attorney General Robert Kennedy, who minutes earlier had bolted up the front steps of the plane, rushed to the back, and simply told his sister-in-law, "Hi, Jackie. I'm here."[31] Melancholy dignitaries gather near the plane, with Senate majority leader Mike Mansfield and majority whip Hubert Humphrey sobbing openly. Supreme Court Chief Justice Earl Warren feels extreme helplessness as he watches the tableau before him. (He later will remember: "That brave girl, with her husband's blood on her, and there was nothing I could do, nothing, nothing.")[32]

After the coffin reaches the ground and is carried to a waiting ambulance, Jacqueline and Robert Kennedy seat themselves next to the coffin. Once the ambulance departs for an autopsy at Bethesda Naval Hospital, Johnson walks down the front steps. This is not his moment, Johnson knows, but he wants to reassure a shaken nation. With his wife at his side, he approaches microphones a short distance from the plane and slowly delivers a simple speech grounded in humility: "This is a sad time for all people. We have suffered a loss that cannot be weighed. For me it is a deep personal tragedy. I know the world shares the sorrow that Mrs. Kennedy and her family bear. I will do my best. That is all I can do. I ask for your help—and God's."[33] Like so many other people on this day, he seems lost. A large man, he appears strangely dwarfed by the microphones, the bright lights, the huge plane in the background. From this point forward, he takes a supporting role in the drama of the next three days. His highly visible presidency will not truly begin until John F. Kennedy lies in the soft earth at Arlington National Cemetery. Then, he can step onto center stage and lead.

Yet, change is already sweeping through the White House, where workers are taking all of Kennedy's personal belongings out of the Oval Office. Among the memorable pieces are the rocking chair that eased his back pain, the coconut shell that saved his life when he used it to send a message during his heroics in World War II, the silver calendar that marked the thirteen days of the Cuban Missile Crisis, and photos of the wife and children who lightened his load. By 8:46 p.m., NBC anchorman Chet Huntley reports that all of Kennedy's possessions have been removed.[34] With a total absence of personal items, the room echoes the emptiness that JFK's family and friends feel in their hearts.

When they reach Bethesda on this damp and dreary night, Jackie and Robert Kennedy go directly to a seventeenth-floor hospital VIP suite. Waiting for them are close friends and family members. Those in attendance are shocked by Mrs. Kennedy's appearance. ("There was this totally doomed child, with that God awful skirt, not saying anything, looking burned alive," *Newsweek* reporter and family friend Ben Bradlee later will recount.)[35] Over the hours from early evening, past midnight, and into the wee hours of the morning, she mingles with the others, both being reassured and offering support to others. She spends part of the long night sitting in a tiny kitchen with Robert Kennedy and McNamara. Repeatedly, she tells them what they least want to hear—the gruesome details of her day. Returning to the awful moments seems to ease her burden. In a way, this recitation by the nation's chief mourner mirrors the common phenomenon among members of the general public, who often describe where they were when they heard the news. While Mrs. Kennedy is at the hospital, her young children's nanny, Maude Shaw, delivers the bad news under orders from the widow's mother Janet Auchincloss. Caroline is old enough to have some understanding of her loss, but John, who will turn three on Monday, cannot comprehend the permanent nature of his father's absence.

In Bethesda's morgue, Dr. James J. Humes and Dr. J. Thornton Bosley begin the autopsy. Because the widow is intent on staying at the hospital until her husband's body is ready to go to the White House, a difficult task comes with added pressure to work quickly. Despite years of experience as a pathologist, Humes finds this corpse particularly daunting. With eyes and mouth wide open, fists clenched, and a huge head wound, Kennedy's body is startling.[36] Shortly after the doctors' work gets under way, FBI agents who are witnessing the procedure get a call from Dallas. A new development: A bullet has been found on the gurney that delivered Governor Connally to the emergency room. Humes and Bosley find the late president's head wound is so extensive that they can remove his brain without using a saw to cut through the skull. Examining an entry wound in the back, they are puzzled about the bullet's path. (Later in the morning, Humes will talk to the doctors at Parkland Hospital and learn that there was a wound in Kennedy's throat in the spot where an emergency tracheotomy was performed. This conversation clears up misunderstandings in both hospitals. The Bethesda doctors had been seeking an exit wound that was obscured by a subsequent surgical procedure, and the Dallas doctors, who never examined the president's back, had thought the throat wound indicated a bullet entry instead of an exit.) The autopsy concludes that the president was shot twice from behind and above. When the doctors finish their work, embalming begins.

After all of the work at Bethesda is finished, the widow, family, and friends join a caravan that delivers the late president to the White House for the last time. Upon arrival, the military casket team carries the coffin into the East Room and places it on a catafalque that is a replica of the one used for Abraham Lincoln's coffin. A priest immediately sprinkles the casket with holy water and quotes a psalm. Then, the former first lady and her closest friends discuss whether the casket should be open for the state funeral. The late president's face shows no evidence of the massive head wound that killed him, but Jacqueline Kennedy prefers a closed casket. The body in the casket does not look like her husband. Robert Kennedy, who had avoided seeing his brother's body, looks now, as do several friends. Most believe that the casket should remain closed. Two family members are missing. Younger brother Edward Kennedy, along with his sister, Eunice, are in Hyannis Port, where they will perform the difficult task of telling their elderly father, the victim of a stroke in 1961, that he now has lost three of his nine children.

After getting a bit of rest, Jacqueline Kennedy begins to focus on plans for services and public commemoration. Over the coming days, she will reveal "an unerring feel for the architecture of social ritual," in the words of authors Jay Mulvaney and Paul De Angelis.[37] The gatherings begin with a private mass in the East Room for seventy-five family members and friends on Saturday morning. Late in the morning, Robert and Jacqueline Kennedy enter the East Room, and Secret Service agent Clint Hill closes the doors. McHugh folds back the flag, allowing the late president's widow and brother to put a collection of keepsakes inside the coffin. Among them are newly written letters from Jacqueline, Caroline, and John Jr., a PT-109 tie clip, and two gifts that Mrs. Kennedy had given to her husband —a pair of inlaid gold cufflinks and a carving of the presidential seal in scrimshaw. While the casket is open, Jacqueline takes a lock of her husband's hair.[38] With their private moment now passed, the public mourning begins. Dignitaries start arriving at the White House, where they are greeted by a rotating group of Kennedy family members in the Blue Room. They then proceed through the Green Room to the East Room, where the bier lies. Most pause there before departing. The period of visitation lasts seven long hours.

Sunday dawns a brighter day, with clear skies. At 11:45 a.m. Jacqueline Kennedy, dressed in black with a long black veil, stands at the North Portico of the White House. She grasps Caroline's hand on one side and John's on the other. The protective mother who usually attempts to protect her children from the press now places them front and center. She wants to remind everyone that her husband left behind two small youngsters. Mother and children watch military pallbearers carry JFK's coffin out of the White House and place it on an artillery caisson. Six gray horses pull the caisson onto Pennsylvania Avenue on its way to the Capitol. Military drummers follow, filling the mournful silence with the sound of muffled beats. Behind the caisson is a riderless bay gelding; reversed in its stirrups are a pair of military boots. Last in the procession are ten cars carrying the Kennedy family and others to the Capitol. Mrs. Kennedy and her children ride in the first car with Robert Kennedy, as well as Lyndon and Lady Bird Johnson. At the Capitol, the passengers alight, and an artillery battalion in the distance performs a twenty-one-gun salute. Then, the navy band plays a sentimental arrangement of "Hail to the Chief." The casket team, representing all of the military services, carries the coffin up thirty-seven steps to the great rotunda, where they lower it to the catafalque.

Speaker of the House McCormack, Senate Majority Leader Mike Mansfield, and Chief Justice Earl Warren deliver brief eulogies. McCormack, who, like JFK, hails from Massachusetts, comments on the shock and grief blanketing the nation: "Now that our great leader has been taken from us in a cruel death, we are bound to feel shattered and helpless in the face of our loss . . . but as the first bitter pangs of incredulous grief begins to pass we must thank God that we were privileged, however briefly, to have had this great man for our president."[39] After the speeches, Johnson makes a brief public gesture much like an awkward dance. He steps forward as a soldier walks backward in front of him, carrying a wreath of red and white carnations. The wreath's sash says, "From President Johnson and the Nation." Johnson pauses briefly for silent prayer and fades back into the background.

At this moment, Mrs. Kennedy takes Caroline by the hand and tells her that they are going to kiss "Daddy" goodbye. The two kneel beside the coffin and both kiss the flag draped over it. One of Caroline's hands slips under the flag to touch the casket and perhaps be a bit closer to the father she misses. A public viewing of the casket begins at 3:00 p.m. Six hours later, the widow returns on the arm of brother-in-law, Robert. She again kneels and kisses the coffin. Afterward, the two people most stricken by John F. Kennedy's death take a brief walk on the Capitol grounds. About an hour later, the late president's mother arrives with several other family members to pray beside the casket.

On Monday morning at 10:39 a.m., Jacqueline, Robert, and Edward Kennedy arrive with other family members and friends in a procession of six limousines from the White House. Side by side, the three climb the Capitol steps and kneel beside the casket in prayer. The military pallbearers then lift the coffin and carry it to the caisson, which will take it past the White House and on to St. Matthew's Cathedral. The Marine band and drill units from the four U.S. military academies join the procession followed by the limousines. At the White House, those in the cars disembark and prepare to walk behind the caisson to the cathedral. Dignitaries from the United States and nearly a hundred other nations fall into line behind the Kennedy family for an eight-block walk. Caroline, who will turn six this week, and John, who is celebrating his third birthday today, ride to the church in a limousine. They are dressed in matching powder-blue coats and red lace-up shoes, the same clothes they wore the last time their father saw them.

Jacqueline Kennedy walks between her brothers-in-law at the head of the procession. She looks brave and strong, heartbroken and defiant. Jacqueline, Robert, and Edward Kennedy all seem terribly stoic and terribly young. (Robert, who just turned 37, is the eldest of the three.) Leaders of the Secret Service and agencies protecting visiting dignitaries cringe at the idea of so many important people walking openly in the street. Nevertheless, the widow has been adamant about walking to the cathedral. With her in the lead, national and international leaders feel compelled to follow. (Only the elderly, such as former presidents Harry Truman and Dwight Eisenhower, feel free to ride to the church.) Fifteen feet behind Mrs. Kennedy is Lyndon Johnson. Others in the procession are the Soviet Union's Deputy Premier Anastas Mikoyan, Great Britain's Prince Philip, France's General Charles de Gaulle, Ethiopia's Emperor Haile Selassie, United Nations Secretary-General U Thant, and many more.

Richard Cardinal Cushing greets the family when the procession reaches the church. The pallbearers carry the coffin up the cathedral steps. Cushing delivers a eulogy and celebrates a low Mass. After the singing of *Ave Maria*, Mrs. Kennedy begins to cry. Her small daughter tries to comfort her, and Hill hands the grieving widow a handkerchief. More than a thousand people fill the church. Among them are many family members, friends, American politicians, foreign dignitaries, Martin Luther King Jr., and Judge Sarah Hughes.

After the hour-long service ends and as the Kennedys prepare to enter limousines for the ride to Arlington National Cemetery, the military band plays "Hail to the Chief" to honor President Kennedy for the last time. Remembering how her son loves to play soldier, Mrs. Kennedy leans down and tells him: "John, you can salute Daddy now and say goodbye to him." The boy steps forward sharply and raises his right hand in a nearly perfect salute to the flag-draped coffin. For some onlookers, the sight is almost too much to bear.[40] Now, the cortege begins its last journey. A long line of limousines follows the rattle of the caisson, the hoofbeats of the riderless horse, and the haunting whispers of the deadened drums.

As the late president's casket nears its final resting place, Air Force bagpipers wail. Fifty jet fighters, one representing each state, fly overhead in a "V" with a gap to honor the missing man, JFK. Then, Air Force One soars above the mourners at an altitude of only 500 feet and dips its wings. Cardinal Cushing recites a final prayer, and three cannons fire a twenty-one-gun salute. A bugler plays taps. When one note cracks, the sad farewell takes on an added bit of poignancy. Soldiers remove the flag from the casket, fold it, and present it to Mrs. Kennedy. Now, the former First Lady and her two brothers-in-law light an eternal flame, marking the place where John F. Kennedy rests.

After the funeral, Mrs. Kennedy meets with heads of state at the White House, while her son celebrates his third birthday with his nanny and older sister. Around midnight, Robert Kennedy asks Jacqueline, "Should we go visit a friend?" With Secret Service protection, but without the knowledge of the media, the grief-stricken brother and widow cross the Potomac to reach the late president's burial site. Groundskeepers open the gates for them. Once inside, she places flowers on his grave and kneels to pray. Gleaming in the darkness, the vibrant flame is an echo of the spark of life lost on the streets of Dallas.

A TALE OF TWO GUNMEN

Minutes after the president's shooting on Friday afternoon, police and Secret Service agents begin collecting pieces of the assassination puzzle. Several witnesses, including *Dallas Times Herald* photographer Bob Jackson and a local TV reporter, Mel Crouch, report seeing a man with a rifle in one of the upper floors of the Texas School Book Depository, and they provide a partial description. Nature, too, testifies to the likelihood that the shots came from this building: Pigeons on or around the building took flight en masse as the shots were fired. Roy Truly, the building's manager, immediately offers his assistance to Officer Marion L. Baker. The two men begin climbing the stairs to the upper floors of the seven-story warehouse. After passing the second floor, Truly notices that Baker is no longer with him. He retraces his steps and finds Baker holding employee Lee Oswald at gunpoint. Truly verifies that Oswald works there, and Baker sets him free. Soon, officers flood into the building. Oswald chooses to leave and begins circuitous travels through the streets of Dallas. Ten minutes after the shooting, at around 12:40 p.m. Central Standard Time, Oswald takes a seat on a city bus, which makes little headway in congested traffic. After about four minutes, Oswald leaves the bus. He walks to the Greyhound bus station and takes a cab to a corner several blocks from the rooming house where he is staying under the name of O.H. Lee. Oswald walks to the rooming house, picks up a revolver and a jacket, and departs on foot.

Police at the Book Depository find no evidence of a gunman on the roof or on the seventh floor. Soon after an exploration of the sixth floor begins, an officer finds a sniper's nest near the building's southeast corner.

The Biography of Lee Harvey Oswald

Lee Harvey Oswald was the youngest of Marguerite Oswald's three sons. His father, insurance premium collector Robert Edward Lee Oswald, died two months before his birth in New Orleans on October 18, 1939. As a boy, he had an especially strong attachment to his mother, but she had little time for him. She changed jobs and moved often. She frequently asked her sister, Lillian Murrett, and others to care for Lee for long periods of time. When Lee was 2 years old, she put his brother, Robert Oswald, and his half-brother, John Pic, in a New Orleans orphan asylum called Bethlehem Children's Home. The institution would not accept children as young as Lee, but when he was a year older she placed him there, too. He remained in the asylum for a little over a year.

By January 1944, Marguerite Oswald was planning to marry for the third time and to move to Dallas with her new husband, Edwin Eckdahl. Of her sons, she took only Lee with her. Shortly after arriving in Dallas, she apparently changed her mind about marrying Eckdahl, but in June, John and Robert left the orphanage and joined their mother and brother in Dallas. Mrs. Oswald tried unsuccessfully to return the two older sons to the Children's Home in February 1945. She married Eckdahl in May of that year and sent John and Robert to Chamberlain-Hunt Military Academy in Port Gibson, Mississippi. In the summer of 1946, she broke off her marriage to Eckdahl, picked up John and Robert, and moved to Covington, Louisiana, with all three sons. About six months later, she moved the family to Fort Worth, where she briefly reconciled with Eckdahl. Soon afterward, the couple engaged in messy divorce proceedings that required Mrs. Oswald's young sons to testify.

Since the family often had cramped living spaces, Lee shared a bed with his mother until he was almost 11. According to friends and relatives, he was a loud, demanding child. He had a relatively high IQ but sometimes struggled in school, apparently because he suffered from a learning disability. People who knew him considered him to be a withdrawn boy with no close friends. By August 1952, John and Robert had both left school to join the military. Subsequently, Mrs. Oswald and Lee moved to New York, where they lived in Manhattan, Brooklyn, and the Bronx at various times over a period of less than two years. During that time, Lee's behavior became a problem. After a record of truancy, he and his mother were called into court. For a while, Lee lived in a facility for truant youths and underwent psychological evaluations. His doctors believed that he needed regular psychiatric care, but his mother disagreed. Following months of court appearances, she took Lee to New Orleans in 1954. At 16, Lee dropped out of school and tried to join the Marines, but he quickly learned that the Marines would not accept him until he was at least 17. He spent the next ten months doing various clerical and delivery jobs in New Orleans and began reading Communist literature. After that, he moved with his mother to Fort Worth, where he began the tenth grade but dropped out in October, when his seventeenth birthday occurred.

He joined the Marine Corps on October 26, 1956 at the Marine Corps Recruit Depot in San Diego, but he was not prepared for the regimented nature of military service. He reacted badly to taking orders and faced two courts-martial as well as a host of smaller scrapes with authority during his three years of service as a private. He worked as a radar operator and, during part of his tour of duty, he was stationed in the Philippines and Japan, where he may have had access to valuable intelligence information. In addition, he qualified as a sharpshooter with an M-1 rifle. While serving in the Marines, Lee freely voiced his sympathy for the Soviet Union, and that made him memorable to fellow Marines. In September 1959, he got an early honorable discharge after claiming that he needed to care for his mother. He would now be free from daily orders, but he would be required to serve in the Marine Corps Reserve.

After visiting his mother for only three days, Lee told her that he was going to get a job in shipping or in the import/export industry. He immediately left on a transatlantic voyage. He sailed to France, proceeded to Finland and, from there, to the Soviet Union, where he hoped to become a citizen. Soviet officials were suspicious of him and reluctant to grant him citizenship. Consequently, he was told that his visa had expired and that he had to leave. Oswald responded by slitting his left arm above the wrist. Once discovered, he was placed in a psychiatric ward for three days. Later, he went to the U.S. Embassy, turned over his passport, and tried to dissolve his U.S. citizenship. A couple of wire service reporters interviewed him about his actions, and articles about him appeared in American newspapers. Nevertheless, Soviet officials remained wary and left his status in limbo until January 4, 1960, when he was given an identity document for a "stateless person" and was ordered to work in a Minsk assembly plant, the Belarusian Radio and Television Factory. Oswald found the job boring and, once again trapped in a regimented lifestyle, he was confrontational with coworkers. His Russian, which had been elementary, improved as he interacted with people who found it fascinating to talk to an American who had chosen to live in the Soviet Union. Because Oswald was in the Soviet Union and unavailable to complete his promised service in the Marine Corps Reserve, his honorable discharge was revoked, and in its place he received an undesirable discharge, one notch above a dishonorable discharge.

A year after receiving the designation of "stateless" person, the passport office in Minsk contacted Oswald and asked whether he still wanted to become a citizen. Oswald, then in the aftermath of a failed romance, said that he no longer wanted citizenship, but he asked that his temporary residence permit be extended. He contacted the U.S. Embassy in Moscow during February 1961 to request the return of his U.S. passport. The Embassy responded, telling him that he would have to appear in person in Moscow. A month later, Oswald's life changed when he met the beautiful, 19-year-old Marina Prusakova. They were married just weeks later on April 30. Soon, Oswald contacted the U.S. Embassy asking for his passport and seeking approval for his wife to enter the United States. Most importantly, he wanted assurances that he would not face prosecution if he returned to the United States. On February 15, 1962, while the Oswalds still awaited word about entry into the

United States, their first child, June Lee, was born. In May, they finally received all of the proper travel documents, and, after getting a $435.71 loan from the State Department, they paid for transportation to take them from the Soviet Union to the United States.

When they reached the United States, the Oswalds lived in Fort Worth, first with his brother, Robert, and later with his mother. Then, they moved into their own apartment. On more than one occasion, FBI agents interviewed Oswald about his three years in the Soviet Union, and over the years they spoke with his wife, as well. In Dallas–Fort Worth, the Oswalds found a thriving Russian community, and these new friends especially welcomed Marina Oswald, leading to a growing rift between husband and wife. Lee physically abused her.

On April 10, 1963, Oswald took a mail-ordered rifle he had bought from Klein's Sporting Goods in Chicago and tried to shoot General Edwin Walker, a leader in right-wing political activities in Dallas. His shot missed, and within a couple of weeks he was on a bus headed for New Orleans with his family. He got a job in a coffee factory there and apparently constituted the entire membership of the local chapter of Fair Play for Cuba. He handed out literature for the organization on the streets and took part in two radio discussions about Cuba.

In September, Marina returned to Fort Worth to live with Ruth Paine and her children. Later that same month, Oswald went to Mexico City, where he tried to get visas to both Cuba and the Soviet Union, but both embassies denied his requests. On October 2, he returned to Dallas. Eighteen days later, Marina gave birth to their second daughter, Rachel, at Parkland Hospital in Dallas. Marina and her daughters lived with Paine in Irving, while Lee lived in a Dallas rooming house. He had started a new job as a clerk at the Texas School Book Depository on October 15 for $1.25 an hour. Typically, Oswald went to Irving to spend the weekends with his family. Each time, he got a ride from Buell Wesley Frazier, a coworker who lived near the Paines. On Friday, November 15, Oswald did not follow his usual schedule: Because the Paines were having a birthday celebration, Marina suggested that he stay in Dallas for the weekend. On November 18, Lee and Marina had an argument over the phone when she discovered that he was living in Dallas under an alias. Three days later, Oswald altered his schedule again. This time, he asked Frazier to take him to Irving on Thursday, November 21. His arrival was a surprise to his wife. The next morning, he left his wallet containing $170 and his wedding ring in Marina's bedroom. When he met Frazier for the ride into work, he was carrying something inside a long brown paper bag. Oswald told Frazier that the package was nothing special—just curtain rods to decorate his room in the rooming house. What Oswald actually carried to work that day was his rifle.

After shooting President Kennedy, Oswald was quickly arrested, and he was murdered himself two days later by Jack Ruby. As a man who enjoyed attracting attention to himself, he might be pleased to know that he made his mark in history in two ways that weekend—by assassinating the president and by being the first person slain on live TV.

Boxes are stacked to conceal the gunman and to support the rifle barrel. Three spent cartridges are found, but no gun is visible. Following a search of about fifteen minutes, an officer spots the rifle nestling in a crevice between boxes. It has one unspent round in the chamber. Police also find a brown paper bag big enough to conceal a disassembled rifle. Three Book Depository employees report hearing a gun fired and cartridges ejected from a floor above their perch on the fifth floor, directly under the sniper's nest.

Patrolling by car, Officer J.D. Tippit sees Oswald traipsing down Beckley Street and notices that he matches the general description of the assassin. Within minutes, eyewitnesses see Tippit stop, and they watch as Oswald walks over to the car, leaning on the passenger-side window ledge as he speaks to the officer. Then, Tippit gets out of his patrol car with his hand on his gun. Immediately, Oswald pulls a revolver from his pocket and shoots Tippit repeatedly. A female witness screams, and Oswald stares at her before walking away. Other witnesses see him clearing the cartridges from his gun. A used-car-lot manager hears the gunshots and then sees Oswald coming from the same direction. He asks Oswald what is happening, and Oswald responds by saying something unintelligible. A neighborhood resident rushes toward the sound of gunfire and sees Tippit lying on the sidewalk on top of his gun. Another bystander uses the squad car radio to report Tippit's shooting. Picked up by an ambulance, Tippit is dead on arrival at Methodist Hospital. In crosschecking descriptions of the presidential assassin and the man who shot Tippit, police realize that they could fit the same man.

By now, Roy Truly at the Book Depository realizes that he is missing a single employee: Oswald. He gives police access to Oswald's personnel record, which contains his description, telephone number, and address. Captain John William Fritz returns to police headquarters in Dallas's City Hall with plans to track down Oswald. At the same time, police begin rushing into the neighborhood where Tippit was attacked. Oswald hears sirens and steps into Hardy's Shoe Store just as several police cars pass. After police have proceeded past the shop, Oswald walks out the door and onto the sidewalk again. Curious about this quick visitor, the store's manager, Johnny C. Brewer, follows him. Brewer sees Oswald slip into the Texas Theatre without buying a ticket. A double feature is playing, *Cry of Battle* and *War is Hell*. Brewer consults with a ticket-taker, who decides to call the police while Brewer and the concessionaire watch the exit doors. Police race to the scene a little over a half-mile from where Tippit was shot. Under police orders, theater employees bring up the house lights, and Oswald quickly moves to a different row. Hidden by the stage curtain, Brewer points out Oswald to the police. Two officers then step from behind the curtain and march up the left center aisle. They pretend to suspect other audience members, but eventually officers manage to encircle Oswald. His immediate response is, "Well, it's all over now."[41] Oswald strikes one officer and pulls his gun, but he is brought under control after a brief melee that leaves him visibly battered and bruised. As they push Oswald into a car, police discover that his gun is fully loaded. In his pockets, they find two IDs—one says Lee Harvey Oswald; the other, A.J. Hidell. When the arresting officers take Oswald to police headquarters, Fritz is surprised to learn that the man they have brought in is the same one missing from the Book Depository. Slightly more than an hour after Kennedy was declared dead, Fritz begins interrogating the 24-year-old Oswald.

Meanwhile, in the Dallas FBI office, Oswald's arrest sets off alarm bells. Agent James Hosty has been watching Oswald and his Russian wife since their arrival in the Dallas area more than a year ago. Oswald's three-year sojourn as a wannabe Soviet citizen makes him subject to suspicion that he is working for Soviet intelligence, but Hosty and others who have spoken to both Marina and Lee Oswald believe that he is mentally ill. Unfortunately, no one at the FBI told the Secret Service that Oswald was in Dallas. Now, the truth about Oswald will raise questions about the FBI's failure to share critical information that might have saved Kennedy's life.

Recognizing the importance of getting a look at the 8mm color film shot by Zapruder on Dealey Plaza, the Secret Service asks him for a copy. He agrees, but the challenge is getting the film copied quickly. Agent Forrest Sorrels learns that Eastman Kodak Company at Love Field can develop the film immediately, so he and Zapruder climb into a police car and head to the airport. It is already clear that the garment factory owner's film will provide crucial evidence.

Police officers reach Oswald's boarding house between 3 p.m. and 4 p.m. As they step in the door, a woman runs up to the landlady to tell her that "Lee" is on TV being taken into police headquarters. The landlady looks at the image on the screen and identifies the man as O.H. Lee, one of her roomers. Police, who do not have a search warrant, look at Oswald's room, which is a tiny, closet-like space with little room for personal belongings. In the Dallas suburb of Irving, other officers question his wife, Marina. She and her two tiny daughters are living with a friend, Ruth Paine. Mrs. Oswald, who speaks little English, admits that her husband owns a rifle, which is kept in the garage under a blanket. A detective finds the blanket with no rifle swaddled within it.

Oswald's interrogation is ongoing. With Hosty now in the room, Oswald denies killing anyone, and he confronts Hosty about harassing his wife. At the time of the assassination, he claims, he was eating in a warehouse lunchroom. He tells police that he left work under the assumption that nothing would be done this afternoon. He admits to picking up some things from his room before going to the movie, but he has no explanation for his decision to take a pistol to the theater. Fritz grills him about his experiences in the Soviet Union between 1959 and 1962, and seeks information on a more recent trip to Mexico City, where Oswald unsuccessfully sought visas to the Soviet Union and Cuba. When Fritz decides to take a break, Secret Service agent Sorrels asks whether he can question Oswald. Very early in the interview, Oswald asks whether he is supposed to have an attorney, and Sorrels says he is not. Sorrels questions Oswald about his time abroad. Oswald cryptically describes his mundane years as a factory worker in Minsk. Oswald is a cipher to his interrogators: At times withdrawn and evasive, he seems emotionless; in other situations, he babbles propaganda and behaves like a defiant adolescent; and, at odd intervals, he startles his questioners by banging his fists into the table.

A mid-afternoon press conference by two surgeons at Parkland Hospital contributes to the muddle of information. Dr. Clark and Dr. Perry attempt to describe the medical procedures undertaken to save President Kennedy, but they cannot answer many of the reporters' questions, which focus on the number of bullet wounds and the direction from which the bullets were fired. Parkland doctors simply did not examine the president's body that closely. Despite their declaration that they are not sure about the direction of the gunfire, Perry does suggest the throat injury was an entrance wound. Immediately, the press embraces the idea that at least one bullet was fired from the area in front of Kennedy.

By 4 p.m. Central Standard Time, the national broadcast media identify Oswald by name and report details of his attempt to establish Soviet citizenship in 1959. Despite growing national attention to Oswald and anticipated threats against him, the Dallas police follow established policy and place few restrictions on the growing mob of journalists on the third floor of City Hall. In fact, the police make only a superficial effort to check press credentials. Just hours after the assassination, District Attorney Wade declares the case solved, telling reporters that the police have found about fifteen witnesses. He reports that there are no suspects other than Oswald and that Oswald is mentally competent. When asked whether Oswald has legal representation, Wade claims ignorance.

Oswald's mother, Marguerite, leaves for work as a nurse's aide

> As he watched events unfold in Washington, Assistant Attorney General Nicholas Katzenbach feared that, even if Oswald was convicted, the case might be thrown out of court because the Dallas authorities were dashing to conclusions and attempting to try Oswald outside the courtroom without making sure that he had access to legal counsel.

and hears on the radio that her son has been arrested. She calls the *Fort Worth Star-Telegram* and asks for a ride to Dallas. The newspaper's night police reporter, future CBS News correspondent Bob Schieffer, is confused and tells her that the newspaper does not provide taxi service. Then, she makes him understand that she is the mother of the suspect in Kennedy's assassination. The newspaper's auto editor has a Cadillac that he is reviewing for his weekly "road test" column. He offers that car to take Marguerite Oswald to Dallas. Schieffer and Mrs. Oswald ride together in the back seat, and Schieffer interviews her as they head toward the Dallas police station. She tells him that she is sorry about what happened to the president, and she is sure no one will feel sorry for her. She predicts (correctly) that people will sympathize with Lee's wife Marina, but no one is likely to give her any money.[42] (Later, Mrs. Oswald reportedly will try to sell her story to *Life* magazine. Though they agree to pay her food and hotel charges, the editors refuse to pay for an interview.)[43]

As Oswald is moved from the interrogation room to stand in a lineup, he must pass through a third-floor hallway packed tightly with perhaps as many as three hundred journalists. Desperate reporters shout questions at Oswald as photographers and TV cameramen struggle to get new images for their audiences. The atmosphere is unmitigated chaos. One reporter manages to get Oswald's attention by asking whether he shot the president. "No, sir," he replies cavalierly. "Nobody charged me with that."[44] To the TV audience at home, Oswald is hard to read. In a way, he seems more like a young smart aleck than a madman, and yet, what sane man would act so unconcerned when suspected of murdering the president? In the lineup room, Oswald is positively identified by the woman who screamed when Tippit was killed. At about the same time, detectives show up at Oswald's rooming house with a search warrant. They find a great deal of left-wing political literature, a Russian passport with Oswald's photo, and his undesirable discharge from the U.S. Marines.

In the early evening, Marina Oswald reaches police headquarters. Fritz wants to show her the rifle found at the Book Depository. The gun, which has not yet been fully examined for fingerprints, is transported to her location by having a policeman hold it high over his head as he squeezes through the third-floor hallway madhouse. She says it looks like her husband's gun, but she is not sure. Oswald again must wade through the crowd of reporters to get to the lineup room. In all, he will run this gauntlet sixteen times in less than forty-eight hours.[45] In a new lineup, two employees of the used-car lot identify him and later confirm that he was wearing a jacket found in a gas station parking lot along his apparent route. Before 7:00 p.m., police believe they have sufficient evidence to charge Oswald with Tippit's murder. They call a justice of the peace to arraign him.

The Biography of Jack Ruby

Originally named Jacob Rubenstein, Jack Ruby entered the world in March 1911. His exact birthdate is unknown, and there are several gaps in his biography. He grew up in a rough-and-tumble neighborhood on the west side of Chicago. He was the fifth of his parents' eight living children. His father was an alcoholic, and his mother spent time in a mental institution. When Jack was 11, he was placed in foster care along with his younger brothers and sister. A psychiatric report on him said that he was temperamental and disobedient. He often responded angrily when people made derogatory remarks because his family was Jewish. He spent several years in foster homes before eventually returning to his mother's home. At that point, his parents were living separately. His mother began undergoing treatment for mental problems again in 1927, and she was in and out of mental hospitals in the 1930s. Ruby apparently attended school through the eighth grade, after having repeated the third grade. There is no record that he attended high school, although he claimed to have completed at least one year.

When he was young, he got in trouble with police because of ticket scalping, but the charges were dropped. In about 1933, he moved to San Francisco, where he remained for several years. While he was there, he sold newspaper subscriptions and a horse-racing tip sheet. After his return to Chicago, he was out of work for a while and seemed to make ends meet by working as a hustler, scalping tickets and buying items such as watches for resale on the street. From 1937 to 1940, he was employed by Local 20467 of the Scrap Iron and Junk Handlers Union. Ruby's union work may have brought him into contact with Chicago's mob.

During World War II, he sold plaques commemorating Franklin Roosevelt's "Day of Infamy" speech made after the Japanese attacked Pearl Harbor on December 7, 1941. That was the first tangible evidence of his interest in American presidents. One acquaintance described him as "a cuckoo nut on the subject of patriotism" during World War II.[46] He sold busts of FDR and held a variety of other jobs. He was drafted into the U.S. Army Air Forces in May 1943, but served solely at U.S. bases until his discharge in 1946. A year later, he went into business with two of his brothers. They manufactured small products, such as key chains, salt and pepper shakers, and bottle openers. Within about a year, Jack and his brother Hyman left the business, and his brother Earl became the sole owner. At about that time, Earl, Hyman, and Jack all took steps to legally change their last names to Ruby. Jack decided to move to Dallas late in 1947 to help one of his sisters run the Singapore Supper Club. Before and after he moved to Dallas, the Ruby family had contact with Paul Roland Jones, who was reportedly a former Chicago gangster subsequently convicted of trying to bribe the newly elected sheriff in Dallas and of violating federal narcotics statutes there.

During his years in Dallas, nightclub operations represented Ruby's most consistent source of income. He managed several clubs over the years, and in 1959 he became a partner in ownership of the Sovereign, which was later renamed the

Carousel Club. In addition to maintaining his friendship with Jones when he moved to Dallas, Ruby had other contacts with the underworld, and one of his nightclub partners had a criminal record. There were rumors that Ruby, who never married but dated one woman for eleven years, was gay. Ruby was no stranger to violence. During his years in Dallas, he was known to have beaten other men on several occasions, but there is no evidence that he had ever used firearms to resolve disputes.

After shooting Lee Harvey Oswald, he cooperated with police. As he faced trial for murdering Oswald, he hired famed California lawyer Melvin Belli to lead his defense team. Sitting on the bench was Judge Joe B. Brown, a graduate of an already-defunct law school. In December, Brown refused to set bail for Ruby and, on February 13, Brown rejected Belli's plea for a change of venue. Ruby's trial began on Valentine's Day 1964 with jury selection, which lasted twelve days. Belli's defense strategy was to claim that Ruby suffered from brain damage. "He was like an old-time fighter who had his brains scrambled," Belli later said.[47] Among the witnesses for Ruby were strippers with the stage names of Little Lynn and Penny Dollar. The prosecution, led by District Attorney Henry Wade, portrayed Ruby as a man who killed Oswald in the misguided belief that he would become a hero. Following eight days of testimony, the case went to the jury, which deliberated only two hours and nineteen minutes before convicting Ruby of murder. The jury recommended that Ruby be executed by electric chair. The Texas Court of Criminal Appeals reversed his conviction in 1966, concluding that Ruby should have received a change of venue. A new trial was scheduled for February 1967 in Wichita Falls, Texas, and for that trial Ruby had assembled a new defense team. However, Ruby never got his second chance. He died of cancer at Parkland Hospital on January 3, 1967.

At 7:50 p.m., two more witnesses in the Tippit case recognize Oswald in the lineup. A frightened Howard L. Brennan, who saw a gunman aim at Kennedy, says that he cannot positively identify any of the men but that Oswald looks the most like the gunman he saw. (Later, Brennan will tell the Warren Commission that he knew Oswald was the gunman but was afraid that identifying him might bring some kind of retribution, if there had been a conspiracy.) When led through the maelstrom of journalists again, Oswald exclaims, "I'm just a patsy!"[48]

Among those mixing with the journalists on the third floor tonight is a strip club owner named Jack Ruby, a familiar figure to police. He has brought sandwiches for the denizens of this overpopulated work area. When Ike Pappas, a reporter for New York's WNEW Radio, needs a phone to call his office, Ruby asks Wade to find a phone for Pappas, and the district attorney offers his office, telling Ruby to take Pappas there, where he can use Wade's own phone.[49]

Later in the evening, the FBI asks that Oswald's rifle, pistol, and other pieces of evidence be turned over to agents in Dallas for shipment to Washington. Oswald's mother reaches police headquarters, and, as camera flashes temporarily blind her, she tells reporters that her son is a "good boy." At 11:30 p.m., Fritz orders an arrest warrant for Oswald in the murder of Kennedy.

Police have promised the press a good look at Oswald, but Fritz tells Curry that he is worried about Oswald's safety when they put him on display in the assembly room. Curry ignores Fritz's concerns, and Oswald is taken in front of the roiling swarm, where he stands for photographs. Reporters yell questions at him, but he says only what he wants to say. Jack Ruby, who has a gun in his pocket, is one of the people on hand when Oswald tells reporters that he is being denied legal representation. Questioned about the suspect, Wade tells reporters that he does not believe Oswald is "a nut." Curry informs the journalists about Oswald's collection of Communist literature—and says the FBI knew that Oswald was in Dallas. Later, the FBI demands and gets a retraction.

After leaving police headquarters, Ruby decides to close his operations, the Carousel Club and the Vegas Club, for the weekend. The club owner, later described as being depressed by Kennedy's slaying, stops by KLIF Radio and proffers a big bag of corned beef sandwiches to the employees. He chats with reporters and is pleased when he gets credit for a tip in the 2:00 a.m. report. Later, Ruby visits the *Dallas Times Herald* to order a black-bordered advertisement notifying the public that his strip clubs will be closed for the weekend.

Poring over records in the middle of the night, Mitchell Scibor and William Waldman of Klein's Sporting Goods in Chicago find important evidence for eager FBI agents. They discover a record that the weapon used against Kennedy was purchased from their mail-order operation by A. Hidell (one of Oswald's aliases) and mailed to an address in Dallas. The weapon cost $19.95, plus $1.50 for shipping and handling.[50]

The next morning, *Life* magazine regional editor Richard Stolley goes to Zapruder's garment factory because he wants to buy rights to the assassination film. When he arrives at 8:00 a.m., two Secret Service agents are there to view the film, so Stolley watches it with them. He is startled by the images of Kennedy responding to the first wound and by the visible impact of the fatal shot. Other companies try to bid on the film, but Zapruder sells the print rights to *Life* for $50,000, about $350,000 in 2009 dollars.[51]

Under questioning Saturday morning, Oswald assures Fritz that "I have no views on the president." He adds: "My wife and I like the president's family. They are interesting people."[52] Law enforcement officials are planning to move Oswald to the county jail, but details of the transfer remain undetermined. At one point, he yells to the press corps: "They're holding me because I was in the Soviet Union. The police won't let me have representation!"[53]

In the early afternoon, reporters ask Wade whether he expects to call Jacqueline Kennedy or Connally to testify in Oswald's trial. He says that is unlikely and predicts that the case will go to trial as early as mid-January. Wade is a recurring visitor to police headquarters over the weekend and speaks freely to reporters. Some of what he discusses is trial evidence that typically does not dribble out in daily news reports. Some of his "revelations" are either wrong, such as his description of the rifle as a Mauser, or unproven, such as his assertion that Oswald had been practicing to improve his marksmanship. Curry, too, becomes a frequent source of misinformation.

Saturday afternoon, Ruby offers to cover Oswald's transfer as an amateur reporter for KLIF Radio. An on-air announcer agrees, but the arrangement is informal. Ruby has no press credentials; nevertheless, he obviously has no trouble getting in and out of police headquarters. Incorrect reports say Oswald will be moved this afternoon.

As she visits her husband, Marina Oswald can feel two photos that she has hidden in her shoes. They show Oswald holding the rifle used to kill Kennedy. She does not know that police have found the photo negatives and more prints among the Oswalds' belongings at the Paine house. In addition, police retrieve an ad for Klein's Sporting Goods. Later today, Secret Service agents move Marguerite and Marina Oswald, as well as Marina's two daughters, from hotel to hotel because of difficulty guaranteeing their anonymity and safety.

Another witness in the Tippit case and the cab driver who drove Oswald from the Greyhound bus station both identify him after he causes an uproar, claiming that the other men in the lineup are actually teenagers, not easily confused with a man in his mid twenties. At 4:22 p.m., Oswald calls Paine and asks her to try to reach a New York lawyer named John Abt. She tries but is unable to contact Abt, who happens to be out of town. Shortly before 6:00 p.m., the president of the Dallas Bar Association, H. Louis Nichols, arrives at police headquarters to ask Oswald whether he wants legal representation. Oswald is not interested in hiring a Dallas attorney. He tells Nichols that he is trying to hire Abt. Upon his departure, Nichols tells the press that Oswald seems rational and that he has rejected legal representation by anyone except the elusive Mr. Abt.

At 6:15 p.m., a justice of the peace files a formal complaint against Oswald for assault with intent to murder John Connally. Shortly afterward, Oswald is confronted with the photos showing him holding the murder weapon. He claims that his face has been superimposed on someone else's body—not an impossible task in 1963, but a difficult one to carry off flawlessly.

Curry notifies the press that the FBI has located the purchase order for the rifle in Chicago and that an FBI handwriting expert has matched the writing on the order form with Oswald's. That same evening, another key match is found: The handwriting on the postal money order paying for the weapon belongs to Oswald as well, according to a Treasury Department expert. Other evidence released today includes a paraffin test indicating that Oswald may have fired a gun before his arrest and an Oswald palm print found on a box in the sniper's nest. Despite these successes, Fritz becomes frustrated with Oswald's obvious unwillingness to admit his guilt and ends another interrogation session by sending him back to his cell. When Oswald again feels the crush of jittery journalists, he denies any acts of violence.

At 2:30 a.m. on Sunday, November 24, an anonymous source calls Dallas's FBI office and predicts that Oswald will be killed; the sheriff's department receives a similar threat. At 5:15 a.m., the sheriff's department urges that Oswald be moved to the county jail immediately, but police take no immediate action. About four hours later, Curry sets into motion a plan for the police department to move Oswald in an armored car. Captain Cecil Talbert orders a security sweep of the basement garage, where Oswald will be loaded into a vehicle. He brings in extra police squads and insists that the garage be stocked with tear-gas grenades to stop a potential mob that might form spontaneously and attack Oswald. Officers are assigned to guard all doors and the entrance ramp. In final questioning before Oswald's transfer, Fritz asks him about the package that he took to work on Friday morning. (According to Book Depository employee Buell Wesley Frazier, who drove Oswald to work on that day, he was carrying something covered in brown paper. Oswald said the package held curtain rods for his room, but police believe the rifle was inside.) As they press Oswald, Fritz and his men recognize a new inconsistency in his story. Now, he says he was on a higher floor of the warehouse when the shooting occurred—not in the first-floor lunchroom. Nevertheless, he continues to proclaim his innocence. In all, Oswald has undergone about twelve hours of interrogation since his arrest.

Fritz decides to use the armored car as a decoy and to transport Oswald in an unmarked police car. Nervous about violence, Fritz urges Curry to oust TV cameras and lights from the garage, but Curry refuses. Just as Fritz's men are ready to move him to the garage, Oswald asks for something to wear over his T-shirt, and he dons a holey, tattered black sweater that police took from his rooming house. At 11:19 a.m., Detective James

Leavelle handcuffs himself to Oswald as an added security measure. By this time, an angry mob is forming outside the county jail, awaiting Oswald's arrival there.

Ruby goes to the Western Union office to wire money to one of his strippers. He waits patiently in line and, after he wires a $25 money order, he strolls a long block on Main Street and walks into the City Hall garage, either via the Main Street entrance ramp or through an unlocked door along an alley. No one challenges him. Oswald and his guards ride an elevator to the basement and pass through an office area before proceeding into the garage.

"Here he comes!" someone yells as they step into view.[54] Reporters hustle for position to ask Oswald questions. Police have told journalists to stand against a railing, but like a tidal wave they surge forward. The officers escorting Oswald find that they are virtually blinded by the bright lights and have difficulty seeing the people in front of them. At 11:21 a.m., Ruby steps out of the crowd and shoots Oswald once in the abdomen with a Colt .38-caliber, snub-nose revolver. There is a mad scuffle as reporters try to cover the crime and police struggle to restrain the gunman, whom they soon recognize as Ruby. The crowd of journalists appears to be out of control. Oswald doubles over in pain. As soon as police seize Ruby's gun, they extricate both Oswald and Ruby from the crowd and, in the void created by their removal, reporters start to interview each other about what they just witnessed.

The TV networks have been covering the assassination story and national mourning non-stop since the shooting. NBC captures Oswald's murder live, and millions of shocked Americans witness the crime. NBC Reporter Tom Pettit describes the scene: "He's been shot! He's been shot! He's been shot! Lee Oswald has been shot! There's a man with a gun. There's absolute panic, absolute panic here in the basement of the Dallas police headquarters. Detectives have their guns drawn. Oswald has been shot. There's no question about it. Oswald has been shot. Pandemonium has broken loose here in the basement of the Dallas police headquarters."[55] When the shooting occurs, CBS is covering events in Washington, but the network quickly puts its local affiliate's footage on the air. ABC had sent its cameraman ahead to the county jail to film Oswald's arrival there. The only action at the county jail occurs when Sheriff Bill Decker tells the waiting crowd that Oswald has been shot. The mob erupts in jubilation. Cheering and applause celebrate the latest act of violence.

Despite confusion in the garage area, the transport caravan is moved out of the way quickly, and an ambulance picks up Oswald. He is taken to Parkland Hospital, where he is treated in Trauma Room 2 before being transported to an operating room. He dies in surgery at 1:07 p.m.—almost exactly forty-eight hours after Kennedy died in the same hospital. (NBC News, which is covering ceremonies in the great rotunda of the Capitol, waits until that event has ended before announcing Oswald's death.)

Almost immediately after the shooting, police begin questioning Ruby, who is surprisingly open. He says that he acted because he wanted to guarantee that Jacqueline Kennedy would not have to testify in Oswald's murder trial. He tells officers that he has been in tremendous turmoil since the assassination and that he acted impulsively when he saw Oswald looking smug as he entered the garage. He considers himself a patriot. Many Americans, including President Johnson, suspect that Ruby killed Oswald to stop him from revealing details of a conspiracy to kill Kennedy. Ironically, while Ruby may have wanted to bring an end to the chain of events set off by the assassination, his own actions become the gasoline that feeds smoldering suspicions of a conspiracy and makes the assassination a continuing story, even a half-century later.

Secret Service agents, fearing attempts on the lives of Oswald's wife and mother, move them again, this time to the home of his brother Robert's in-laws. As the agents hustle to move Oswald's family, Dallas's FBI office is seeking to keep another secret: The FBI has a file on Ruby as a potential criminal informant. The file is thin because it is the record of a single agent's efforts to develop a relationship with Ruby and the collapse of those efforts when the FBI transferred that agent to another city. The Ruby file holds four pieces of paper, one of which is misfiled and has nothing to do with the nightclub owner, but revelation of this secret still has the potential to raise questions about FBI involvement with Ruby. Consequently, Kenneth C. Howe, a supervisor in the Dallas office, decides to keep this news quiet.

On Monday, police move Ruby to the county jail without fanfare, and when he gets there he faces fresh interrogation—this time, by the FBI. Few Americans consider Ruby a hero, and the nation is discombobulated by events in Dallas. Over the last three days, several forces have planted seeds in fertile soil for future conspiracy theorists: The media's eagerness for any kind of details, whether confirmed or not; Dallas authorities' efforts to prove Oswald's guilt before getting all of the facts right; and the FBI's attempts to protect its secrets. (The CIA's secrets will provide reasons for doubt, too, but they will remain under cover for another decade.)

On this day when the late president is buried in Washington, two notable funerals occur in Texas. Officer Tippit's funeral service at Dallas's Beckley Hills Baptist Church attracts about two thousand mourners, and Dallas TV stations broadcast it live. In his eulogy, the Reverend C. D. Tipps Jr. tells the congregants that Tippit, 39, was slain by "a poor, confused, misguided assassin, as was the president."[56] At a much smaller gathering, Oswald is laid to rest in Rose Hill Cemetery outside of Fort Worth. His family had difficulty finding a cemetery and minister for his service. The minister who finally agrees to perform the service also refuses to conduct it inside his church, so a graveside ceremony is planned. At the appointed time, that clergyman fails to appear. The Reverend Louis Saunders, executive secretary of the Fort Worth Council of Churches, leads the service.[57] Because only family members attend, journalists must act as pallbearers.[58]

POSTSCRIPT

Within sight of Washington, a flame on a hill bears witness to the fact that John F. Kennedy passed this way, but to a pair of fatherless children there is only loss and confusion. When they grow older, they will understand the meaning of two notes that await them:

> Dear John—It will be many years before you understand fully what a great man your father was. His loss is a deep personal tragedy for all of us, but I wanted you particularly to know that I share your grief— You can always be proud of him.

> Dearest Caroline—Your father's death has been a great tragedy for the Nation, as well as for you at this time. He was a wise and devoted man. You can always be proud of what he did for his country.

Someday, they will know that one of the first actions of the thirty-sixth president of the United States was to sit down and write to them about their father. He wrote these notes, his first since assuming the highest office in the land, in the vice president's office on November 22, 1963, as soon as he returned to Washington from a place called Dallas. Both are signed, "Affectionately, Lyndon Johnson."[59]

CHAPTER 3

Mourning in the Shadows

"Exult O shores, and ring O Bells!
But I with mournful tread,
Walk the deck my Captain lies,
Fallen cold and dead."

Walt Whitman, "Oh Captain,
My Captain"[1]

Information about John F. Kennedy's shooting and subsequent death radiated through the American population like an electrical shock jolting the nation's nervous system. Just thirty minutes after shots reverberated through Dallas's Dealey Plaza, 70 percent of American adults knew about the sniper attack.[2] In an age before cell phones and internet connections, this fast transmission of information was astonishing, particularly in comparison to the diffusion of news about similar events in the past.

The first reaction, almost without exception, was disbelief. This generated a need to verify the news via broadcast media. ABC interrupted local programming at 1:38 p.m. Eastern Standard Time, becoming the first television network to report the attack. The other networks quickly followed. CBS's Walter Cronkite initially interrupted the soap opera *As the World Turns* with an audio-only report, because news cameras of that era required twenty minutes to warm up. As the news proliferated among those who were out and about, strangers spoke to one another as they never had before. Around the country, people on the streets huddled in small groups, especially around parked cars with radios broadcasting the news. Others lined up in appliance stores to watch the latest reports on rows of television sets.

To ground themselves on an unsettling day, many Americans communicated by telephone with family members and close friends. The volume of calls in Washington was so great that it disrupted phone service. In Chicago, Illinois Bell Telephone Company experienced a similar surge. "We haven't seen anything like this since the death of President Roosevelt and the end of World War II," a company official said.[3] In a post-assassination study conducted in San Jose, CA, one third of participants reported talking to fifteen or more people about the assassination on that day.[4] A Greenwich, Connecticut, postal carrier described meeting a long succession of sobbing housewives, each one imparting the news as if she had lost a member of her family.[5] Many Americans felt the need to talk with loved ones; others wanted to be alone. Many children learned the news in school, either heard as raw radio reports broadcast through school intercom systems or filtered through the sensibilities of teachers or principals.

The San Jose survey found that almost 90 percent knew about the gunshots before the president's death was confirmed about an hour later.[6] Two-thirds found out about the shooting in the first half-hour,[7] and even among those who heard about the shooting after Kennedy's death, one third knew about the assassination within fifteen minutes after the announcement of Kennedy's demise.[8] In Denver, a study found that 9 percent got the news on television, 13 percent from radio, 30 percent from a good friend, 35 percent from an acquaintance, and 11 percent from a stranger.[9] A Minnesota analysis found that 60 percent of women and 40 percent of men heard about the 12:30 p.m. attack before 1:00 p.m. Central Standard Time; three-fourths of participants knew by 1:15 p.m.; and all had heard about the assassination by 3:30 p.m.[10] At 6:00 p.m., 99.8 percent of adult Americans knew they had a new president.[11]

A Dallas study showed earlier and more widespread knowledge in the city where the crime occurred. Two-thirds of the city's population heard about the attack within fifteen minutes. When doctors declared the president dead thirty minutes after the shots had been fired, 84 percent of Dallas residents already were aware of the shooting. An additional 11 percent found out in the next hour, and by 6:00 p.m., all respondents knew Kennedy had died in their city.[12]

The news was virtually impossible to miss if you were on terra firma, but even on airliners, some pilots announced the assassination to shocked passengers. Journalist Keith Crain, of Crain's Business, had boarded a flight from Denver to Chicago, and, as a young reporter returning from covering a large broadcasters' convention, he looked forward to an easy flight. The plane departed on schedule, and just after the "no-smoking" sign was extinguished, the pilot announced, "Ladies and gentlemen, I am sorry to announce that the president of the United States has been assassinated." For three hours, Crain and everyone else on that plane lived in a news blackout. "Stewardesses were sobbing. Because of the era, the on-board speculation was the Russians had killed Kennedy, and it was the beginning of a nuclear war. None of us was certain Chicago would be there when we arrived. I can only imagine the conversations between the pilots . . . I'll never forget the sensation of flying in a news blackout."[13]

Harry McPherson, deputy undersecretary of the Army for international affairs, was in Tokyo when the assassination occurred. A friend called him in the middle of the night to relay the news. In shock, he wandered into the hotel's hallway, where other Westerners stood in their pajamas listening to English-language stations on transistor radios.[14]

The rapid diffusion of this news within the United States was unprecedented, partially because of the technology available. When John Wilkes Booth shot Abraham Lincoln, the fastest means of communication was by telegraph; James Garfield was slain after the patenting of telephones but before they were commonly in use; and William McKinley succumbed to his wounds more than twenty years before radios became fixtures in many American homes. With telephones, radio, and television spreading the news of Kennedy's assassination, the explosion of information was unmatched in American history. And there were other forces at work. "Rarely are all channels of communication—both the mass media and person-to-person channels—focused at the same time on the same event," explained Bradley S. Greenberg, an assistant professor in Stanford University's Institute for Communication Research. "Even more rare are events of great magnitude unanticipated."[15] The confluence of events surrounding the assassination tapped into all of Americans' communications pathways at once. Those at home depended mostly on television and, because televisions were not common in the workplace in 1963, those at work relied more heavily on radio reports. Most drivers had access to radio, and many who were on foot chose to exchange information with passersby.

When they got the news, many Americans felt a kind of paralysis. More than a million chose to be part of the nation's farewell to John F. Kennedy. They flooded the streets of Washington, while their fellow citizens became one gigantic congregation connected by the magic of television and sharing a common experience, whether they were rich or poor, black or white, Catholic, Protestant, or Jew. By designating Monday, November 25, as a national day of mourning, President Johnson gave the nation's citizens a chance to become a part of this dark and memorable episode in American history.

Other Presidential Assassination Attempts

Name: President Andrew Jackson
Date: Jan. 30, 1835
Attacker: Richard Lawrence
Outcome: Both pistols misfired
Attacker's fate: Sent to mental hospital

Name: President Abraham Lincoln
Date: April 14, 1865
Attacker: John Wilkes Booth
Outcome: Lincoln died within hours
Attacker's fate: Escaped, killed days later by soldier

Name: President James Garfield
Date: July 2, 1881
Attacker: Charles Guiteau
Outcome: Garfield died two months later
Attacker's fate: Captured immediately, later hanged

Name: President William McKinley
Date: Sept. 6, 1901
Attacker: Leon Czolgosz
Outcome: McKinley died eight days later
Attacker's fate: Captured, electrocuted

Name: Former President Theodore Roosevelt
Date: Oct. 14, 1912
Attacker: John Schrank
Outcome: T. Roosevelt finished speech, saw doctor
Attacker's fate: Sent to mental hospital

Name: President-elect Franklin Roosevelt
Date: Feb. 15, 1933
Attacker: Giuseppe Zangara
Outcome: Shots missed F.D. Roosevelt, killed Chicago mayor
Attacker's fate: Electrocuted

Name: President Harry S. Truman
Date: Nov. 1, 1950
Attackers: Oscar Collazo, Griselio Torresola
Outcome: Police shoot gunmen, killing Torresola
Attacker's fate: Truman commuted Collazo's death sentence

Name: President Gerald Ford
Date: Sept. 5, 1975
Attacker: Lynette "Squeaky" Fromme
Outcome: No bullet in chamber
Attacker's fate: Sentenced to life in prison, now paroled

Name: President Gerald Ford
Date: Sept. 22, 1975
Attacker: Sara Jane Moore
Outcome: Shot missed
Attacker's fate: Sentenced to life in prison, now paroled

Name: President Ronald Reagan
Date: March 30, 1981
Attacker: John Hinckley
Outcome: Reagan seriously wounded, survived
Attacker's fate: Sent to mental hospital

WEEPING ON THE SIDELINES

When John F. Kennedy's coffin arrived at Andrews Air Force Base on November 22, 1963, television cameras focused on the high and the mighty, but beyond the bright lights, lost in the darkness of a cool, wet night, 3,000 nameless Americans stood together behind a fence, silently paying their last respects. After TV correspondents reported that the late president's body was on its way to Bethesda Naval Hospital, similar rows of quiet mourners stood along the streets between the Air Force base and the hospital, and by the time the ambulance carrying the coffin had arrived at 6:55 p.m., thousands had gathered on the hospital grounds. Almost ten hours later, when the Kennedy party left the hospital at 3:56 a.m., all along the route from the hospital to the White House were individuals, looming in the night and living a wakeful nightmare. In the words of William Manchester, members of the official party looked out and saw "men in denim standing at attention beside cars halted at intersections, and in all-night filling stations attendants were facing the ambulance, their caps over their hearts."[16] Many unofficial automobiles joined the quietly anonymous caravan bound for the White House.

Late on Sunday morning, as the caisson carried Kennedy's body to the Capitol, the sidewalks overflowed with an estimated 300,000 mourners, many of them weeping. At 3:00 p.m. Sunday, the rotunda was opened

Figure 3.1 Kennedy's body lies in state in the White House. Photograph by
     Abbie Rowe. John F. Kennedy Presidential Library and Museum.

so that members of the public could walk by the bier. The public response
was awe-inspiring. About two and a half hours before the viewing began,
the cars of ordinary mourners were bumper to bumper from Washington's
New York Avenue all the way to Baltimore, thirty miles away. More than
250,000 people filed past the casket between 3:00 p.m. Sunday and 9:00
a.m. Monday. Some waited in line as long as ten hours. For much of the
day, the strangely peaceful mass of humanity extended thirty blocks on
East Capitol Street all the way to the Anacostia River, and then it doubled
back toward the Capitol. There was little conversation in line. Most
engaged in sad, solitary contemplation. It was a cold night, but families
did not remain tucked warmly in their beds. Instead, parents stood for
hours while holding well-bundled children in their arms. Among those
who joined the line was Adlai E. Stevenson, twice the Democratic
candidate for president and the U.S. Ambassador to the United Nations
at that time. Overnight, all three of the TV networks broadcast scenes of
these mourners with little or no commentary. It was a silent vigil shared
by a nation. To allow as many people as possible to pass by the bier, those
responsible for the funeral arrangements decided to expand the single-file
line to two abreast, three abreast, and finally four abreast. At least 5,000

people were turned away Monday morning when police realized that those at the back of the line could not reach the Capitol before 9:00 a.m. Among the last to pass the bronze casket were several nuns, who had been in line since 1:00 a.m. Standing stiffly erect around the bier were military guards who fought to maintain expressionless faces. When one stone-faced young man's guard duty ended, he broke into tears.[17]

Later Monday, more than a million people lined the streets of Washington for the chance to see a page of history unfold. In some places, the crowd was ten people deep; in others, it was twice as dense. Standing quietly, reverently, they saw the coffin travel from the Capitol to the White House. With amazement, they watched a parade of national and world leaders walk from the White House to St. Matthew's Cathedral. Most never expected to see such a majestic scene in their lifetimes. And, despite security concerns about this part of the day's events, no one raised a hand or lifted a gun against the official mourners, because the people on the sidewalks were members of the funeral party as well.

Among the millions watching the funeral on television were many American children who had never attended a funeral, so this pageant of tears became their first. With televisions serving as outreaching hands, Americans united in a ring of worshipers. Because most Americans were Protestant, this service offered an introduction to the Roman Catholic Latin Mass of that era.

After the funeral party left the church and went to Arlington National Cemetery, the sidewalks were again filled with tear-streaked faces. When the burial service ended, many cars attempted to visit the cemetery, but were unable to enter before the gates closed at 4:45 p.m. Drivers were advised that the cemetery would reopen at 8:00 a.m. Tuesday.

In all its maudlin splendor, the nation's farewell to John F. Kennedy had been unmatchable. The *New York Times* called it "a hero's burial," and that was an understatement. In the first year after the assassination, Americans visited the gravesite more often than the Lincoln Memorial and the Washington Memorial combined.[18]

In the weeks immediately after the assassination, Kennedy's death carried unexpected symbolism. "We have been present at a new crucifixion," Dean Francis Sayre of the Washington Cathedral proclaimed. "All of us have had a part in the slaying of our president. It was the good people who crucified our Lord, and not merely those who acted as executioners. By our silence; by our inaction; by our willingness that heavy burdens be borne by one man alone; by our readiness to allow evil to be called good and good, evil; by our continued toleration of ancient injustices . . . we have all had a part in the assassination." The comparison between

Kennedy and Jesus Christ was not unique. Many thought that JFK had sacrificed his life as a martyr for the greater good. "Spiral of Hate," a memorable *New York Times* editorial, declared that "none of us can escape a share of the fault for the spiral of unreason and violence that has now found expression in the death by gunfire of our martyred president and the man being held for trial as his killer."[19]

Kennedy's opponent in the 1960 election, Richard M. Nixon, hailed the slain leader, saying that "President Kennedy . . . wrote the finest and greatest chapter in his *Profiles in Courage*. The greatest tribute we can pay is to reduce the hatred which drives men to do such deeds."[20] In this way, Nixon perpetuated the idea that Kennedy made a conscious sacrifice for his nation. It was a comforting idea. Still, Kennedy did not dive on a live hand grenade to save the nation; he did what every president since Lincoln has done—appeared in public with the knowledge that gunmen sometimes kill presidents. Less popular presidents, like Rutherford B. Hayes, William Howard Taft, Nixon himself, and Jimmy Carter, all did the same thing. Were they being heroic, or is this kind of heroism something endowed by the killer who chooses to slay one president and not another? Perhaps Kennedy had more reason to fear than most because of the volatile political atmosphere during his administration. I do not belittle his sacrifice in any way, but as a World War II hero he probably would not have considered being gunned down in a motorcade a heroic death. Viewing him as a martyr was one "coping mechanism" many Americans employed to rebound from this tragedy.

COPING WITH SADNESS

Americans across the United States experienced the death of Kennedy in a personal way. A National Opinion Research Center survey taken within a week of the assassination showed that the majority of respondents said they could not recall a previous occasion in their lives when they had experienced the same feelings of grief.[21] Seventy-nine percent reported the same deep feeling that they would have experienced in "the loss of someone very close and dear."[22] During the four days beginning with the assassination and ending with the burial, 68 percent of those interviewed said that they felt nervous and tense. Many reported symptoms such as sleeplessness. Fifty-seven percent felt "sort of dazed and numb," 43 percent said they had no appetite, and 42 percent experienced unusually high levels of fatigue.[23] A study of reactions among students at Connecticut's Wesleyan University concluded that "the magnitude of grief was as great, if not as enduring, as would be expected for the death of a family member or a very close friend. Clearly something about the president's symbolic position and the public's repeated exposure to him leads people to incorporate him into their private worlds, into their selves."[24] And certainly because of Kennedy's mastery of the burgeoning medium of television, the public had greater day-to-day exposure to him than to any of his predecessors. Even FDR, a dynamic president who served four times as long as Kennedy, was essentially a voice on the radio in the daily lives of Americans.

Kennedy was, indeed, a frequent visitor to American homes, holding sixty-four live televised news conferences during thirty-four months as president, and a 1961 poll showed that 90 percent of Americans had seen at least one in the first year of his presidency.

"The sting of death has a more intense sense of tragedy when it is out of place," sociologist Arthur G. Neal contends. "The death of the president was seen as a senseless event that should never have occurred by the standards of what is normal, natural, and just within the social realm."[25] Psychiatrists reported false heart attacks and temporary amnesia as symptomatic responses to the assassination. "Why do I react so strongly to this man's dying when I never knew him?" one man reportedly asked his doctor. The psychiatrist told him that in a highly mobile nation, where extended families are widely scattered, the president and his family played an expanded role in people's lives.[26] Clearly, the rapid expansion of communication resources since Kennedy's death has made long-distance relationships with family and friends more vital, as cell phones and social networking have minimized the distances separating loved ones. This may have lessened the symbolic importance of the president and his family as unifying figures. Most Americans do not carry around mental pictures of the children of George W. Bush or Barack Obama, but almost everyone knew Caroline and John.

On the day of the assassination, the *Philadelphia Inquirer* reported men and women weeping in the streets, and reported that "the populace reacted as next of kin, informed without warning of a tragic and untimely death."[27] Other sources described Death Row prisoners crying when they learned Kennedy was dead.[28] "I feel like I've lost a real friend," said a Los Angeles shoeshine man.[29] A month after the assassination, 54 percent of adult Americans questioned by Louis Harris's pollsters said that they felt as though they had lost a member of their own family. Even twenty-five years later, 62 percent told Associated Press/Media General interviewers that they experienced a personal loss when JFK was slain.[30]

Coping with the complex set of feelings caused by Kennedy's assassination may have been easier for his supporters than it was for his opponents. The NORC study showed that, even in the South, where Kennedy's most fervent opponents dwelled, 62 percent of whites reported feeling "a loss of someone very close and dear."[31] Governor George Wallace of Alabama, who had defied Kennedy, trying to block integration of the University of Alabama earlier in 1963, said he felt "a deep sense of personal tragedy."[32] When the *Idaho Falls Post Register* talked to residents of the largely Republican state to collect their memories of the assassination in 1993, one woman recalled a strange sense of isolation during the long weekend of mourning: "If we hadn't been ambivalent, the whole community would have come together and we would have had something at the Civic Auditorium. Let's say the town was apathetic."[33]

Post-assassination interviews with young men at Wesleyan University demonstrated that "one consequence of the assassination was to reveal even to students who had opposed Kennedy's politics—who would not have voted for him—the strength of their *personal* attachment, their fascination with him," concluded political scientist Fred I. Greenstein. Because the 1960 election represented a "coming of age" experience for a generation of young people, Greenstein argued that the loss of Kennedy had a profound effect on that age group.[34] A small National Institute of Mental Health survey showed widespread shock among members of both parties, but there were differences between those who strongly supported Kennedy and those who strongly opposed his policies. Among supporters, 75 percent said they were extremely upset, and the remaining 25 percent said they were fairly upset. Among opponents, 45 percent described themselves as extremely upset; 10 percent, as fairly upset.[35]

During those four days and in the weeks that followed, it became apparent that Kennedy's personal charm broke through barriers and had a lasting impact on many who knew him and many more who did not. "I had no idea that I loved him," said syndicated columnist and Kennedy friend Joseph Alsop months later.

> I don't go in for loving men. But nothing in my life has moved me as it did, not even the death of my father. And everyone has said the same. [Deputy Secretary of Defense] Roz Gilpatric—now Roz doesn't go in for men, don't you know—Roz said he's never got over it. And [Secretary of Defense] Bob McNamara said the same thing. And [National Security Adviser] Mac Bundy. As though he were the one thing we most valued and could never replace.[36]

In a 1964 article in the *Saturday Evening Post*, Alsop expanded on this theme. "Even [Franklin] Roosevelt did not command the love of his closest collaborators, who saw the real man behind the public personage. They admired him; they believed in him; they sought to aid him by all means in their power; but Harry Hopkins himself, who was FDR's closest friend, cannot quite be said to have loved his chief." One close associate of JFK said, "I minded more than when my father died, and I loved my father." Another added, "It is the worst thing that has ever happened to me, and that is how I shall remember it as long as I'm alive."[37]

Across the country, JFK had an especially strong following among African Americans. After more than two years of crisis-driven federal intervention, he had earned their loyalty by telling the nation that civil rights was a moral issue, and he had sent to Congress the strongest civil rights bill in almost a hundred years. Hearing about Kennedy's death, Martin Luther King Jr. was saddened, and he prophetically told his wife, Coretta, "This is what is going to happen to me also."[38] *Ebony* told its readers in early 1964 that Kennedy had done more for African Americans than Abraham Lincoln. "President Kennedy, heralding the dawn of a new era of public respect (if not love) for Negroes in America, surpassed President Lincoln with regard to personal attitudes toward their dark brothers," wrote Simeon Booker.[39] Indeed, no one could argue that Lincoln was more progressive than Kennedy. Like most forward-thinking white men of his era and geographic background, Lincoln condemned slavery, but he doubted that true racial equality was possible. And in death, Kennedy's previous foot-dragging on this issue was forgotten. A survey of 172 African Americans in Detroit showed they were more likely than white Americans to display symptoms of physical distress following the assassination. Measuring emotions at the "very deepest level," 82 percent felt nervous and tense, as compared to 68 percent of the general population; 65 percent cried, in contrast to 53 percent among all races; and 65 percent had trouble sleeping, while just 48 percent of all respondents reported sleeplessness.[40]

Why was Kennedy's appeal so strong for many Americans? Perhaps, a clue lies in the comment of a Washington cab driver taking a fare to the White House about a week after the assassination. He told his passenger that he would not charge her for the trip. His explanation was simple: "Lady, Jack Kennedy had class, and he made me think I had class, too."[41] The conservative *National Review*, which often had opposed Kennedy's policies, particularly on the domestic front, struggled to explain the deep feelings of grief that held much of the nation in a stranglehold:

> The grief was spontaneous and, in most cases, wholly sincere. Not because Mr. Kennedy's policies were so universally beloved, but because he was a man so intensely charming, whose personal vigor and robust enjoyment of life so invigorated almost all who beheld him. The metabolism of the whole nation rose on account of the fairyland quality of the first family. After all, no divine typecaster could have done better than to get JFK to play JFK, Jackie to play the first lady, and the children to play themselves.[42]

An early supporter of Barry Goldwater offered a different reason for the national shock, as she said in a shaky voice, "Oh, I never thought anything could happen to him. He always looked so lucky."[43] Thirty-five years later, Theodore C. Sorensen, Kennedy's special counsel and friend, wrote that he was "the quintessential American. He could loft a pass, swap a joke, hoist a beer, hurt his back, and hug his kids like millions of other Americans. Ordinary people identified with him."[44] While many ordinary people may have identified with JFK, it is doubtful that many envisioned him as the guy next door. His life and his lifestyle shimmered with the stardust of glamour. Large numbers of Americans saw him as someone special, a friendly face among the nation's elite. Others more cynically viewed him as an elitist who led the privileged life available only to the nation's wealthiest citizens.

Magazine magnate Henry Luce, often a Kennedy antagonist, said,

> I would like to pay my personal tribute to this memorable figure, this young man who occupied the White House for nearly three years, and I do it just in a personal way, but it is the kind of personal way in which no doubt thousands and even millions of people in this country and elsewhere in the world felt about it. For my part it was a great privilege to know him for himself and to have had the privilege of knowing him when he was president of the United States, as president of the United States. Whatever may be the balance sheet of his achievement, it is certainly favorable on balance.

Although Kennedy's time in office was short, the publisher of *Time* and *Life* concluded, "there is no question that he made a tremendous contribution to the intangible attitude of the American people—toward government, toward life, toward the things that mattered."[45] Here, a longtime Kennedy opponent makes an exceptionally cogent analysis of his unquantifiable power to affect people.

To many, the president's death seemed like a life-changing event. When journalist Mary McGrory hosted a dinner party on the evening after the assassination, she spoke through a veil of tears. "We'll never laugh again," she moaned. Liberal policymaker Patrick Moynihan replied by telling her that she was wrong: "Oh, we'll laugh again, Mary. But we'll never be young again."[46]

Although commentators at that time believed Kennedy had been the target of more enmity than many of his predecessors, Americans' trust in government was much higher then than it is today. In 1960, about 75 percent believed that they could trust the government to do the right thing "just about always" or "most of the time;[47] by 2010, a mere 22 percent of Americans expressed that much trust, according to a survey by the Pew Research Center.[48] As faith in government has declined, belief in a conspiracy to kill Kennedy has risen. Perhaps, the later willingness to accept a helter-skelter array of conspiracy theories is the result of guilt and shame long buried, or perhaps it is the product of a pop culture that often obscures history. What seems obvious is that Kennedy's violent death jarred the nation with emotional tremors, tossing the United States out of its complacency and opening the doors to change—both good and bad.

FACING SHAME

Profound grief held the nation hostage, but with it came shame as well. Writing in the *New York Times* immediately after the assassination, James Reston asserted:

> America wept tonight, not alone for its dead young president, but for itself. The grief was general, for somehow the worst in the nation had prevailed over the best. The indictment extended beyond the assassin, for something in the nation itself, some strain of madness and violence, had destroyed the highest symbol of law and order."[49]

In the National Opinion Research Center study, 83 percent of respondents admitted feeling shame "that this could happen in our country."[50] Uncannily, children shared shame at exactly the same level as adults, 83 percent, according to another study.[51]

For the most part, John F. Kennedy's America had been sunny and prosperous. His youth, his vigor, and his wit had sharpened the nation's appetite for change. The prospect of nuclear war was a haunting presence in modern life, but in 1963 there were new signs of hope in the Cold War. Racial conflict, an out-of-control scythe slicing a path through America's history from its beginnings, remained a potent issue, but changing public attitudes offered hope. Whether or not they supported the late president, Kennedy's constituents, with very few exceptions, were proud to call themselves Americans.

In one afternoon, that changed for many Americans. After the gunshots, shame stained Lyndon Johnson's nation as vividly and indelibly as the blood spatters on the widow's pink suit. The message rang out from clergymen, TV commentators, and newspaper editorials: America tolerated a culture of violence. Like original sin, it was a seed we carried with us. Perhaps only one man pulled the trigger, but the culture that made him and the shame that followed him belonged to all of us.

While most Americans felt shock and a great sense of loss at the president's sudden death, a nasty undercurrent in American politics heightened speculation that sharp political divisions had created an atmosphere conducive to assassination. Fanaticism on the far left and far right often dominated center stage, shoving aside those Nixon later called the Silent Majority. There were scattered examples of Americans rejoicing that Kennedy had been slain, and, for many, these incidents added to the burden of shame. The details are difficult to revisit. Soon after the president's murder, Americans heard reports of a class of fourth-graders in north Dallas cheering when they heard the news.[52] An Austin, Texas, fifth-grader recalled a student shouted, "Someone killed Kennedy!" and half the class rose to applaud.[53] A Wisconsin minister remembered that a young man was arrested at Capitol Square in Madison for carrying a Nazi banner and announcing, "I'm celebrating the death of a nigger lover."[54] An Elkhorn, Wisconsin, seventh-grader later noted shamefully that his response to news of Kennedy's death was, "Good!"[55] A teenaged boy called WQXI Radio in Atlanta just hours after the assassination to say, "I'm sure that the majority of the people of Alabama feel, that Mr. Kennedy got exactly what he deserved . . . any man, any white man, who did what he did for niggers should be shot."[56] Michael Ensley, who was 17 at the time, remembers one student in his Arlington, Virginia, class saying that he was happy the president was dead. Some of his classmates "packed him in a locker, but I think they had to go to the hospital with him later on."[57]

Young people were not alone in expressing joy about the president's death. On the day of the shooting, the news triggered shouts of approval from a crowd standing across from Dallas's City Hall.[58] Even twenty years later, a District of Columbia resident bragged to the *Washington Post* that he had "leaped up and cheered and cheered and started delivering a heartfelt toast to the person killing what I considered an unelected president put in office by stolen votes from south Texas and Cook County [crucial spots where Kennedy victories ensured his election and where voter fraud was suspected]."[59] Right after the announcement of Kennedy's death, CBS reporter Roger Mudd heard a jubilant roar at the far side of the Capitol Plaza.[60] One man recalled coming home from work on the day of the assassination and telling his politically conservative wife that the president had been slain: "She said, 'Good!' then asked me what I'd like to have for dinner."[61] In fact, the more one studies the polarization present in American society in 1963, the less surprising Kennedy's assassination seems. If he had not been killed by a man with ties to the left, a man with right-wing sympathies might have stepped forward to do the job. The nation was facing massive changes, and that generated fear-driven hatred and anger. And yet, no one fired a gun at Kennedy's immediate successors, Johnson and Nixon, both of whom experienced crushing blows to their popularity.

Historian James W. Hilty was a college student at Ohio State University in November 1963. As he left a political science class, it became clear to him that something big was happening.

> [I] stepped inside a tobacco shop, and there were several people grouped around the counter listening to the proprietor's radio. He turned up the volume so we could hear. Then he said, "Kennedy has been shot and it doesn't look good." We all leaned forward over the counter trying to get all the details. Then, I remember the shop owner said, "Good, well I'm glad someone shot him." All of us recoiled from the counter. We were all younger people, and I remember literally backing out of the shop staring at this guy. I don't think anyone said a word to him. We just left. I never went back in there again. I always thought of that guy afterward as one of the enemy.[62]

Many Americans were ashamed of their fellow citizens' actions. A high school student in New Haven, Connecticut, was asked to type a paper on random thoughts about Kennedy, and he or she wrote, "In some way or another we helped to kill the president with the hate and anger we had for other people at some time or another."[63] Readers writing to the *New York Times* expressed similar feelings. "Assassins may be caught and punished, but are they more guilty than irresponsible men who inflame the ignorant for their own selfish reasons?" wrote one reader.[64] Another asserted, "There is far too much selfishness and violence in our civilization. Differences of color and ideology make too many men think of killing. We badly need understanding and give-and-take negotiation before it is too late."[65] A seventh-grade parochial school student in McAllen, Texas, wrote that "all the people never thought it could happen in a civilized country like the United States."[66] Historian Arthur M. Schlesinger Jr., a member of Kennedy's White House staff, was asked by his weeping daughter, "Daddy, what has happened to our country? If this is the kind of country we have," she said, "I don't want to live here anymore."[67]

Episcopal priest Robert Cromey of San Francisco was assistant to the bishop of California at the time Kennedy was slain. He says,

> Being in the ministry . . . and looking at the Old Testament, I got the idea of corporate guilt because God in the Old Testament often blames the whole people of Israel. I then remember reflecting on that. There is a sense in which the nation is responsible for the things it does, and even for the people within the nation . . . I can see how people of a certain kind of stripe that don't like liberals or don't like a certain kind of people would strike out like that. I think that's part of the American way. The American culture is very violent. If you don't like something, pull out a gun, just like Hopalong Cassidy, Roy Rogers, and all the people I saw as a kid in movies.[68]

Margaret Glose, who was a Sister of St. Joseph in St. Paul, Minnesota, taught sixth grade in an urban parochial school. She recalls uneasiness about the youngsters' response to violence. News of the assassination came at lunchtime.

> When we got back into the classroom, I did not want to be with the children. I wanted to be where I could hear what was going on, and I was disappointed that some of the children just couldn't grasp the enormity of what was going on and they were *excited* by it in the sense of shooting guns, with finger motions. That was very disturbing to me. I tried to remember that they were only eleven or twelve years old.

While she believes many Americans experienced "a recognition after death what this man could have meant for the country," she added in reflection, "I think these kids were not thinking of him as a person or a politician. They were just thinking of the shooting and the gore."[69]

Janet Fishburn was a young mother of two in Potomac, Maryland, in 1963. She recalls, "I didn't know this could happen on American soil." Her reaction to the assassination was similar to her response on September 11, 2001, when hijackers seized four airliners, crashing two into the World Trade Center, one into the Pentagon, and one in western Pennsylvania. "It was, again, a feeling of hopelessness and despair. And also kind of a wake-up call of how much democracy depends on people being trustworthy, and that our freedoms take big chances." Fishburn believes the tendency to adopt conspiracy theories about JFK's assassination satisfies "the need to explain bad things that happen, but it doesn't do that for me. I guess that may be because I think individuals are capable of doing really bad things." As a retired modern church historian, Fishburn sees the shock of the assassination as a strangely beneficial force in American life. She argues that it "opened up the culture to begin to acknowledge more of what we really were like and give us new freedom in terms of what we then called 'lifestyles' . . . It made a difference in our consciousness and somehow dynamited us out of a whole country who wanted to stay as traditional as we had been." On issues such as racial equality, she thinks the assassination caused Americans to "rip away the veil. I think it helped us to see more clearly what was really there." She believes that, while the turbulence of the 1960s brought tragedies, it also "inaugurated a major cultural transition and we're still trying to come to terms with it." She notes that, in the wake of the 1960s, conservatives voice continuing concerns about family, morals, and sexuality, "but there are the other folks who see the Sixties as having called America back to our original values as a people."[70]

The Reverend Karel Ramsey, a Baptist pastor, celebrated her twentieth birthday at Kansas State University on the day President Kennedy died. As a teenager, she had met Kennedy when she had played the piano at a Democratic Party event in Ellis County, Kansas, where then-Senator Kennedy was building grassroots support for a budding presidential campaign. She recalls the assassination as "an experience that really shakes your understanding of who you are and who you think your country is, and who you think the people around you are . . . It shakes your sense of identity and your sense of who other people are." Now recognizing that violence against African Americans was common at that time, especially in the South, she said her parents shielded her from the seamier side of life. The president's assassination marked "the first violent event that the nation could not avoid looking at." She sees it as the first of a series of violent events, including the assassinations of King and Robert Kennedy in 1968 and the killing of four students at Kent State University two years later. "I think things are better now," she said, in that we do face somewhat more honestly those real things in the darkness that for a long time we preferred not to look at. But it comes with a cost—and this is the downside. The cost is that I think most of us have a sense that we live in a less stable, less safe, less secure, less predictable environment. It's much harder for us to see ourselves as somehow connected to a bigger enterprise than ourselves. I think that there's been a lot of loss of confidence in institutions, in the church and a lot of other things that we used to just assume were stable parts of life that we could rely on . . . It would be nice if we could have truth *and* a sense of connectedness.[71]

The Reverend Adrianne Carr was a postulant in the Roman Catholic order of Maryknoll sisters when Kennedy was shot. As a postulant, she generally was shielded from the outside world; however, when the assassination occurred, "we all were invited to the recreation room where we watched television for seventy-two hours straight, just like everybody else in the country." Now a minister in the United Church of Christ, she believes that Americans at that time were "totally blind to the inequities in the system." In the Cold War culture, she thinks, Americans focused so much on Communists that they did not see the flaws in the United States. "If we opened our eyes, we could see the . . . ghettoes. We could see inequities between rich and poor." She viewed the violence of the 1960s and the thousands of American deaths in Vietnam as signs of American fallibility.

In 1963, we were living in an unreal world. I think everything that happened—not that Vietnam was good, not that violence surrounding the peace movement or the civil rights movement was good, not that the riots were good—but they were the growing pains that got us from that age of innocence. We'd come out of World War II which was "the good war." We were feeling very good about ourselves as a country. We had technology. We had the answers to everything, and there was nowhere but upwards into space we could go. The sky was the limit. We got taken down a number of pegs and got a dose of reality. We are, as a people, better for it.[72]

In 1963, Father Richard McGowan was teaching at a parochial school near the scene of Kennedy's assassination, and he says his school was the only one in Dallas that closed so that students could see the motorcade. Some Dallas residents were unhappy about the way the assassination colored the city's reputation, he recalls. Kennedy was not popular there: "I had a lot of friends who disliked the Kennedys beyond a political thing. It was a hatred that was very persistent." After the assassination, he believes, behavior in Dallas changed. Some citizens felt negligent in allowing an atmosphere of hate to prosper. "There was a big resurgence of people in political activity . . . and saying, 'I haven't been participating in the political system and now this has happened. This is bad for everybody.'"[73]

Violence in American culture worried American clergymen of many faiths. What they saw was hatred empowering extremists on the right and left, while most Americans watched silently or fell prey to heated rhetoric. On the Sunday after the assassination, the Reverend George A. Buchanan of Shannondale Presbyterian Church in Knoxville told his congregation the plain truth, as he saw it: "The man who killed the president did not come from Mars; he is the product of our society and culture, and therefore we all contributed according to our involvement or non-involvement in the structure of our society and our culture."[74] In the bulletin of Chicago's Anshe Emet synagogue, Rabbi Seymour J. Cohen wrote in December 1963, "We live in an age which, tragically, is brutal and violent." He blamed two world wars for creating openness to savagery and "contempt for human dignity."[75]

"Either we will search our hearts, confess our sins and turn back to God; or else we shall continue to plunge down the toboggan of evil which leads over the precipice to oblivion," warned the Reverend H.H. Hobbs at the First Baptist Church of Oklahoma City two days after the assassination.[76] The Reverend O.H. Closter of Trinity Lutheran Church in Faribault, Minnesota, told his congregation:

> We Americans must today bow our heads in shame . . . Our reaction should indeed be one of anger, but anger, not at the assassin, rather anger at ourselves. It should be one of mourning, not only for a dead man and his family, but mourning over ourselves. It should be one of shock, not so much at what someone else has done, but shock over our own sinfulness and at what we have permitted to happen.[77]

Speaking of Oswald, the Reverend Barry M. Carter of St. John United Methodist Church in Greenville, South Carolina, said, "The man was simply the executioner. He was under orders from a sentence handed down by millions of accomplices who must now stand before the bar of judgment and submit to the scalpel-edge of that inescapable query: 'Where is your brother?' The twisted man nested in a cluttered room was but the logical

The Aftermath in Dallas

In the waning weeks of 1963, many Americans saw Dallas, much like Lee Harvey Oswald, as bearing responsibility for the assassination of President Kennedy. The subsequent murder of Oswald intensified the view of Dallas as a haven for extremists who clung to Wild West codes of violence. This indictment came from a Dallas minister's wife: "We think it's this Western tradition. They are used to shooting at everything they don't like."[78] A New York Times article about the assassination began simply by asking, "Was Dallas to Blame?" The article's writer sensed arousal of a new "mass conscience" in the city as waitresses, cab drivers, politicians, and businessmen expressed concern about the city's image.[79]

On the Thanksgiving weekend following the assassination, Dr. James R. Allen, one of Dallas's leading Baptist ministers, argued that Oswald and Ruby were not representative of Dallas but, he said, they were examples of "an element in our city . . . The white heat of a hate-filled atmosphere allowed the necessary warmth for this element to crawl out from under the rocks to be seen." There was no way to hide from the physical evidence of Dallas's venom: The city remained littered with thousands of "wanted" leaflets carrying Kennedy's photo and accusing him of treason. Memories of the full-page attack ad in November 22's *Dallas Morning News* remained fresh. CBS correspondent Robert Pierpoint later said, "The whole general tone of that particular paper was as if Kennedy was the devil incarnate."[80] Rejecting the label "city of hate," Dallas Mayor Earl Cabell declared, "There are maniacs all over the world and in every city of the world. This was a maniac. It could have happened in Podunk as well as in Dallas,"[81] but many agreed that haters in Dallas felt no need to hide in the shadows.[82]

More than one minister spoke about the city's shame from the pulpit. "There has been brought forth in our town in the last few weeks a force of hatred that has erupted like a flame in two different instances," Dr. Walter A. Bennett told his congregation at Westminster Presbyterian Church. A Methodist minister, the Reverend William H. Dickinson Jr., contended that the climate of hostility was not an aberrant sentiment affecting a small, irresponsible part of the city's population. Dickinson told his congregation: "At a nice respectable dinner party only two nights before the president's visit to our city, a bright young couple with a fine education, with a promising professional future, said to their friends that they *hated* the president of the United States—and that they would not care one bit if somebody did take a potshot at him."[83] Condemning extremist literature, Dr. Thomas A. Fry of the First Presbyterian Church declared,

We are proud of our heritage and our image. But something has happened like a cancer you cannot quite put your finger on. We have allowed the apostles of religious bigotry and the purveyors of political pornography to stir up the weak-minded. These events should cause us to see to it that never again will we allow persons to brand a president a Communist unless he can back up his charges in court with facts.[84]

Another minister described a more complex picture of Dallas: "I think it is significant that the president received a warm and genuine reception by thousands of its residents before he was shot by a single emotionally disturbed man. Dallas cannot be explained in a few words. It is a lot of things."[85]

In an editorial, the *Dallas Times Herald* urged city residents to "pray to God to teach us love and forgiveness." The editorial reflected Dallas's sense that it was being condemned by the rest of the nation: "Terrible history has been made in Dallas, and the magnitude of our city's sorrow can only be measured by the enormity of the deed. John F. Kennedy, president of the United States of America, is dead. Killed in Dallas. No matter what the explanation of the act, the awful reality of it overwhelms us. He died here."[86] Jack Krueger, managing editor of the *Dallas Morning News*, issued a directive to his staff on November 22. It said, "We must handle this story with the best of taste in the next few days. We are sort of on trial because it happened in our city.[87] Two days later, a Dallas businessman said that the murder of Oswald "makes it worse than ever for Dallas."[88] During the two years immediately after the assassination, the city's murder and suicide rates increased significantly more than they did in other American metropolitan areas. The death rate from heart disease increased 4 percent in Dallas over the next four years when the number of deaths nationwide dropped by 2 percent.[89]

Clearly, Dallas was caught up in fears that its reputation would be forever blackened, but the city was not without sorrow for the Kennedys or the nation. Interviews of 212 Dallas residents within ten days of the assassination showed that 90 percent felt deeply sorry for the president's wife and children, while 86 percent were ashamed that the crime had occurred in their city.[90] City residents placed wreaths and other fond remembrances of JFK in Dealey Plaza, many on what would later become known as the infamous "grassy knoll." The *Dallas Times Herald* published a letter dated November 22 in its November 24 editions. Titled "My Dear Caroline," the letter was written by a Dallas man who took his two daughters to see the presidential motorcade. In his letter, he attempted to explain the horror of the assassination to almost-6-year-old Caroline Kennedy. It stated, "No one can erase this day . . . You will cry. (My children did, my wife did, and I did.) You will miss him. (We will.) You will be lonely for him."[91] It is doubtful that Caroline Kennedy ever saw this maudlin letter, but friends of Jack Ruby later said it had a profound effect on his state of mind.[92]

The country's grievances against Dallas did not fade quickly. A few months after the assassination, James Chambers Jr., president of the *Dallas Times Herald*, was in Detroit on business when a cab driver noticed his southern accent and asked where his home was. When Chambers said that he was from Dallas, the cabbie stopped the car and told him to get out.[93] Despite the city's image problems, there was no obvious shift in Dallas politics. In the immediate aftermath of the assassination, School Superintendent W.T. White had seemed ready to fire a teacher who told her students that she longed to spit in JFK's face, but he changed his mind. On the other hand, he did suspend another teacher just two weeks later because she wrote to *Time* about "the seed of hate being planted by our newspapers and many of our leaders of Dallas."[94] The United States Information Agency's 1964 film tribute to Kennedy, *Years of Lightning, Day of Drums*, drew huge audiences in many places, but was "a complete flop" in Dallas.[95]

Unlike other cities around the nation, Dallas did not rush to name buildings or streets after JFK, but a surprisingly high portion of the city budget over the following years was earmarked for keeping the city clean, and in the period 1962–68, Dallas residents gave significantly more to charities like the United Way. These special behaviors diminished after 1968, when the assassinations of Martin Luther King Jr. and Robert Kennedy diverted attention from Dallas.[96]

conclusion of the hatred of us all."[97] And the Reverend Loring D. Chase, pastor of the New Haven (Connecticut) Congregational Church, recalled with horror seeing footage of the president's motorcade as it rushed to the hospital, passing a teenager holding a sign that read, "Yankee, Go Home."[98]

Journalists and historians, too, looked at Kennedy's assassination and saw something frightening about American culture. Television anchorman Chet Huntley spoke with passion just hours after the assassination:

It is a logical assumption that hatred . . . far left, far right, political, religious, economic, or paranoiac . . .moved the person or persons who, today, committed this combined act of murder and national sabotage.

There is in this country, and there has been for too long, an ominous and sickening popularity of hatred. The body of the president, lying in Washington, is the thunder testimonial of what hatred comes to and the revolting excesses it perpetrates.

Hatred is self-generating, contagious. It feeds upon itself and explodes into violence. It is no inexplicable phenomenon that there are pockets of hatred in our country—areas and communities where the disease is permitted, or encouraged, or given status by those who can and do influence others.

You and I have heard, in recent months, someone say, "Those Kennedys ought to be shot." A well-known national magazine recently carried an article saying Chief Justice Warren should be hanged. In its own defense it said it was only joking.

The left has been equally extreme.

Tonight, it might be the hope and the resolve of all of us that
we have heard the last of this kind of talk, jocular or serious; for
the result is tragically the same.[99]

America the Beautiful, this was not. And after watching Jack Ruby
kill suspected assassin Lee Harvey Oswald, Americans found even more
reason to question their society. Clearly, all Americans did not plan the
assassination or pull the trigger, but many wondered about the celebration
of violence, so much a part of popular culture, and whether it had
become an American birthright—
or an American curse. Writing an
analysis for the *Washington Post*,
historian Henry Steele Commager
saw several explanations for American violence. "What we have
here is deeply ingrained vanity and
arrogance—vanity and arrogance
fed by isolation . . . It is fed, too,
by histories which exalt everything
American; which brush aside our
wars of extermination against the
Indians . . .; which paint slavery as a kind of fortunate accident for the
African Negro."[100]

> Celebration of American exceptionalism
> became particularly pronounced during
> the Cold War years, when the United
> States juxtaposed its democratic
> values and the totalitarian government
> of the Soviet Union; the assassination
> reduced Americans' faith in the nation's
> goodness.

For a few weeks, much of the nation was open to questions about
American culture. Norman Cousins declared in *Saturday Review*,

We can re-examine the indifference to violence in everyday life.
We can ask ourselves why we tolerate and encourage the
glorification of violence in the things that amuse us and entertain
us. We can ponder our fascination with brutality as exhibited hour
after hour on television or on the covers of a thousand books and
magazines. We can ask why our favorite gifts to children are toy
murder weapons.[101]

In an editorial, the *New York Times* told its readers: "The shame all
America must bear for the spirit of madness and hate that struck down
President John F. Kennedy is multiplied by the monstrous murder of his
accused assassin while being transferred from one jail in Dallas to
another."[102] The *Sacramento Bee* reported that Kennedy "came to the
presidency . . . in an hour of rising extremism and in an hour when the
preachers of hate were spreading their gospels of fascism across the land

and because this is a free land they were permitted to speak."[103] Columnist Richard Starnes wrote, "Indecency took the country by the throat in a raw, too-rich, too-soon Texas city, and none can say what the ending will be."[104] The *Christian Science Monitor* argued that Kennedy's assassination had taken place "in a mental climate of conflict between fanaticism in a godless cause on one side and proscriptive, hate-filled zeal on the other. True devotion to one's country consists in servicing it through peaceful processes, striving to improve it but relying on the verdict of the electorate where debate and suffrage are free."[105] And the *Nation* concluded, "Oswald, as much as America, had a soul, or character, and it was a part of the vast collective soul of America."[106]

National leaders joined in the proclamations of shame. Chief Justice Warren, a frequent target of right-wing extremism, said that Kennedy died "as a result of the hatred and bitterness that has been injected into the life of our nation by bigots, but his memory will always be an inspiration to Americans of goodwill everywhere."[107] Representative Hale Boggs of Louisiana issued a statement bemoaning his belief that "the radicals and haters in politics and everywhere have had their way. They are the ones who really pulled the trigger which killed a great American."[108]

Despite widespread expressions of shame and demonstrations of shamelessness, the idea that society was responsible for Kennedy's assassination gradually faded from American memory, just as initial shock waned and tears dried. In annual newspaper articles marking the anniversary of the assassination, expressions of shame disappeared over the course of a few years. Many people simply rejected the idea that Americans as a whole had any responsibility for the president's death. As the body count of social and political leaders rose over the next five years, with the deaths of Malcolm X, Martin Luther King Jr., and Robert F. Kennedy, the idea of American shame gained currency in the peace movement, while conservatives considered it unpatriotic slander.

WATCHING THE WORLD STAND STILL

In recollection, that four-day weekend in November 1963 seems like a rare interlude when everything else stopped, as Americans took time to absorb the assassination, Oswald's murder, the riderless horse, the eternal flame, and the toddler saluting his father's flag-covered coffin—and that feeling is not entirely a trick of memory. Much of typical American life did stop in the hours and days immediately following Kennedy's death when activities related to the president's death captivated the nation.

Consider Friday in New York City: Less than an hour after the shooting in Dallas, the New York Stock Exchange and the American Exchange both stopped trading. Horse racing at the Aqueduct Track ended after the seventh race. Broadway theaters and Radio City Music Hall in Manhattan closed, as did Harlem's Apollo Theater. New York's Mayor Robert F. Wagner ordered all flags flown at half-staff. Manhattan's Fifth Avenue Association urged member stores to turn off all Christmas lights and to lower their flags as city offices had done. By the end of the day, Best and Co. and Saks Fifth Avenue had changed their window displays to honor Kennedy. At the United Nations, all other member flags were taken down to draw attention to the American flag at half-staff. Through the course of the afternoon, more than 20,000 people went into St. Patrick's Cathedral. The cathedral's bells began to toll five minutes after announcement of Kennedy's death, and 2,500 people attended an impromptu Mass in Kennedy's memory. Psychologist Monroe J. Miller and sociologist Roger S. Zimmerman described a "frantic quiet" in the usually bustling city.[109]

In Chicago, everything seemed to come to a standstill in the city's shopping area. Some customers went home when they found out about the attack; others gravitated toward TV departments. In some stores, music coming through the intercoms was interrupted by radio news updates. Philadelphia's City Hall was quiet as all work came to a stop, while city workers turned their attention to gathering the latest news. Conductor Eugene Ormandy stopped the afternoon concert of the Philadelphia Orchestra. On the city's streets, pedestrians flagged down passing cars and trucks, asking the drivers to stop for a moment and turn up their radios.[110] In Baltimore, city workers and police officers descended on the Associated Press bureau to read the latest bulletins. On the West Coast, the streets of Los Angeles were filled with people carrying transistor radios.

Fifty-four percent of Americans did not continue their usual activities when they heard the news, the National Opinion Research Center post-assassination study found.[111] A similar study in Dallas indicated that 58 percent suspended what they were doing.[112] Because the shooting occurred on a Friday, Americans had the opportunity to extend their period of inactivity through the weekend. In cities and in small towns, there were fewer people on the streets and more Americans sitting in front of their TV sets. Immediately after the assassination, many employers, ranging from factory owners to retailers, closed their doors and sent their workers home. At the same time, a large number of universities interrupted or canceled classes. On Monday, the official day of mourning, most businesses closed. A newspaper dealer in New York left a sign on his kiosk that said, "Closed because of a death in the American family."[113] The *New York Times*'s R.W. Apple wrote that the city was "like a vast church."[114] At noon, as Kennedy's coffin was scheduled to enter St. Matthew's Cathedral, the standstill became even more profound. To honor the late president, all U.S. telephone and cable communications with the outside world were suspended for five minutes. Most means of public transportation stopped service for those few minutes. Airliners stood still on airport runways. Automobile traffic came to a halt in New York's Times Square as teenage Eagle Scouts played taps from the top of the Astor Hotel's marquee. At Grand Central Station, a huge crowd watched the funeral Mass on a gigantic TV screen. No trains were leaving the station, and those already in transit stopped in their tracks on rural rails and in cities. A Pennsylvania Railroad local halted at noon in Narberth, Pennsylvania, for one minute. During the break, the passengers stood and bowed their heads while the train's conductor played taps on a bugle. The Panama Canal, a small strip of American territory in Central America, suspended operations, and even as far away as Athens police officers stood in the middle of the streets to halt all traffic for a brief moment of remembrance.

For those not attending the funeral services in Washington, there were local services across the country. New York's Temple Emanu El's service attracted more than 5,200 people—the most ever in its 118-year history—filling every seat. About 1,000 people were turned away. In Massachusetts, Kennedy's home state, most businesses closed all day, and even the exceptions to that rule, such as establishments that sold food, closed from 11:00 a.m. to 2:00 p.m.

As the flow of everyday life paused, the nation, in its despair, seemed more connected than ever before. Watching the same scenes unfold on TV screens from coast to coast tied Americans together through a unique manifestation of how communications technology could forge social ties. Just as strangers shared the news and the accompanying horror on Friday, mourners on Monday felt an ecumenical connection, whether they were New York Jews, Atlanta Baptists, or Boston Catholics. In this momentarily close-knit nation, it seemed quite normal that twenty-eight New York police officers who went to Washington to mourn the president's death found themselves serving as part of the security force for the funeral. All of the things that might tend to

> The sense of community provided by television after the assassination represented an early and somewhat primitive precursor to twenty-first-century social networking.

divide Americans—racial prejudice, political vitriol, regional tensions, religious differences—were tabled by most of the population. They would return soon enough. And yet, for those four days, they were placed on hold, like much of daily life.

AROUND THE WORLD

Many people around the world mourned for Kennedy, and condolences poured into the United States from six continents. Television had made it easier for Kennedy to be seen in other lands, and jet technology had simplified his travel to nations in distant corners of the world. "How shall we explain this worldwide reaction which united emotionally people so different as Bolivian Indians, black men in South Africa, and 'the man on the street' of Warsaw?" a *New York Times* editorial asked. "It came from President Kennedy's projection to all the world of his and his country's deep concern for humanity, for freedom and for peace."[115] The funeral was broadcast live in twenty-three other nations. Kennedy was a familiar figure to America's allies as well as its enemies.

When news of Kennedy's death reached the Soviet Union, Moscow Radio stopped broadcasting a concert and filled the airwaves with funereal music. Over the weekend, Soviet Premier Nikita Khrushchev visited the U.S. Embassy in Moscow to discuss the negative effect Kennedy's death would have on U.S.–Soviet relations. During televised coverage of assassination news, one Russian newscaster struggled to hold back tears. And the Soviet Union was among the nations that broadcast live coverage of Kennedy's funeral, the first time Soviet citizens had been allowed to see a live broadcast originating in another country.

At his post in Washington, General Maxwell Taylor was startled to see the assassination's impact on German officials meeting with him at the Pentagon. The general, then chairman of the Joint Chiefs of Staff, learned about the shooting while taking a break from meetings with the German chief of staff and his aides. Taylor called a meeting of the Joint Chiefs and then went to explain to the German officials why there would be a delay in resuming their talks. "I've never seen a man more stricken than the German chief of staff," Taylor said. "I assured him there was nothing we could do." Later, when Kennedy's death had been announced, Taylor was struck by the Germans' outpouring of emotion. He said he realized that Kennedy "had become a symbol of a sort to people that really seized their imagination . . . Here was a young hope coming forward, and with all the strength of the United States behind him, every country felt it had a stake in him."[116]

Kennedy had a special affinity for the divided city of Berlin situated within Communist East Germany. He had delivered a memorable speech there just months earlier. Dismissing the prophets of doom who saw democracy as a weak, decrepit form of government, he proclaimed, "Let them come to Berlin!" When his death occurred, two university student councils spontaneously organized a solemn candlelight march through the city in his memory. Mayor Willy Brandt was among the 60,000 people who memorialized Kennedy that night. "A flame went out for all those who had hoped for a just peace and a better life," he said.[117] On the other side of the Berlin Wall, East Germany's Communist Party organ allotted a large percentage of its news space to coverage of the assassination.

Shortly after midnight on Saturday, a crowd of Italians, some of whom were weeping, stood outside the U.S. Embassy in Rome. The next day, thousands of Italian soccer enthusiasts observed a moment of silence in JFK's memory. Pope Paul VI took the unprecedented step of inviting an American TV crew into the papal apartments so that he could express his sorrow and promise his prayers. Even the Communist Party's headquarters in Rome lowered its flag to half-staff. Because he had fallen victim to the flu, Italian President Antonio Segni could not attend services in Washington, but he attended a Mass in Rome and collapsed in sobs.

In London, when the news first broke, citizens pressed against the glass facade of the U.S. Embassy to read the latest bulletins, which embassy employees had taped to the windows. Queen Elizabeth's coachmen wore black armbands to reflect a state of mourning. British flags flew at half-staff, and the House of Commons adjourned, a sign of respect usually reserved for prime ministers.

In many nations, American embassies drew long lines of people who wished to sign a book acknowledging their grief. Nearly 6,000 Spaniards poured into the embassy in Madrid. Crown Prince Asfa Wossen signed the book of condolences at the embassy in Ethiopia. Among Yugoslavian messages left in a condolence book was this one: "I am one of 19 million Yugoslavs who sincerely admired his dynamism and efforts for the preservation of peace. With his death, we lose a great friend."[118]

Meeting in the presidential palace when word of the shooting arrived, the Peruvian Cabinet ministers rose and took a moment to silently contemplate Kennedy's memory, and the Peruvian House of Representatives voted unanimously to nominate the late president for the Nobel Peace Prize. Five thousand Kenyan tribesmen sent their condolences to the United States, and on the streets of Portugal people donned black ties as well as black armbands. Buddhist priests in Tokyo prayed before a portrait of Kennedy; Swiss mourners joined a torch parade in Bern; and in Trinidad, nightclubs and hotels ceased all dancing and other forms of entertainment. Citizens of Kennedy's ancestral home, Ireland, felt special ties to the American lad who had visited their island earlier in 1963. Townspeople who had met him worshiped together in Ballykelly Church in New Ross. "Never again will we see his smiling face," one farmer said.[119]

Interest in the news was so high that, in Munich, fighting erupted among men waiting to buy the first newspaper editions to report the assassination, and in Rio de Janeiro circumstances forced police to provide protection for newsstands, *Time* magazine reported.[120] The Israeli government designated three days of mourning, as did the government in Indonesia. In Algeria, a week of mourning was set aside, while Liberia ordered thirty days of mourning.

Patricia C. "Kathy" Connelly, one of the first to heed Kennedy's call to service, was a Peace Corps volunteer in Bolivia when he was shot. She taught at the National School of Nursing in La Paz. On November 22, she took her boss to the La Paz airport, which is the highest in the world at 12,000 feet. "So as I was descending from the Altiplano [a large Andean plateau], I could see the black flags going up. They were mourning . . . so I got to my students and they were weeping. They were just very, very moved. It was my American president, and I was in shock." The day after the shooting, two residents of the Altiplano invited Connelly and another volunteer to join a memorial service. They were seated "up front and everybody in the village came to greet us and express their mourning to us. It was very moving . . . They were grieving with us." The following day, there was a mass at a cathedral, and "there was a silence in La Paz." That afternoon, she and a couple of volunteers decided to climb a mountain facing the city, Muela del Diablo, or Tooth of the Devil. "So as a tribute to Kennedy, we hiked up with the flag and put it on top . . . We felt that we were the American representatives in Bolivia at the time, and people did have a great deal of respect for Kennedy. It was through Kennedy that we were brought there."[121]

CHILDREN AND THE DEATH OF THE PRESIDENT

For many American children in November 1963, death was totally abstract, something that happened in other people's families. Many had fought back tears in films that portrayed noble deaths. No one could watch Walt Disney's 1942 animated classic *Bambi* without feeling a tug at the heartstrings when Bambi's mother died. And 1957's live-action Disney film *Old Yeller* elicited tears when the title character, a feisty and heroic yellow dog, contracted rabies and had to be shot. Death seemed horrible at those times, but on almost a daily basis children saw television's Western heroes, policemen, and private detectives killing bad guys with seldom a second thought. Since most youngsters had never lost a member of their immediate families, they simply did not know what to think about death. This reality amplified the shock of Kennedy's assassination.

JFK was well known to children. He often had televised news conferences in the late afternoons, when children were at home. In addition, youngsters knew that Kennedy had set the goal of sending Americans to the moon by the end of the decade, and many had undergone testing on school playgrounds to see whether they met the standards of the President's Physical Fitness Program. Moreover, Kennedy had small children of his own, so youngsters could relate to him as a father figure. In 1960, when children in the third through eighth grades were polled after the presidential election, younger children were most likely to say they were pleased about Kennedy's election to the White House. More than 61 percent of third-graders told researchers that they were either very happy or happy about Kennedy's victory. This figure declined as grade levels rose. Only a little more than half of the eighth-graders surveyed were very happy or happy about Kennedy's victory over Nixon.[122]

During this period, children's attitudes toward the presidency differed significantly from adults' views. In 1958, researchers presented a questionnaire to fourth- through eighth-graders in New Haven, Connecticut, and found that most children lacked their parents' skepticism about politicians; instead, they tended to see presidents as benevolent figures.[123] The study's findings showed that the president was the most prominent leader in most children's worldview.[124] Ninety-six percent of fourth-graders could name the president (then Dwight D. Eisenhower or simply "Ike") and, by eighth grade, 100 percent could name him. Interestingly, 92 percent of children believed that the president's job performance was either very good or fairly good.[125] Obviously, these findings might have simply reflected good attitudes toward the grandfatherly Eisenhower, but a 1963 study by Robert D. Hess showed that children's opinions about the presidency changed little between the Eisenhower and Kennedy years.[126] Political scientist Roberta S. Sigel noted in the early 1960s that "the president, being far away, enjoys an added advantage over local authority figures: The child has no opportunity to check against reality the idealized image taught him by the adult world."[127] A follow-up paper on this topic in 1975 showed that, as a reflection of widespread political discontent in the late 1960s and 1970s, fewer children attached the quality of benevolence to politicians. Political scientist Fred I. Greenstein, who publicized the 1958 study and updated it in 1975, wrote that "as more than one commentator has noted, some of the same pre-adolescents who blithely 'idealized' Eisenhower and

Kennedy in the early studies may well have been the leaders of protest against 'the system' a few years later."[128]

After the assassination, many parents tried to talk to their children about what had happened, but because they were stunned themselves they could offer no easy answers or guarantees that this violent weekend had been an aberration rather than the first indication of growing political violence in the United States. One study found that parents were more likely to offer an explanation if they had high emotional involvement in Kennedy's death as well as political knowledge. Social status mattered much less than an understanding of politics. Of those parents who did attempt to explain the assassination, the largest number focused on the "diseased or wicked character of the assassin."[129] At the time they were questioned, 62 percent of the parents believed that the assassination had been a conspiracy, but there were no indications that they had shared these suspicions with their children.[130] The older the child, the more likely parents were to try to frame the event in a political or historical context.[131]

When psychologists and social scientists asked children about their reactions to the assassination, what they found was that children's feelings were not terribly different from the feelings of the adults around them. As one might expect, more children than adults thought this event had generated feelings they had never previously experienced, and that logically made the event more central to children's memories of national events. Like adults, many children became consumed by news about the assassination, and they reported similar levels of sadness. In considering Kennedy's death, 68.6 percent of white children and 80.7 percent of black children said they felt "the loss of someone very close and dear."[132] Like their parents, most children recalled initial feelings of disbelief. And children and adults also shared many of the same nervous symptoms— difficulty sleeping, headaches, upset stomach.[133] Nevertheless, there was one striking difference: Children sometimes remembered other people crying over Kennedy's death, but most denied that they had cried themselves. Fifty-three percent of adults admitted shedding tears, while only 39 percent of children recalled weeping. This reflects a taboo among children about openly crying.[134] On average, children worried somewhat more than their parents about how the assassination would affect the nation's future.[135] Nevertheless, idealization of the president grew after this crisis, while an understanding that a president could be killed predictably lessened children's belief in presidential power.[136]

A third-grader in Bristol, Maine, recalled the shock of seeing his "hard-boiled" teacher weeping as she delivered the bad news to her class, and he attributed his later fascination with politics and history to that single weekend in November 1963. "I've been a newsaholic ever since," said Norm Chase thirty-five years later. In college at the University of Maine, he majored in political science, and later moved to Dallas, where his taste in reading remained rooted in history. "I think the reason I feel such a connection to the event is because it led to an awareness that bad things can happen to someone without warning. Maybe that was the beginning of the end of some kind of innocence for me and for the country."[137] Journalist Jeff Rivers looked back thirty years to when he was 9 years old, and wrote:

> Earlier that year, my teacher had told us about James Garfield. He had been president in the olden days. He'd been fatally shot in 1881. But, the teacher had said, "that kind of thing couldn't happen today." She explained that the nation had changed, grown up, become more civilized, an assassination such as Garfield's could only have happened in our "cowboy past" . . . Like many children, I had loved Santa Claus and the Easter Bunny, but I didn't learn the truth about them until I was ready. I hadn't been ready for this—the assassination of President Kennedy.[138]

Among a generation of youngsters, most of whom had never attended a funeral, the televised services in Washington became the best-remembered event of the weekend, and the death announcement ranked second.[139] Children were more likely to blame Oswald alone and less likely to cast blame on a political faction or American society as a whole. Forty-one percent of children hoped that Oswald would be killed, while very few adults admitted to sharing that sentiment. Survey results indicated that younger children were more likely to adopt vengeful attitudes.[140]

While sharing adults' sense of shame that such a crime could happen in the United States, some children apparently had particularly strong feelings of personal guilt about the assassination. In letters to Kennedy's widow, Jacqueline, children voiced remorse. One Iowa girl blamed herself because she had experienced bad luck in the two years she had lived in her new house, and for her, Kennedy's death was just one more sign that two was her unlucky number.[141] A Chester, Pennsylvania, teenager felt responsible, too: "I prayed every night for God's help for the president so that he would always remain a perfect example as a Catholic and a leader," she wrote. "But I neglected these prayers last week, intending to make up for it during retreat this week. Consequently, I feel extremely guilty for, if I hadn't been so negligent, it might have rained and the hood [on Kennedy's limousine] would have been down."[142] A more chilling letter reached the White House from a youngster in Lodi, California. As a Seventh Day Adventist, she admitted that she was unhappy when a Catholic had been elected president, and she added that when she heard he had been shot, she had said, "I hope he dies."[143]

AFTERMATH

Some people questioned their own emotions; some lost faith in the goodness of the United States; others saw this shocking event as a reason to rededicate their lives to something more meaningful. No one in the United States was able to put much distance between the assassination and their own lives. The intensity of feelings about Kennedy was a problem for some. Glose remembers that

> my only feeling of guilt or shame was that this was touching me more than any death in my past. Although I didn't have a parent die yet in life, I guess Grandmother was closest, and two uncles. But I just felt this was closer to me, and I felt I should have felt worse at the death of my own family.[144]

In 1983, when *Newsweek* asked Americans about Kennedy, Hector de la Rosa, then a community worker in Salinas, California, wrote about his life as a migrant farm worker in 1963. He believed in the War on Poverty and saw it as Kennedy's legacy:

> I think Kennedy had a great inspiration that if Americans want to do it, we can do it. And up till today, almost every home that I go to that's Hispanic, I see a picture of Kennedy—a picture cut out of a newspaper or a magazine . . . And there's no pictures of any other president in the home. So it keeps reminding me, and I sort of relate to them, also because I have a picture of him also over at my house, in my bedroom.[145]

Kennedy's handsome visage has become an icon of hope to some people. For them, it retains the almost sacred quality that many applied to Kennedy in the days immediately following the assassination. This holy aura survives despite Kennedy's growing reputation as a sinner. His image is like an intricate stained-glass window to this group: It can be admired repeatedly without losing its power to instill uplifting emotions.

The Making of a Myth

A common response to the death of a loved one is to remember solely the goodness of the person who has died and to want other people to relish that person's best traits. Like many bereft people, thirty-four-year-old Jacqueline Kennedy wanted people to have fond memories of her murdered husband, but there was a difference between her and other people: She had the prominence to transform her warm memories of JFK into a myth, the myth of Camelot.

It all began with an interview she gave to Theodore H. White on November 29, 1963. In that interview, she recalled how her husband loved music from the Broadway hit *Camelot*, starring Richard Burton, Julie Andrews, and Robert Goulet. Specifically, she drew a connection between her husband's presidency and the last lines of the title song as it is sung at the end of the play: "Don't let it be forgot, that once there was a spot, for one brief shining moment that was known as Camelot." White published her words in *Life*, and he reinforced her message, ending his article by saying, "For one brief shining moment there was Camelot."[146]

From that point forward, a myth grew, tying Kennedy's administration to the glorious days of Camelot. Rather than being seen as a pragmatic leader or even a good man, JFK became an epitome of perfection: handsome and brilliant, witty and wise, gallant and regal. The propagation of this portrayal was accelerated by the fact that the first two prominent posthumous books to examine Kennedy's life and his service as president were written by Kennedy loyalists Theodore C. Sorensen and Arthur M. Schlesinger Jr. Though neither author explicitly embraced the Camelot imagery or claimed to be a Knight of the Round Table, each described Kennedy as a great president with few flaws. And, at a time when it seemed improper to speak badly of a president who had been gunned down at 46, the imagery of Camelot permeated media reprises of the Kennedy years.

Consequently, when more objective historians sought to revise the public face of Kennedy in the late 1960s and afterward, they felt the need to specifically target the Camelot myth. In a period when most people scorned the idea of heroes, the myth of Kennedy's Camelot increasingly seemed like nonsense. Reports of Kennedy's many infidelities, his misleading statements about his health, and his occasional stumbles as president competed with the Camelot myth for prominence. Attacks on Camelot benefited, too, from a legal scuffle between the Kennedys and author William Manchester over his book *The Death of a President*.

While it is well documented that as a boy JFK loved to read about King Arthur and his knights and that, as a man, he did indeed enjoy (former classmate) Alan Jay Lerner and Frederick Loewe's *Camelot*, it is equally well documented that many of his friends believe he would have scoffed at applying the Camelot myth to his administration. A cynic himself, he likely would have been embarrassed by the suggestion. Nevertheless, adopting that myth became a part of the mourning process for many Americans. The revisionists did their best to tear down every remnant of that mythical association, but some people did not care for revisionism. And, interestingly, the latest wave of JFK histories tends to paint a more human individual than the mythical JFK but also a better president than the early revisionists depicted.

For Ramsey, the assassination changed a lot more than who was sitting in the White House: "It clearly was a major loss of innocence."[147] Almost fifty years later, former Peace Corps volunteer Connelly still believes Kennedy was unique:

> There would never be anything like John F. Kennedy again . . . It doesn't happen anymore—that kind of leadership, that kind of charisma. It was joy; it was fun; it was interesting. He did appeal to us: "Ask not what your country can do." We kind of got into that. We felt a whole new world opening up for us because of the Peace Corps.[148]

Many Americans felt that Kennedy's death signaled the end to an era of hope, but others heard a call to duty as they mourned. A mother of nine children in Minnesota wrote a condolence letter to Jacqueline Kennedy, saying, "Your husband has not died in vain; because I know many Americans . . . are ready to rededicate their lives & ask God to help us build strong, unselfish, God-fearing, good Americans, who would proudly die for their country and their God as he did."[149]

Between one quarter and one third of the participants in a post-assassination study in Chicago believed that they had an obligation to rededicate their lives. This feeling was strongest among those who classified themselves as grief-stricken. Christopher J. Hurn and Mark Messer, both research associates in the Center for Metropolitan Studies at Northwestern University, concluded that "the assassination of President Kennedy brought the respondents, some of them for the first time perhaps, into an intense involvement with a public event." Those who felt a calling to rededicate their lives "perceived a relationship between a public event and the manner in which they and others had hitherto conducted their lives. They did not feel merely that 'something should be done' or that people like themselves should rededicate their lives, but that they themselves should attempt to be more tolerant, promote brotherhood, and become better citizens."[150] A second-year law student in Washington, D.C., in November 1963, Frank Heller lost faith in the government and the system during that long weekend. "It literally was a shattering of innocence, nobility, and idealism," he concluded many years later. "The assassination was like the atomic bomb that wasn't dropped before. It was as shocking as we had imagined it might be." Over that weekend, Heller met with friends to discuss the possibility that a conspiracy had taken Kennedy's life, but for him the assassination's most compelling result was to highlight Kennedy's ideals about how the government should attack social problems. Therefore, instead of seeking a high-paying job after law school, he played a part in Johnson's grand schemes to continue Kennedy's legacy and bolster equality. Heller worked in the War on Poverty and Head Start, and, in 1972, he threw himself into the presidential campaign of Democratic Senator George McGovern of South Dakota. Four years later, he left the political rat race and moved to Maine, where he built a life around his own small businesses. "There actually was a romance to a lot of the Great Society programs. Government now only does things it can win," he said in 1998.[151] Johnson himself witnessed a post-assassination turn toward better living. "I think that following the assassination, the people of the nation engaged in some introspection," he said. "And as a consequence, they became more concerned with their fellow human beings than they did with themselves."[152]

Kennedy's calls to activism and his tragic death fired the passions of many Baby Boomers who participated in the movements for peace, civil rights, feminism, and environmentalism. It is impossible to know how many activists traced the roots of their involvement to Kennedy, but we know that some members of one of the most well-known radical political groups, Students for a Democratic Society, saw Kennedy as the catalyst for their organization's formation and drive.[153] Widespread activism faded over time as the protesters of the late 1960s and early 1970s disappeared into the conformity of the 1980s. Nevertheless, they had profound effects on American public policy and on the lives of American citizens, including many who did not share their movements' goals. Among the eventual results of their struggles were elimination of the military draft, federal requirements for schools to provide equal funding for girls' sports, use of unleaded gasoline to limit air pollution, business incentives supporting diversity in the workplace, and the election of the first African American president—an event more unimaginable in the 1960s than landing a man on the moon. If Kennedy's life and death provided the spark that inspired even 10 percent of these activists' achievements, then his impact, indeed, stretched far beyond November 1963.

CHAPTER 4

Life after Death

*"The whole earth is the sepulcher of famous
men; and their story is graven not only on
stone over their native earth, but lives on far
away, without visible symbol, woven into the
stuff of other men's lives."*
  Pericles' Funeral Oration from Thucydides[1]

As he squinted into the bright sunlight of a November day in Dallas, Lyndon Johnson had no way of knowing that his life and the nation's history were about to change. A mail-order gun took John F. Kennedy's life, but his memory would burn brightly in the minds of many Americans for years to come. In death, he would become an enticing chimera who would never grow old, never make another mistake, never stumble into an unwinnable war.

Even after JFK died and Johnson became president, LBJ's relationship with Kennedy did not end. Day after day, in Johnson's mind, the ghost of JFK stood beside him, judging him and beckoning Americans to a mythical world far better than anything Johnson could offer. Kennedy remained a colleague who could not be forgotten, a rival who could not be beaten, a ghost who could not be dispelled. Tying his legislative package to JFK's martyrdom bolstered Johnson's masterfully directed legislative initiatives, and as a result Johnson continued to link himself to the Kennedy legacy. Through years of careful and respectful interactions, the two men had prepared the groundwork for Johnson's transition to the presidency. What could not be anticipated was Kennedy's lasting hold on the American imagination and that phenomenon's effect on Johnson's presidency and his place in history. Johnson found himself haunted by Americans' rosy memories of JFK and by a living apparition in the form of Kennedy's brother and confidant, Attorney General Robert Kennedy.

NOT THE SAME

As Johnson became president, he was keenly aware of how the broad differences between JFK and himself might affect Americans' impressions of him. The pairing of Kennedy and Johnson had been an inspired ticket-balancing gambit. Its regional component was most obvious, but it would have been difficult to find two leading politicians who were more different in appearance, personality, and style. On political issues they were much closer than many Americans would have guessed; nevertheless, they moved in different social circles and claimed divergent alliances.

Kennedy had the glamorous aura of a youthful movie star with a stinging wit. His wife was gorgeous and stylish. Even his adorable children looked like products of central casting. His family seemed perfectly packaged for the golden age of picture-laden magazines and TV's rise to prominence within the news media. Though he could be a charmer, JFK was a man who tended to put distance between himself and those around him. Bright and spirited, he enjoyed human companionship but preferred reading to long group discussions. Dean Rusk, who served as secretary of state under both men, suggested that Kennedy was skeptical about everything and everyone, including himself.[2] He took money for granted and often carried an empty wallet. However, because he knew that his appearance gave his political career a boost, he never went out without a manicurist's pencil during the 1960 campaign and, while serving in the Senate, he always changed into a clean suit between day and evening sessions.[3] Recognizing the power of television to bolster an enviable image, he invited its challenges.

Johnson was neither handsome nor witty, but he was profoundly memorable. Everything about him was super-sized—from his height and his ears to his personality and his ego. He was an in-your-face, in-your-space politician. When he was happy, that elation was contagious; when his cheeks sagged in a hangdog grimace, his sadness and frustration were palpable. He was a doer more than a thinker. Like a bounding golden retriever, he loved people and was impossible to ignore in his natural state. In the vice presidency, he typically restrained himself to fit within the bounds of the job, but it was a struggle. A mercurial fusion of emotion and cunning drove him to success. Naturally boisterous, he could be the life of the party and the tyrant of the office. Seeing himself as the perpetual underdog, he could range from arrogance to self-pity on any given day. He learned more through conversational exchanges than he did by reading. And he was, in every sense of the term, a political animal.

Orville Freeman, who served both men as secretary of agriculture, said Kennedy was a more congenial boss, but in social situations he felt closer to Johnson.[4] In his diary, after the assassination, Freeman noted that Kennedy "was never really outgoing in a sense with people that felt close to him, but yet he had a peculiar quality that so endeared him and commanded such loyalty and devotion." He recalled a conversation with Franklin D. Roosevelt Jr., who had told him that he had witnessed Kennedy's strangely dispassionate charisma even when they were schoolboys together.[5] As a 2-year-old stricken with scarlet fever and confined to a hospital with no visits from his mother, JFK had learned the value of charming those around him;[6] as the son of an alcoholic, Johnson grew up seeking validation of his worth in a lonely battle to find love in a complicated childhood.

Kennedy compartmentalized his life, a skill he undoubtedly learned from his promiscuous father and his pious mother. He could be a crisis-solving president in one minute and a fully engaged father to a rambunctious toddler in the next. He was not a workaholic and, just like flipping a switch, he could change from professional to casual. This unusual knack for separating the parts of his life seems to explain his ability to behave recklessly in the sexual arena while remaining a cautious leader.

Johnson, on the other hand, was a politician twenty-four hours a day. Surrendering to impulse, he called people at all hours to talk about issues. At his dinner table, he shocked guests by calling on them to analyze political events. His persuasive powers were awesome. During his years as Senate majority leader, many colleagues wilted with a sigh under the heat of what they called "the Johnson treatment." One politician said, "Being won over by Johnson is a rather overwhelming experience. The full treatment is an incredibly potent mixture of persuasion, badgering, flattery, threats, reminders of past favors and future advantages."[7]

With the help of speechwriter Ted Sorensen, Kennedy's oratory soared. Johnson's speeches were more evangelical, driven by emotions that sometimes gave his simple words unexpected power. Kennedy spoke quickly with a clipped New England accent; Johnson had a rich Southern drawl often oozing with heavy doses of melancholy. Growing up in a wealthy, politically active family, Kennedy had traveled abroad from an early age. Between 1939 and 1941 alone, he had visited twenty-two nations in Europe, the Middle East, and South America. Johnson never enjoyed that luxury. When he became vice president, he had taken two trips to

Europe and one brief military mission to the South Pacific. Beyond that, his international travel had been limited to visiting Acapulco.

While Kennedy was low-key, Johnson was markedly aggressive. In a masterful attempt to draw distinctions between the two men without angering the still-living, still-powerful Johnson, Louisiana's Senator Allen J. Ellender said in 1967, "President Kennedy was a lovable character. He was easy-going, and he didn't try to twist anybody's arm. I'm not saying now by indirection that Lyndon Johnson does that, but I've heard it often said that he does . . . [Kennedy] didn't go to you and say, 'Well now, I expect you to do this.' Not that he said, 'If you don't, you can expect punishment from me,' or anything like that, but President Johnson has a peculiar way of getting people to work with him, and he's very successful at that."[8] Johnson's persuasive skills made the task of working with Congress easier for him than it had been for Kennedy.

JFK sometimes disagreed with the people who worked for him, and he did not hesitate to overrule them. He could be stern and sarcastic, but he was not a screamer. Johnson's staff often felt his wrath, and he

Figure 4.1 With his wife, Lady Bird, at his side, the new president, Lyndon B. Johnson, speaks upon arrival at Andrews Air Force Base. Photograph by Cecil Stoughton. John F. Kennedy Presidential Library and Museum, Boston.

occasionally launched into unbridled tirades against underlings whose only sin was disagreeing with him. Kennedy was a private person, who shrank from physical displays of affection and refused to be seen wearing funny hats, but Johnson sometimes invited officials to brief him when he was sitting on the toilet.[9] Johnson once disrobed and changed clothes during a press briefing in Saigon, and in Bangkok he gave a press conference in his pajamas.[10]

A document at the Lyndon B. Johnson Library lists Kennedy's favorite books as *Lord Melbourne* by Lord David Cecil and *John Quincy Adams* by Samuel Bemis. The same list identifies the naval veteran's favorite song appropriately as "Anchors Aweigh."[11] (We know he liked "Camelot," too.) On the library's website, a page is dedicated to Johnson's favorites, which begin with food and include no books. He loved coconut macaroons, Mexican food, and Scotch. His favorite songs included "The Battle Hymn of the Republic" and "Raindrops Keep Falling on My Head." He wore Old Spice, and all of his favorite activities involved being with people.[12]

They were, indeed, an odd couple. Their differences accentuated the shock of Johnson's sudden rise to the presidency. Kennedy's death heightened his standing as an American hero and deepened Johnson's discomfort about comparisons between the two men.

LBJ'S FIRST WEEK

Johnson stood one step away from center stage during his first four days as president. He ascended to the nation's highest office under the worst possible circumstances. He hated the mind-numbing purgatory of the vice presidency, but its gory end came drenched in horror, disbelief, and doubt. He could offer the nation a quiet sense of stability, but until Kennedy's burial the late president and his family still claimed the hearts of most Americans. Confused and frightened like many of his countrymen, Johnson could offer no answers.

"I found it hard to believe that this nightmare had actually happened," he later wrote. "The violence of the whole episode was unreal, shocking, and incredible. A few hours earlier, I had been having breakfast with John Kennedy—alive, young, strong, and vigorous. I could not believe that he was dead. I was bewildered and distraught."[13] His grief and shock were genuine. He had liked JFK and had enjoyed a cordial relationship with him. Moreover, Johnson was horrified that this tragedy had occurred in the worst possible place, his home state of Texas, where the spirit of the Wild West still showed signs of life and where schoolchildren applauded the president's murder.

Perhaps, there was unexpected comfort in having those first few days to get his bearings, while the widow, the children, and the coffin held the nation spellbound. Without commanding the spotlight, Johnson began planning his administration. He knew that much of Kennedy's staff held him in contempt. The awkward flight from Dallas to Andrews Air Force Base had reinforced those feelings. In a plane full of people in shock, the Kennedy and Johnson teams had clearly divided into camps. Johnson's rise to the presidency seemed like a brutal insult to some. "It was almost as if they were angry at Johnson," *Newsweek*'s Charles Roberts later recalled.[14] Remembering that awful flight, Johnson wrote that "along with grief I felt anguish, compassion, and a deep concern for Mrs. Kennedy and the children."[15]

According to his own recollections, Johnson made a silent commitment during the flight: He would do his utmost to fulfill JFK's goals, especially in Vietnam. "Rightly or wrongly, I felt from the very first day in office that I had to carry on for President Kennedy," he explained. "I considered myself the caretaker of both his people and his policies. He knew when he selected me as his running mate that I would be the man required to carry on if anything happened to him. I did what I believed he would have wanted me to do."[16] Aboard Air Force One, he called Kennedy's mother Rose in Hyannis Port. She responded warmly to his condolences, saying, "I know you loved Jack, and he loved you."[17]

After the plane reached Andrews and before workmen had finished pushing portable stairs up to the jet's front door, Robert Kennedy was dashing up those steps. He bounded onto the plane and wordlessly brushed past Johnson on his way to find Jacqueline Kennedy. Johnson had hoped to escort Mrs. Kennedy and the coffin off the plane as a sign of continuity, but she asked Kennedy's Secret Service detail to carry the coffin from the back of Air Force One, leaving the Johnsons uninvolved and isolated in the front of the plane. As the nation caught its first glimpse of the grieving widow, Robert Kennedy was the person standing beside her.

Hoping to convey to the country that government would go on despite this tragedy, Johnson had rejected the idea of banning the press from Andrews. After departure of the ambulance carrying Jacqueline Kennedy, Robert Kennedy, and the late president's body to Bethesda Naval Hospital, the Johnsons descended from Air Force One's front exit. Johnson made a brief, somewhat meek statement, and spoke briefly with dignitaries gathered there. He then boarded a helicopter to the White House along with his wife Lady Bird, National Security Adviser McGeorge Bundy, Secretary of Defense Robert McNamara, and Undersecretary of State George Ball. The president's key foreign policy advisers (minus Secretary of State

Dean Rusk, who was en route back to Washington from his aborted trip to Japan) told Johnson that there were no signs of international trouble and no Soviet troop movements to suggest that the assassination had been the opening maneuver in a military conflict. Ball later recalled that Johnson talked primarily about his admiration for Mrs. Kennedy's strength, dignity, and courage. After arriving at the White House, Mrs. Johnson rode to her home, known as The Elms. Johnson stepped briefly into the Oval Office and then went to his office in the Executive Office Building.

In a phone call to Supreme Court Justice Arthur Goldberg, the new president conveyed his trepidation. "I want you to be thinking about what I ought to do to try to bring all of these elements together and unite the country to maintain and preserve our system in the world," he said. "Because I—if it starts falling to pieces—and some of the extremes are going to be proceeding on the wrong assumption, why we could deteriorate pretty quick."[18] When he went home that night, Johnson's 16-year-old daughter Luci thought "he looked like he'd been run over by a truck and yet was very strong."[19] The Secret Service agents accompanying her father had lost one president that day, so as they approached The Elms they openly brandished their guns. At 1:00 a.m. November 23, the new president retired to his room with longtime associates Jack Valenti, Bill Moyers, and Clifton C. Carter. The four men talked until 3:00 a.m. about the day's events and likely public perceptions of a Johnson presidency.

A day after the assassination, journalists had already begun speculating about how Johnson's new role might affect the 1964 elections. Because Johnson was a southerner, some predicted that he was likely to choose a liberal running mate, and others expected his incumbency to give Republican liberals an advantage in the fight for the GOP nomination. Though Johnson's presidential re-election was a hot topic, he was still working in the vice president's office and living in his own home.

Transfixed by her brave beauty, Johnson wanted to treat Jacqueline Kennedy with the utmost respect and kindness; he also feared that negative reactions from Robert Kennedy could become a stumbling block to his presidency. Valenti wrote thirty-five years later that, on November 22 as he waited on Air Force One at Dallas's Love Field, "LBJ foresaw that [if he left] he would be maligned for being so eager to be president that he left behind his predecessor's body."[20]

> Despite pleas from the Secret Service and others, LBJ did not move into the Oval Office until after Kennedy's funeral, and he delayed taking up residence in the White House until December 7, the day after Mrs. Kennedy and her children moved out.

Johnson himself feared what RFK had in mind. "During all of that period, I think [Robert Kennedy] seriously considered whether he would let me be president, whether he should really take the position [that] the vice president didn't automatically move in. I thought that was on his mind every time I saw him the first few days," Johnson later told an interviewer.[21] In fact, when the State Department originally planned a reception for foreign dignitaries attending the funeral, the original scenario called for Robert Kennedy, not Lyndon Johnson, to serve as host to visiting heads of state.[22] Kennedy's unique role during his brother's presidency created confusion, as did Johnson's sudden move toward the spotlight. (It is unclear whether Johnson knew that, in 1961, Attorney General Kennedy had written an analysis of the constitutional grounds for vice-presidential succession to the presidency. In it, he concluded that the Founding Fathers had never meant for a vice president to be anything more than acting president following a president's death. He believed the vice president's service as acting president was intended to end with the election of a new president. RFK felt that the convention's clarity on this point had been lost when a five-man committee on style made revisions to the constitution.)[23]

On November 23, Johnson lived a day in fast-forward mode, losing himself in frantic activity. His daily diary entries list thirty-six telephone calls and thirty-two meetings, including a five-minute breakfast with his wife. He received intelligence briefings, conferred with former presidents Harry S. Truman and Dwight D. Eisenhower, held a Cabinet meeting, talked to congressional leaders, met with Mrs. Kennedy briefly in the White House living quarters, spoke by telephone with FBI Director J. Edgar Hoover about the murder investigation in Dallas, and went to St. John's Episcopal Church for a few minutes. One of Johnson's first recorded actions as president was declaration of November 25 as an official day of mourning for JFK. His daily diary, now located on the website of the Lyndon B. Johnson Library, shows traces of dishonesty in the official report of his activities. A couple of unexpected encounters are misrepresented as meetings with benign purposes. The diary shows a meeting with President Kennedy's private secretary, Evelyn Lincoln, and another with Attorney General Robert Kennedy between 8:40 and 9:20 a.m. The purpose listed for both meetings is expression of regret. In reality, Johnson, who had planned to move into the Oval Office that morning at the recommendation of McNamara and Rusk, asked Mrs. Lincoln to quickly clean out her desk. Kennedy, who was nearby, interceded and told Johnson that it would take time to make JFK's work areas ready. Johnson retreated to his domain in the Executive Office Building, where he stayed until November 26.

Looking back on that day, Eisenhower described the new president as being overwhelmed, and noted that LBJ repeatedly commented that he must fulfill Kennedy's agenda.[24] Eisenhower noticed that Johnson "suggested nothing new or different. He wanted to talk about Laos, Cuba, and so forth. He seemed to be less informed about foreign policy than about domestic policy."[25] Rusk asked all assistant secretaries of state to prepare notes for Johnson about any anticipated repercussions of the assassination, and Marshall Green's response stated plainly what the biggest problem would be in the Far East: "President Kennedy's personal touch will be gone; so will his influence and prestige."[26] Many of the foreign dignitaries who attended the funeral requested one-on-one sessions with Johnson over the following days, because he was not well known among world leaders. European leaders who had met him during his vice-presidential trips or on other occasions "thought that his manners were bad. They thought of him as a rustic," said NBC newsman John Chancellor. The more cosmopolitan Kennedy, by comparison, was extremely popular among them. When Kennedy died, Chancellor placed European officials in two groups: "one, who . . . said, 'Well, who's Lyndon Johnson? We don't know anything about him.' And another smaller and probably more influential group, a tiny group who said, 'Oh, my God, not him!' So he started way behind with the Europeans, *way behind.*"[27]

During those first few days, Johnson met privately with many members of Kennedy's Cabinet and staff. His message was simple: He wanted to keep Kennedy's team. He needed their help, Johnson told them, and the nation deserved a sense of continuity. In his meeting with Arthur Heller, chairman of the Council of Economic Advisers, Johnson heard details of the stock market's 3 percent plunge on Friday after news of the Dallas shooting and got his first briefing on JFK's request for recommendations on conquering poverty, a cause that Johnson embraced enthusiastically. After his meeting with Johnson, Arthur M. Schlesinger Jr. wrote that LBJ described Kennedy's staff as superior to his own: "He said all this with simplicity, dignity, and apparent conviction. I am a little perplexed as to what to do. I am sure that I must leave, but I can see the problem of disengagement is going to be considerable."[28]

On Sunday, November 24, Johnson conferred with U.S. Ambassador to South Vietnam, Henry Cabot Lodge, who had been scheduled to meet with Kennedy. "I am not going to be the president who saw Southeast Asia go the way China went," he told Lodge.[29] Subsequently, LBJ announced to the public that he would continue assistance to the war-ravaged nation.

In the eyes of some, Johnson represented a step backward from the bright future promised by Kennedy's youth and élan. "I took the oath.

I became president," Johnson told Doris Kearns Goodwin, "but for millions of Americans I was still illegitimate, a naked man with no presidential covering, a pretender to the throne, an illegal usurper. And then there was Texas, my home, the home of both the murder and the murder of the murderer."[30] As the days of mourning unfolded, Johnson, like the widow, became a subject of sympathy among those who saw a shaken man facing an enormous task. Even journalists, who usually shy away from shows of support for politicians, found themselves blessing Johnson. Roberts was somewhat surprised to hear himself say, "God be with you, Mr. President," as they flew back to Washington on Air Force One.[31] During the funeral Mass three days later, Ben Bradlee, a Kennedy friend from *Newsweek*, briefly stood alongside Johnson. "I knew he would live in Kennedy's shadow for the rest of his life, and that he needed help," Bradlee later said, so he whispered, "God bless you" in Johnson's ear.[32] On the day of the funeral, as they rode to the Capitol, even Jacqueline Kennedy said, "Oh, Lyndon, what an awful way for you to come in."[33]

After the funeral, Johnson hosted the State Department reception for foreign dignitaries and met with about thirty governors in attendance. He told the governors that he would push for approval of Kennedy's civil rights bill and his proposed tax cut. And he reported that all Cabinet officials and high-ranking appointees had offered their resignations, although he wanted them to stay.

The earliest quantifiable judgment of Johnson's first days as president was a sharp rise in stock prices when the markets reopened on Tuesday, November 26. In deference to Robert Kennedy's feelings, Johnson delayed his first address to a joint session of Congress until 12:30 p.m. on Wednesday, November 27. When he spoke, he began with a simple declaration: "All I have ever possessed I would have gladly given *not* to be here today." Johnson praised President Kennedy's leadership and urged Congress to enact his proposals. "The greatest leader of our time has been struck down by the foulest deed of our time," he said. "Today John Fitzgerald Kennedy lives on in the immortal words and works that he left behind. He lives in the mind and memories of mankind. He lives on in the hearts of his countrymen." The finest memorial to Kennedy, he argued, would be approval of his civil rights legislation. "We have talked long enough in this country about equal rights. We have talked for one hundred years or more. It is time now to write the next chapter, and to write it in the books of law," he declared. His major theme ran parallel to an exhortation in Kennedy's inaugural address: "Let us begin."[34] As he spoke in November 1963, Johnson's message was: "Let us continue." In a Thanksgiving Day address on the following day, Johnson told Americans that he wanted "to ask that you remember your country and remember me each day in your prayers."[35] At that time, opinion polls showed that 70 percent of Americans voiced uncertainty about how the nation would proceed without Kennedy,[36] but Johnson was beginning to allay concerns.

In his syndicated column, Joseph Alsop recalled a 1960 conversation with John F. Kennedy. In it, Kennedy said something like this: "If I didn't want the job myself, I'd get behind Lyndon. He's the ablest man I know in American politics and he really cares about this country as I want a president to care."[37] Those words, published days after Johnson took office, bolstered his position. A week after Kennedy's death, the *Wall Street Journal* reported that LBJ had "done much to command respect and encourage confidence."[38]

After a difficult week, Kennedy's cabinet and staff remained unsettled. Some would adjust to new leadership and become members of Johnson's team. McNamara, Rusk, and Bundy were the most obvious members of this group. Others, like Schlesinger and Sorensen, would politely exit. A third group, best represented by Robert Kennedy, would remain at the White House for months or years without ever accepting Johnson as president.

PRESIDENT JOHNSON

In his notes for *The Making of the President 1964*, Theodore White wrote a memo to himself dated February 28, 1964:

> When did politics resume? It was as if the nation was madly, purposefully, seeking distraction. Perhaps it was when the Beatles came—and never, ever, has more commotion been rouse [sic] by more meager characters; or perhaps it was the Liston–Clay bout; for radio almost came into its own again as it offered the nation the insane bellowing of "I am the greatest, I am the King." But always in the forefront was the sense that things were not right, as if Johnson were an usurper. A taximan in New York called Emanuele Damioni carried in front of his cab where cab drivers normally carry a St. Christopher medal, a black-edged portrait of John F. Kennedy.

Then, a handwritten addendum by White: "What would Kennedys have done with Beatles?"[39]

It was not the Beatles or Cassius Clay aka Mohammad Ali who reset the nation's mood. Time and Johnson's steady hand helped to restore normalcy. Hubert Humphrey once compared Johnson's dogged determination to "a tidal wave,"[40] and LBJ's tsunami quickly began to sweep away the logjam that had blocked Kennedy's bills in Congress— an outcome Kennedy almost certainly would not have accomplished before winning a second term. Kennedy's death had generated a desire to honor his memory, and that simplified some battles. However, Johnson's mastery of the process was crucial, too. JFK's eloquence had never translated into success in Congress. He was not comfortable wading knee-deep into legislative battles, while Johnson flourished in a congressional tug of war and enjoyed identifying the tactics that would guarantee success. "Everything I had ever learned in the history books taught me that martyrs have to die for causes. John F. Kennedy had died . . . I had to take the dead man's program and turn it into a martyr's cause. That way Kennedy would live on forever, and so would I," he said.[41]

Johnson, who considered Franklin Roosevelt his political "daddy," hoped to remake America as FDR had.[42] In his January 1964 State of the Union address, he dramatically proclaimed that his administration had declared "unconditional war on poverty."[43] He placed Kennedy in law Sargent Shriver in charge of the offensive and tied it to JFK's legacy. Johnson told Shriver that "the sky's the limit," as long as no program resorted to simply handing out money to the poor.[44]

Johnson put his initial legislative effort behind Kennedy's proposed tax cut. To win passage, Johnson promised to keep the federal budget below $100 billion. In February 1964, despite strong opposition from Senate Finance Committee Chairman Harry Byrd, the bill passed.[45] After its enactment, the economy heated up, and unemployment dropped.[46]

> The tax cut proposal was controversial because it came at a time of prosperity and because it guaranteed a budget deficit; nevertheless, Kennedy's financial advisers had convinced him that it was necessary to reduce the unemployment rate, which exceeded 5 percent.

The magnitude of Johnson's support for civil rights legislation surprised some observers, who had considered its passage impossible until after the 1964 presidential election. The legislation faced no significant challenge in the House: The big threat, as always in civil rights struggles, was in the Senate. One reason that no strong civil rights measure had won congressional approval since Reconstruction was conservative lawmakers' ability to block Senate votes by launching filibusters. Breaking a filibuster requires the votes of three-fifths of the Senate. As long as conservative Republicans and southern Democrats stuck together, the Senate would never vote on civil rights legislation unless it had been watered down to avoid a filibuster. Johnson refused to weaken his bill, which was stronger than what Kennedy had proposed in June 1963. Cannily, LBJ decided to target the Republican leader in the Senate, Everett Dirksen. Johnson was willing to give government contracts to Dirksen's home state of Illinois, and he was happy to praise Dirksen loudly as long as the lawmaker supported ending a filibuster. Dirksen agreed. One lawmaker thought he could sink the bill by adding a provision against sex discrimination, but the bill passed with that provision intact. As a result, the newly created Equal Employment Opportunity Commission had orders to root out discrimination based on race or gender. With much fanfare, Johnson signed the bill on July 2, 1964.

Despite his legislative victories, Johnson was not at peace. In what some aides considered obsessive behavior, he constantly tried to anticipate what Robert Kennedy might do. Within the Kennedy circle, whispered accusations quickly arose that Johnson wrongly delayed Air Force One in Dallas so that he could take the presidential oath. Early in 1964, the new president feared a pro-Kennedy stampede might deny him the presidential nomination at the 1964 Democratic National Convention. Later, as Johnson registered legislative success after success, Kennedy allies pushed to make RFK the vice-presidential nominee. LBJ rankled at the idea. Complaining about "the Bobby problem," he voiced fears that his presidency might be a space-filler between two Kennedy administrations. "I'd waited for my turn. Bobby should have waited for his. But he and the Kennedy people wanted it now. A tidal wave of letters and memos about how great a vice president Bobby would be swept over me. No matter what, I couldn't let it happen." Johnson's biggest reason for opposing RFK's nomination was not his attitude or his record: He did not want RFK as his running mate because "with Bobby on the ticket, I'd never know if I could be elected on my own."[47] Ultimately, although Kennedy led in polls gauging the popularity of possible vice-presidential nominees,[48] Johnson skirted the issue by announcing that no Cabinet member would be considered for vice president. He enjoyed telling people that when he informed RFK of his decision, Kennedy's mouth dropped open. Kennedy later apologized to a fellow Cabinet member for "taking you all with me."[49] He decided to run for the U.S. Senate in New York and, with Johnson's help on the campaign trail, he won. Johnson may have felt awkward about helping Kennedy, but having his rival on Capitol Hill was far better than having him inside the administration. Johnson chose Senator Hubert Humphrey, a gregarious liberal warhorse, as his running mate.

The strength of Bobby Kennedy's hostility toward Johnson is clear in a 1964 interview in which he referred to Johnson as "mean, bitter, vicious—an animal in many ways."[50] Journalist Stewart Alsop, who was a close friend of President Kennedy, believed that Robert Kennedy treated Johnson like "he was a Macbeth, that his claim to the presidency was inherently illegitimate—always that kind of instinctive sub-level feeling about Johnson." Alsop believed that, on a "subconscious" level, many Kennedy supporters saw Johnson as usurping power.[51] Clark Clifford, Johnson's friend and second secretary of defense, noted the same phenomenon: "It seemed to irritate Bobby Kennedy when he saw President Johnson as president. His attitude was almost—and I think to a certain extent the attitude of the Kennedy family—was that President Johnson was an interloper of some kind."[52] Clifford told an interviewer that almost all of Johnson's attempts to make friendly contact with the Kennedy family "were rejected in a manner that was thoroughly offensive and insulting." Clifford believed Johnson "was gracious and courteous and handled it in statesmanlike fashion and they repulsed him at every turn."[53] Once, Johnson invited longtime Kennedy aide Kenneth O'Donnell to join him when he attended a birthday party for Jacqueline Kennedy at a Washington club. O'Donnell and Johnson arrived in street clothes, but many of those attending wore white ties and tails because they planned to attend an embassy event later. "We stood there," O'Donnell recalled. "We had a drink. We wandered around, almost trying to get somebody to talk to him. It was just outrageous . . . He still was vice president to most of those people. They were fluttering around Jackie and Bobby was there, and they were fluttering around Bobby."[54] Johnson friend and aide Liz Carpenter believed that "Lyndon Johnson had come on stage before a black curtain, and the Kennedys made no move to lift the darkness for him, or for the country."[55]

In the 1964 election, Johnson won what he wanted more than any-thing—the American presidency in a landslide victory. The Republicans made his chore easier by nominating Barry Goldwater of the party's extreme right wing. Johnson knew that he would lose southern votes because of white backlash caused by his civil rights bill, but his campaign tried to initiate "frontlash," which was abandonment of the GOP by liberal and moderate voters who were uncomfortable with Goldwater's radicalism. Johnson received 43,129,484 votes; Goldwater garnered only 27,178,188. It represented the biggest vote margin in history and the highest percentage of the vote ever won by a president, 61 percent. At the same time, Democrats won a 68–32 split in the Senate and a 295–140 margin in the House of Representatives.[56] Nevertheless, turning that victory into a successful presidency would not be easy.

On Capitol Hill, Johnson continued to triumph. Congress approved only 27 percent of Kennedy's legislative package in 1963, but LBJ had a 58 percent success rate in 1964, 69 percent in 1965, and 56 percent in

1966.[57] During 1965, LBJ won passage of two items that had been on the Democrats' agenda since Harry Truman's presidency—medical insurance for the elderly and aid to public education. The Voting Rights Act of 1965 opened the way for African Americans to cast ballots in southern states where questionable literacy tests had stopped them from registering for nearly a century.[58] In another social initiative, the government launched Head Start to help underprivileged children get ready for first grade. LBJ signed legislation establishing the Department of Housing and Urban Development and became the first president to nominate an African American to a Cabinet post when he chose Robert Weaver as HUD's first leader. Johnson won approval of the Water Quality Act, the Highway Beautification Act, and the Immigration Act, which repealed an immigration quota system in effect since 1921. Passage of the Higher Education Act set aside more federal money for universities and added scholarships and low-interest loans. Furthermore, in this busy year, Johnson managed to get his old friend, Abe Fortas, a seat on the Supreme Court. The following year, Johnson signed two more important pieces of legislation, the Freedom of Information Act and a bill establishing the Department of Transportation. His legislative bandwagon hit a few bumps in 1967, but he signed into law the Food Stamp Act, the National Product Safety Commission Act, the Air Quality Act, and the Public Broadcasting Act, which led to formation of PBS and NPR. In another historic first, Johnson named an African American, Thurgood Marshall, to the Supreme Court. Unfortunately for LBJ, winning legislative battles represented just one facet of his job.

In April 1965, Johnson sent military forces into the Dominican Republic, a Caribbean nation where rebellion had erupted against pro-American dictator Donald Reid Cabral. The rebels wanted to renew a constitutional government. There was violence in the streets, and Johnson ostensibly sent troops to evacuate American citizens. Less than a week after the troops' arrival, a cease-fire was declared, and a five-man Government of National Reconstruction was formed. Cabral no longer was a key figure, but a year later a pro-American candidate was elected to lead the country. In all, 14,000 U.S. soldiers took part in the initial invasion, and Americans participated in an Inter-American Peace Force to prevent more violence before the June 1, 1966 election. This intervention generated political opposition, although it was not widespread.

In the summer of 1965, Johnson watched helplessly as six days of rioting in Los Angeles' Watts area took thirty-four lives, sent 1,000 to hospitals, and led to almost 4,000 arrests. Johnson, who had hoped to win a special place in the hearts of African Americans, saw black rage consume a neighborhood. In July 1967, he sent U.S. military forces to quash rebellion in the Congo and in Detroit, where forty-three people died in rioting. In the aftermath of Detroit's violent eruption, he named a special panel, the Kerner Commission, to investigate racial conflict and civil disorder in the United States.

Meanwhile, in the Senate, Robert Kennedy had begun drifting to the left. His first speech in 1965 was about the dangers of the nuclear arms race, and he opposed the murders of 100,000 suspected Communists in Indonesia. The following year, he encouraged U.S. pressure on many Latin American countries to take land away from the wealthy minority and redistribute it to aid the impoverished. Traveling internationally, he often was treated like a head of state rather than a member of the Senate. At home, he had inherited African American support from his brother. When asked why he was so excited to see Robert Kennedy in his neighborhood, one youth explained, "His brother, the president, was like a father to me."[59] Johnson, who felt he should have won minority support for his legislative efforts, resented seeing black, Mexican American, and poor white constituents bestowing their love on RFK. Everything about Robert Kennedy made him a nightmare for Johnson.

VIETNAM

The defining issue of Johnson's presidency was Vietnam. He maintained a policy that was solidly grounded in his vice presidency. In 1961, he had traveled to the struggling nation and met with its leader, Ngo Dinh Diem, to offer reassurances of U.S. support for South Vietnam following American acceptance of neutrality in Laos. Johnson established a favorable opinion of Diem, and U.S. diplomats believed that he left Diem feeling optimistic about ongoing American support.[60] In a report for President Kennedy, Johnson argued that America must take a leadership role in Southeast Asia. However, he told Kennedy, "American combat troop involvement is not only not required, it is not desirable." At this time, North Vietnamese infiltration into South Vietnam mainly consisted of South Vietnamese citizens returning home to join the Viet Cong. The rebels' weapons supply source was material stolen from the South Vietnamese government— conditions that changed as Ho Chi Minh's North Vietnamese troops and his supply line became a big factor later in the decade. In his 1961 report, Johnson contended that the struggle for control of Southeast Asia was challenging, but "it is by no means inevitable that it must be lost."[61] In a rare press conference as vice president, he reported that some Asian leaders feared the U.S. commitment to liberty around the world had been weakened by the threat of nuclear war.[62] At this time, just a few hundred

The Death of a President

Months after the assassination, Jacqueline Kennedy urged William Manchester to write the story of the four dark days beginning with her husband's murder. Manchester had authored a flattering book about JFK—1964's *Portrait of a President,* and he accepted the task, which came with promise of exclusive interviews with family members. Mrs. Kennedy had expected the book to be a slim volume on her library shelf. What Manchester turned in to Harper & Row in March 1966 was a 1,287-page tome that used intimate details to paint Lyndon Johnson as a vulgar oaf who bore some responsibility for Dallas's atmosphere of violence. Mrs. Kennedy was surprised to learn in August 1966 that *Look* had paid more than $600,000 for the book's serialization rights. Kennedy associates, such as Arthur M. Schlesinger Jr., had seen the book and were appalled by its disrespectful portrayal of Johnson, and Mrs. Kennedy, who had spoken a bit too frankly with the author, was concerned about her own loss of privacy.

On August 29, 1966, the *Washington Post* carried an Associated Press report that Manchester's book would contain "200 page-one stories." Johnson mobilized his staff to make a record of his contacts with Mrs. Kennedy after the assassination and tracked down the truth about one of the leaked bombshells—the loss of a Kennedy family Bible used by Johnson at his swearing-in. (It was a Catholic missal, which Lady Bird Johnson had kept as a memento.) Johnson was embarrassed by the book's revelations, but late in the year he wrote to Mrs. Kennedy, saying, "We [he and his wife] hope you will not subject yourself to any discomfort or distress on our account . . . We do not want you to endure any unpleasantness on our account."[63] She responded, telling Johnson that she was "deeply touched" by his letter, and she added, "I am sick at the unhappiness this whole terrible thing has caused everyone."[64]

As Johnson braced for attack from the Kennedys through Manchester's work, the Kennedys themselves were concerned that the book might create backlash against them because of the way Johnson was described. There were fears in Robert Kennedy's camp that the negative characterization of the president might hurt RFK's political future. Jacqueline Kennedy feared, too, that her openness with the author might produce an unflattering portrait of her. Consequently, she went to court in late 1966 to block the book's publication. Reaction to the court battle and Robert Kennedy's loud attack on Manchester in a hotel lowered the senator's popularity and lessened public admiration for Mrs. Kennedy.[65] Eventually, an agreement was reached, and 1,600 words were deleted to remove details that Mrs. Kennedy opposed on personal grounds.[66] Even after the changes, she felt it contained "historical inaccuracies and unfair references."[67] In an oral history interview conducted for the Lyndon B. Johnson Library, she expressed regrets about the book, which finally was released in the spring of 1967.[68]

Despite the Kennedys' efforts to stop the book, Johnson saw its publication as evidence that he was right about Robert Kennedy's schemes to sabotage his presidency. Johnson told Bill Moyers, "I think they're gonna write history as they want it written, and as they can buy it written. And I think the best way we can write it is to try to refrain from gettin' into an argument, or a fight, or a knockdown."[69] Johnson adviser John P. Roche saw one positive side to the controversy at a time when questions about the Warren Commission report were gaining steam. "The Manchester caper," he wrote, "should have as an accidental benefit the overshadowing of the nasty attacks on the Warren Commission."[70]

U.S. troops served as advisers in Vietnam. By the end of the year, more than 3,000 advisers had been deployed there as America's long march into the quagmire of Vietnam picked up speed.

Johnson's trip played an important part in the development of U.S. policy toward Vietnam, at least in part because Johnson became the ultimate decision-maker just thirty months later. Johnson's statements reflect total acceptance of Cold War dogma. Most revealing are his comments before the House Foreign Affairs Committee on June 5, 1961. He testified, "I am for standing with South Vietnam and Thailand, for I have seen as a boy that when you start running from a bully he keeps you running, and if he doesn't respect the line you draw out in the pasture he isn't going to respect the line you draw at your front yard." Here we see Johnson conflating the tangled and complicated issues of poverty, political repression, foreign interference, and proliferating violence in Vietnam with the largely metaphorical two-nation contest between the United States and the Soviet Union. Johnson went on to say, "The only generalization that I am going to accept [about Asians] is that these people are just like you and I are, and that they share the same hopes and dreams."[71] In a fundamental statement of goodwill, Johnson unveiled his belief that what was best for Americans was best for everyone, and he demonstrated a total failure to recognize that the villagers in the rice paddies of South Vietnam were nothing like him or the lawmakers he addressed. By seeing all Asians as being just like him, Johnson ruled out the possibility that Ho Chi Minh might understand the Vietnamese better than he did.

In 1963, when the Kennedy administration tacitly accepted the overthrow of Diem, Johnson disapproved. Although Kennedy had hoped that Diem would be removed peacefully, the Vietnamese leader was assassinated. Despite the Diem regime's massacre of protesting Buddhists earlier that year, Johnson believed that he was a solid leader. By playing even a passive role in displacing him, LBJ felt the United States had deepened its responsibility to South Vietnam. Almost immediately after ascending to the presidency, Johnson made Vietnam a priority. In February

1964, he asked Bundy, McNamara, and Rusk to put together proposals on Vietnam for a Tuesday luncheon meeting, and from that point forward the civilian decision-making process became primarily isolated among these four men. Making choices without the benefit of outside questioners tended to limit options and eliminate debate.[72] Logistical details rose to the top of the agenda, and policy questions slipped away in the routine of managing a war. In the summer of 1964, Johnson won congressional approval of the Tonkin Gulf Resolution after an alleged North Vietnamese attack on U.S. Navy ships. It granted him power "to take all necessary measures to repel any armed attack against the forces of the United States and to prevent further aggressions."[73] This resolution, based on questionable evidence, became Johnson's blank check to expand U.S. involvement in Vietnam.

With South Vietnam's military position worsening, Johnson launched systematic bombing of North Vietnam and sent in the first American combat troops in 1965. On July 30, Johnson announced that the 75,000-man American force would grow to 125,000 troops. By the end of 1966, the total number of American troops had reached 389,000. Late in 1967, McNamara resigned as secretary of defense after unsuccessfully questioning the policy he had helped to shape. By the end of that year, 486,000 American troops were in Vietnam. The American death toll was 206 in 1964, 1,863 in 1965, 6,144 in 1966, and 11,153 in 1967.[74] In addition to killing thousands of Vietnamese, the United States raped their countryside by using eighteen million gallons of herbicide, code-named Agent Orange. Over the years, American aerial attacks on North Vietnam added up to the biggest bombardment in history.

Johnson's policies triggered growing discontent among a burgeoning peace movement. At the same time, conservative complaints about excessive spending and the ever-expanding federal government led to Republican victories in the off-year elections of 1966. Johnson's domestic policies, labeled the Great Society, began to suffer under spending cutbacks. Moreover, Johnson's pursuit of guns and butter—war in Vietnam and expensive domestic initiatives—threatened to cause economic disaster. Inflation became a hot issue, beginning in 1966. Johnson's approval rating, which was 70 percent in June 1965, dropped 22 percentage points by September 1966.[75] By the end of 1966, it had slid an additional 5 percentage points, leaving him with an approval rating of only 43 percent.[76]

Television helped to shape Americans' perceptions of the war. The conflict played out in American living rooms, with nightly reports becoming far more powerful than any written accounts could be. The *New York Times* and other leading newspapers distinguished themselves by revealing the false claims and artful omissions in Johnson administration accounts of the war. Anti-war protests gained momentum in 1966, and in 1967, with more and more politicians opposing the war, the anti-war movement expanded, massing huge numbers of demonstrators. In April, a New York City rally attracted about 100,000 and another in San Francisco drew 50,000. During October, more than 50,000 protesters marched on the Pentagon and staged a whimsical attempt to levitate the building. A confrontation between protesters, troops, and U.S. marshals produced a memorable image of a peace advocate putting a flower in the barrel of a soldier's gun.

As on many other issues, Johnson contended that his Vietnam policy sprang from JFK's legacy. "I've tried my best to play fair with Jack Kennedy," he told Lawrence O'Brien in 1967. "I think I have; my conscience is very, very clear on that point and I think on Vietnam that he's right where I am and I'm carrying out his policy."[77] In reality, Kennedy's likely course is unclear. In a September 2, 1963 interview with CBS's Walter Cronkite, Kennedy said that, in the end, "it is their war. They are the ones who have to win it or lose it."[78] A week later, Chet Huntley and David Brinkley interviewed Kennedy on NBC. In that discussion, he defended the domino theory in relation to Southeast Asia. "I believe it," he said. "I think that the struggle is close enough. China is so large, looms so high just beyond the frontiers, that if South Vietnam went, it would not only give them an improved geographic position for a guerilla assault on Malaya, but would also give the impression that the wave of the future in Southeast Asia was China and Communists."[79] One of Kennedy's last major policy decisions was to order withdrawal of 1,000 troops from Vietnam. Explaining his reluctance to dive too deeply into the Vietnam conflict, Kennedy prophetically told one aide, "The troops will march in; the bands will play; the crowds will cheer; and in four days everyone will have forgotten. Then we will be told we have to send more troops. It's like taking a drink. The effect wears off, and you have to take another."[80] Kennedy never forgot one fact: He had met with General Douglas MacArthur twice, and on both occasions the general, who had vast experience fighting in the Pacific, had warned Kennedy to avoid a land war in Asia.[81]

Initially, Johnson heard little opposition to his Vietnam policy. In 1964, George Ball of the State Department was a voice in the wilderness when he expressed concern about the dangers of expanding U.S. involvement, and, a year later, Vice President Hubert Humphrey earned virtual political exile by writing Johnson a private memo about his misgivings. As others supported U.S. withdrawal in 1966 and 1967, LBJ felt trapped. "The idea of opening this yawning issue, this chasm under your feet, is a horrible thing," said Johnson aide Harry McPherson. "Imagine! Christ, you put

550,000 Americans out there; you've lost 25,000 of them dead! What if it's wrong? What if we've made an error?"[82]

In 1967, senators Robert and Edward Kennedy aggressively voiced outspoken opposition to the war, and in the eyes of some Kennedy loyalists they abandoned the foreign policy position of their late brother. Still, by late 1966, a Harris poll showed that 54 percent of Democrats favored Robert Kennedy for the 1968 presidential nomination.[83] In 1967, for a time, Johnson led Kennedy, thanks to some political missteps by RFK, but over time the tide turned back in Kennedy's direction. Johnson had become fixated on Robert Kennedy's actions and blamed RFK for almost everything. In December 1966, he told Abe Fortas, "I believe that Bobby is having his governors jump on me, and he's having his mayors, and he's having his Negroes, and he's having his Catholics . . . and he's having 'em just systematically, one after the other, each day [jump on me]."[84]

1968

The last year of Johnson's presidency was among the most turbulent in American history. Violence in multiple forms—military, racial, and political—contributed to the sense that civil order was disintegrating in the United States. When he advocated change in his presidential campaign eight years earlier, JFK never could have anticipated the change-driven turmoil of this raucous year.

The year's first big event occurred on January 23, when North Korean patrol boats captured the USS *Pueblo*, a U.S. Navy intelligence-gathering ship. The Koreans claimed the *Pueblo* and its eighty-three-man crew had violated North Korea's territorial waters. The Communist regime held the crew for eleven months, and this incident became yet another thorn in Johnson's side as a growing segment of the U.S. population distrusted the military.

On the last day of January 1968, almost 70,000 North Vietnamese troops and thousands of Viet Cong launched the Tet offensive during a holiday cease-fire. On the first day of the weeks-long campaign, a Viet Cong suicide unit invaded the U.S. Embassy compound in Saigon and controlled the courtyard for six hours before all were slain. Blitzkrieg-like attacks hit targets throughout South Vietnam within hours. As the rebels seized cities and strategic positions, U.S. troops, South Vietnamese soldiers, and other allies fought to oust them. A counterattack virtually wiped out the ancient city of Hue, where about 7,500 enemy troops had taken cover. A combined force of 11,000 American and South Vietnamese troops fought for three weeks to rout 1,000 Viet Cong from Cholon. Civilian casualties were high: A month after it had begun, troops found the bodies of about

2,000 civilians executed by Communists. An estimated 33,000 enemy troops died, while the United States and its allies lost only 3,400 soldiers. The numbers indicated a U.S. victory, but Americans at home smelled defeat. Many were stunned after watching bloody scenes on the evening news and seeing the vulnerability of the most secure U.S. outposts. Voters' support for the war plummeted."The terrible quality of the war in Vietnam came home to people," said McPherson. "It appeared . . . that our crowd was caught off guard as ever."[85] Subsequently, the percent of Americans supporting Johnson's Vietnam policy dropped from 40 percent to 26 percent.[86] In February, in a television special, journalistic icon Cronkite urged the United States to pursue a negotiated settlement.

That winter, hundreds of college students went to New Hampshire to campaign for a long-shot anti-war candidate for president, Minnesota Senator Eugene McCarthy. In the Democratic primary on March 12, McCarthy shocked the White House by almost matching the sitting president's vote total. Encouraged by McCarthy's good showing, Robert Kennedy, who had been waiting in the shadows unwilling to run for president until victory seemed possible, decided to enter the race. "The thing I feared from the first day of my presidency was actually coming true," Johnson later told Doris Kearns Goodwin. "Robert Kennedy had openly announced his intention to reclaim the throne in the memory of his brother. And the American people swayed by the magic of the name, were dancing in the streets."[87]

Many observers believed that Robert Kennedy had undergone a dramatic change after his brother's murder. He emerged as a more fervent advocate of the disadvantaged and a more vocal opponent of injustice. He favored shifting government spending from military to domestic programs Because of his priorities and his kinship to JFK, he attracted emotionally charged allegiance from minority groups, but some Democrats turned against him because he had not taken the risk of challenging Johnson earlier, when pacifists first urged him to run.

In March, the Kerner Commission issued its report concluding that the United States was "moving toward two societies, one black, one white—separate and unequal," and Johnson chose not to respond to the panel's recommendations.[88] Also in that month, a Gallup Poll showed that 49 percent of Americans thought the Vietnam war was wrong.[89] In one day, an American company of soldiers killed more than 300 unarmed civilians in My Lai. Although news of the assault did not become public until the following year, its barbarism fits neatly into the period when it happened. On March 31, Johnson announced a partial bombing halt in North Vietnam in a nationally televised address and surprised his audience by dropping out of the presidential race.

At this moment in history, Martin Luther King Jr., Robert Kennedy, and to a lesser extent, Eugene McCarthy represented the best leadership available to dissident Americans who wanted peace in Vietnam and racial equality at home.[90] On April 3, King confided to an aide that "truly, America is much, much sicker . . . than I realized when I first began working in 1955." In a speech that evening, he told his followers, "I may not get there with you, but I want you to know that we as a people will get to the promised land." The following evening, he was shot to death on a hotel balcony. As Robert Kennedy faced a crowd of black Indianapolis voters who were unaware of King's death, he delivered a powerful, extemporaneous eulogy, begging his audience to "tame the savageness of man and make gentle the life of this world."[91] Though Kennedy struck an emotional chord in Indianapolis, within hours race riots broke out in about a hundred American cities, including Washington, Boston, Chicago, and Detroit. Forty-six people lost their lives in this conflagration. The riots unsettled many white Americans and weakened the Democratic liberal coalition by strengthening racial fears among white southerners and white ethnic populations in the north.

Later in April, Columbia University students protested the university's connection with the defense industry by occupying five buildings for seven days. Police ended the protest by storming the buildings and ousting the demonstrators. In May, Robert Kennedy won Democratic primaries in Indiana and Nebraska but faced defeat in Oregon, where McCarthy triumphed. And Humphrey, who competed in no primaries, joined the race.

On June 5, Kennedy prevailed in the California primary and was shot in the head moments after delivering his victory speech. He died a day later. Some believed that the grief over his assassination nearly matched the nation's feeling of loss in November 1963. It seemed like a ghastly rerun. "Too horrible for words" was how Lyndon Johnson described it.[92] Robert Kennedy's funeral, like his brother's, was memorable. Engulfed by emotions, Ted Kennedy delivered a moving eulogy at St. Patrick's Cathedral and tenor Andy Williams beautifully sang "The Battle Hymn of the Republic." Then, a train carried Kennedy's casket to Washington along tracks lined with mourners. He was buried at the same Arlington site where his brother lay. Kennedy's death put the presidential nomination easily within Humphrey's grasp.

In August, the Republicans conducted a relatively unremarkable convention in Miami, where Richard Nixon, freshly repackaged as the "New Nixon," denied the nomination to Ronald Reagan on the right and Nelson Rockefeller on the left. On August 20, the Soviet Union invaded Czechoslovakia and used the full weight of its powers to repress the citizenry and end a period of reform, but violence closer to home quickly dominated the headlines. In Chicago, during the Democratic National Convention, police attacked anti-war protesters. Officers beat many youths in what was later characterized in an official report as "a police riot."[93] Humphrey's nomination seemed like a footnote to the atmosphere of brutality. "These were our children," Tom Wicker of the *New York Times* wrote.[94] Even newsmen on the convention floor were bullied by Mayor Richard Daley's minions. After viewing a film memorial to Robert Kennedy, the furious and demoralized convention delegates sang "The Battle Hymn of the Republic" repeatedly for more than twenty minutes. Convention organizers attempted to regain control, but those on the convention floor wanted to be heard.

In September, women's liberation groups protested at the Miss America Beauty Pageant in Atlantic City. Vietnam veterans organized a peace protest in San Francisco in October and two American medal winners at the

> More than 14,000 U.S. military personnel died in Vietnam during 1968, and by the time U.S. troops stopped fighting in mid-1973 more than 58,000 had been killed.

summer Olympic Games in Mexico City controversially raised their fists in a black power salute as the "Star Spangled Banner" was played. In November, Nixon edged out Humphrey to win the presidency, and Vietnam peace talks began in Paris. The year ended on a somber note as the Apollo 8 astronauts became the first humans to orbit the moon. Their photos of a beautifully fragile Earth invited contemplation at the end of a contentious year.

As Johnson prepared to leave the White House, Nixon promised what turned out to be an illusory plan for peace. When Johnson departed, the drive to complete JFK's legacy ended as well. Frustrated and defeated, Johnson hated what his own legacy had become in comparison to the gleaming vision associated with his predecessor. Kennedy was tied to American potential; Johnson, to American failure.

GHOST

In life or in death, Johnson could not escape the shadow cast by JFK. Among his constituents, he felt that his achievements could never measure up to Kennedy's memory. For Johnson, the situation was unsettling and puzzling. He liked Kennedy but never really understood Kennedy's power over people and once asked a friend, "Tell me, just what is it that people like so much in Jack Kennedy?"[95] What had been a mystery to Johnson before Kennedy's assassination later became a haunting source of dismay.

Johnson was in a strange position: JFK was more than just a memory. On a regular basis, LBJ had to face what Wicker called "living and breathing reminders, the flesh and blood heirs of the Golden Age." The handsome and youthful Robert and Edward Kennedy seemed to offer Americans something that Abraham Lincoln's supporters could not have imagined after his assassination—the possibility of a restoration. JFK's ghost loomed large at the 1964 Democratic National Convention, where he was to have been renominated for president. On the last night of the convention, when Robert rose to introduce a film about his brother, he received a twenty-two-minute ovation. He tried repeatedly to stop the cheers, but Senator Henry "Scoop" Jackson told him, "Let it go on . . . Let them get it out of their system."[96] With great forethought, Johnson had scheduled Kennedy's appearance to come after approval of his nomination for president and Humphrey's nomination for vice president so that no emotional response could affect the convention's outcome. As he stood there with tears in his eyes, Robert Kennedy seemed far removed from his "ruthless" reputation. He read an excerpt from *Romeo and Juliet*:

> When he shall die
> Take him and cut him out in little stars
> And he will make the face of heaven so fine
> That all the world will be in love with night,
> And pay no worship to the garish sun.

Immersed in the imagery, some Democrats saw the excerpt's last line as a reference to Johnson. Unfortunately for Johnson, Kennedy's address was memorable, a moment frozen in amber, and LBJ's acceptance speech was not.[97] Wicker wrote in *Esquire* in 1965, "It is a sad and terrible likelihood that Lyndon Johnson will not live down the fact that he followed John Kennedy."[98] Often when Johnson spoke before Congress, TV cameras alternated between views of the president and reaction shots of the two brothers-in-waiting, especially Robert.

Johnson found unexpected reminders of JFK's aura in his travels. To bolster citizens' sense of continuity early in his presidency, the White House distributed photos of both Kennedy and Johnson to members of the public when LBJ spoke outside the capital, but the practice was abandoned because Kennedy's photos disappeared ten times as quickly as Johnson's.[99] In 1965, Johnson visited a poor family in Appalachia as a way of dramatizing his War on Poverty. Later, he said, "They seemed real happy to talk with me and I felt real good about that. Then, as I walked out, I noticed two pictures on the wall. One was Jesus Christ on the cross. The other was

John Kennedy. I felt as if I'd been slapped in the face."[100] As Johnson struggled to escape negative comparisons with Kennedy, the production of detailed tallies comparing Kennedy's achievements and Johnson's became almost a cottage industry within the Johnson White House. Memos compared statistics on vote totals among suburbanites and city dwellers,[101] numbers of African Americans appointed,[102] press conferences held,[103] foreign dignitaries welcomed,[104] and press criticism received.[105]

Although John and Robert Kennedy were very different people, many Americans felt that RFK embodied his brother's essence. Some noticed that Robert began to adopt some of his late brother's mannerisms and seemed to redefine himself as an emerging intellectual in the 1963 assassination's wake. Johnson found himself in the difficult position of wanting to tie himself to JFK's legacy without bolstering the career of his nemesis, the heir-apparent to that legacy. Johnson reached out to Jacqueline Kennedy and Ted Kennedy in an effort to maintain good relations with the family. Tapes at the Lyndon B. Johnson Library document polite interactions between LBJ and Jacqueline Kennedy, although she repeatedly disappointed him by saying that she could not return to the White House for any event. Among Johnson's recorded conversations are warm exchanges with Ted Kennedy. Johnson worked hard to maintain a cordial relationship with Robert's younger brother. The two extroverts seem to have maintained a totally friendly relationship, at least until Kennedy decided to take a stand against the Vietnam war. In a 1965 telephone conversation, Johnson told Ted, "This business about my being at crossways with the Kennedys is just a pure lot of crap. I started out here to keep faith, and I'm gonna do it."[106] O'Brien saw that relationship as "the most significant and probably the best evidence that the president was making a real effort to see if he couldn't bridge this. And he felt that having this pleasant relationship with Teddy would lead to Bobby not having that glare on his face all the time."[107]

Robert Kennedy was just one manifestation of Johnson's troubling Kennedy connections. Jack Kennedy had friendly relations with members of the press corps, despite occasional charges of "news management" on his part, and many of those journalists had a correspondingly negative response to Johnson. Columnist William S. White said many saw LBJ as "essentially a raw frontiersman lacking sophistication." In addition, Johnson did not take criticism well and often responded to reporters' questions without tact.[108] Journalist Stewart Alsop thought that Kennedy loyalists in the press caused "considerable" trouble for Johnson.[109] Shoveling salt into Johnson's wounds, reporters made a habit of seeking comments from RFK on many of Johnson's proposals, a practice that symbolically treated Kennedy as a government in exile.

McPherson thought the press favored the Kennedys and under-estimated Johnson's sophistication, categorizing his speaking style as corny. "He would rage against 'the Georgetown crowd,' particularly those who needled him in their columns and editorials; their devotion to John Kennedy's memory made them incapable, Johnson thought, of fairness to him."[110] McPherson believed that reporters minimized Johnson's successes. "The press, to be sure, recorded those achievements with dutiful appreciation, but as Grand Prix drivers might appreciate a good tractor. An inimitable part of the fun was gone. A distinguished reporter told me, 'I don't hate Johnson. I just hate the fact that all the grace and wit has gone from what the American president says.'" McPherson said he understood that LBJ's self-justifications were less fun than Kennedy's banter, but he added, "it was hard to be fair in a climate of hurt feelings."[111]

Stepping into a position previously filled by a legend would be difficult for any man, and Johnson carried a particularly heavy burden because of his own insecurities. "Unable to admit his own shortcomings, he lied and exaggerated to avoid blame for his failures," according to historian Paul R. Henggeler. "Despite his legislative brilliance, he felt intellectually inferior in the company of academicians. Although he was a charming and entertaining storyteller, he feared being a social outcast. He dreaded loneliness, clamored for attention, and sometimes displayed behavior that some of his closest aides called 'paranoid.'"[112] Arthur Krim, finance chairman of the Democratic National Committee, recalled hearing Johnson bemoan "a problem he had following in Kennedy's footsteps imagewise. It was in that context that he downgraded the accomplishments of the Kennedy presidency and felt that with a lesser record of accomplishment [Kennedy] had been able to project the image of a better president."[113]

Marking the third anniversary of Johnson's presidency, the Associated Press's James Marlow noted that Kennedy had become "a magic figure" to many Americans and that "he ranks far higher in popular favor than his successor." Marlow wrote that Johnson "has not much wit, not much grace in the Kennedy sense, his utterances are not poetic but prosaic. And he wears his egotism like a green beret, with 'I this' and 'We this' and 'My that.'" Marlow's analysis concluded that Johnson worked harder than Kennedy and probably exceeded him in the ability to push legislation through Congress. Though Marlow was not ready to draw a historical judgment, he made it clear that Johnson could not compete with Kennedy in the judgment of many Americans.[114]

Of course, there were many Kennedy haters both before and after JFK's assassination, but, as Johnson knew all too well, that did not diminish the hero worship many Americans directed toward the late president. During Kennedy's life and after his death, some critics noted his many setbacks in Congress, and JFK's detractors often attacked with ferocity. Many of the verbal assaults were equally as passionate as tributes delivered by his greatest admirers. Kennedy played both the hero and the villain. During one week in 1964, the bestseller list held both a reissue of Kennedy's *Profiles in Courage* and Victor Lasky's negative Kennedy critique, *JFK: The Man and the Myth,* which had been published before the president's death.[115] Even some people who admired Kennedy disliked the tendency to mythologize him as a white knight. They thought Jacqueline Kennedy's comparison between his administration and Camelot had gone too far. As Pete Hamill wrote in 1988, the Camelot campaign was "too insistent, too fevered, accompanied by too much sentimentality and too little rigorous thought."[116]

In the end, JFK won—again and again. In the awful August of 1968, Johnson's approval rating hit an all-time low of 35 percent, while Kennedy's approval rating never sank below 56 percent. Although he won the White House with the support of less than 50 percent of the population, more than half of the nation's voters backed him throughout his presidency. Johnson watched his rating drop 44 percentage points from a high of 79 percent.[117] Despite his poor legislative record, most Americans believed in JFK, and most lost faith in Johnson.

After leaving the White House, Johnson admitted to Cronkite that comparisons to Kennedy had been a daily trial during his presidency:

> I had many problems in my conduct of the office being contrasted with President Kennedy's conduct of the office, with my manner of dealing with things and his manner, with my accent and his accent, with my background and his background. He was a great public hero and anything that I did that someone didn't approve of, they would always feel that President Kennedy wouldn't have done that—that he would have done it a different way, that he wouldn't have made a mistake , , , There was a group in the country, a very important, and influential molders of opinion who I think genuinely felt that if President Kennedy had been there, those things wouldn't have happened to him. And I hoped it wouldn't have. And maybe it wouldn't have. But it was a problem for me.[118]

Both friends and foes have characterized Johnson as paranoid at times, but in this case he was not imagining or exaggerating the forces that stood against him. Many who mourned Kennedy condemned Johnson for matters as petty as his accent and his mannerisms. Henggeler concluded that "like the television character Jed Clampett [of the 1960s TV hit *The*

Beverly Hillbillies] he seemed suddenly thrust into a situation for which he lacked the proper refinement. Each idiosyncrasy was proof of his 'backwardness.'"[119] A 1964 Gallup Poll showed that, in rating Johnson's qualities, Americans ranked him highest on being "well-qualified," "experienced," and "intelligent," and they gave him the lowest marks on having "an attractive personality" and being "intellectual."[120]

As Johnson asserted, denunciations of his policies often were yoked to assertions that Kennedy would have acted more wisely. Because many believed that Kennedy had grown during his presidency, his imagined potential remained unlimited. Many Johnson critiques came from Kennedy loyalists who never accepted LBJ's leadership, but others came from less biased political observers, who believed that Kennedy's experiences during his brief presidency would have prepared him more effectively to avoid some of the pitfalls in Johnson's path.

Among Kennedy loyalists was former appointments secretary O'Donnell, who attacked Johnson's 1965 military intervention in the Dominican Republic. He contended that Kennedy never would have dispatched troops without conferring with the Organization of American States.[121] Robert Kennedy joined opposition to Johnson's action, arguing that U.S. opposition to Communist revolution in the western hemisphere "must not be construed as opposition to popular uprisings against injustice and oppression."[122] This approach is more in line with JFK's evolving Cold War rethinking, which he unveiled in his American University speech in the spring of 1963.

By far the most common argument about JFK's superior decision-making relates to Vietnam. Many Americans believed that Kennedy never would have mired U.S. combat troops in Southeast Asia. McNamara, one of the architects of U.S. policy in Vietnam, went on the record in the mid-1990s, saying, "I think it highly probable that, had President Kennedy lived, he would have pulled us out of Vietnam."[123] Ed Guthman, who worked in the Justice Department under Robert Kennedy, thought that JFK supported the idea of sending a minimal number of troops, but "he would never have taken the Vietnam war up as Johnson did."[124] O'Brien, who served throughout both the Kennedy and Johnson administrations, thought Kennedy would have "found a way of disengaging before it became all-out . . . But that's only the nature of the guy, that he would have come to the conclusion at an early date that it was a lost cause."[125] In his book *JFK: A Hero for Our Time*, Ralph G. Martin quotes Kennedy as telling a neighbor that, as soon as he was re-elected, he was "going to get the Americans out of Vietnam."[126] While many projected JFK's growth along a skyrocketing trajectory, it is interesting that RFK never suggested that his brother would have handled Vietnam more effectively. Ted

Sorensen, who was extremely close to JFK, wrote in 2008, "Because of my own strong opposition to the subsequent escalation in Vietnam under Johnson, I would like to believe that Kennedy would have found a way to withdraw all American instructors and advisors. But even someone who knew JFK as well as I did can't be certain."[127]

Some historians have postulated that Kennedy, who had proven his foreign policy toughness and proficiency in the Cuban Missile Crisis, would have felt free to back away from a U.S. commitment to Vietnam during a second term. In comparison, Johnson had no foreign policy credentials and probably felt a stronger drive to demonstrate his toughness as a leader. Historians James G. Blight, Janet M. Lang, and David A. Welch argue in their book *Vietnam if Kennedy Had Lived: Virtual JFK* and in a companion documentary, *Virtual JFK*, that Kennedy rejected the option of engaging in warfare all six times when he confronted the choice during his presidency—at the Bay of Pigs, in Laos, in Berlin, during the Cuban Missile Crisis, and twice in Vietnam. They insist that this is clear evidence of what he would have later done in Vietnam if he had lived. "A close look at 'Virtual JFK,' we believe, shows us that this is not a utopian dream. It actually happened, not in some fantastic Camelot, but in the White House occupied by John F. Kennedy."[128] The authors make a fascinating case that past actions can be used as evidence of future behavior.[129] In a source that carries far less historical weight and a far greater role in popular culture, Oliver Stone's 1991 film, *JFK*, famously asserts that JFK was slain because he would never have escalated American involvement in Vietnam.

Others have suggested that Johnson might have been well served by gathering his own group of foreign policy decision-makers instead of closeting himself with Kennedy men whose knowledge and experience may have intimidated him. McPherson noted that the near unanimity of these advisers was a key element in Johnson's decision-making, and he said that Johnson was swayed by "the mere existence of this superb and skillfully managed power that we had which seemed to be sufficient to handle any kind of problem."[130] Clark Clifford agreed with this analysis: "These senior advisers to President Kennedy all felt that we were headed correctly in Vietnam. And then when President Johnson inherited them, he encountered a practically unanimous sentiment."[131] One of those advisers, Dean Rusk, believed that Johnson had little choice in Vietnam. He argued that "any decision by President Johnson in 1963 and 1964 to abandon Southeast Asia would have been a decision to abandon the fidelity of the United States under its commitments."[132] This may well be true, and yet Johnson had far greater flexibility after his landslide re-election.

Another big issue of the 1960s was the expensive race to the moon, which consumed money that might have been spent on easing the nation's domestic problems. In 1961, Kennedy established the goal of reaching the moon by the end of the decade, but historian James W. Hilty has argued that Kennedy probably would have dropped the moon goal to spend that money on more pressing matters. The Kennedy administration suggested this idea to the Soviet Union as early as 1961, but the proposal generated no serious discussions. On September 20, 1963, the cost-conscious Kennedy departed from the idea of the space competition when he spoke before the United Nations and expressed American willingness to consider a joint U.S.–Soviet mission to the moon. Audiotapes released in 2011 show that, in 1963, he discussed the prospect of shelving the project, although he still believed that it was important.[133] It seems likely that spiraling costs would have led Kennedy to abandon or delay the moon-landing goal if the United States had to bear the entire cost; after the missile crisis, his chances of convincing Soviet leaders to pursue a joint effort probably were higher than Johnson's. As the years passed, Johnson maintained spending on space even as the War on Poverty and the war in Vietnam drained the budget. He, no doubt, felt that the public would disapprove if he abandoned Kennedy's goal, but JFK, after re-election as president, probably would have felt secure enough to decelerate the project or to push for a joint mission.

On the planet Earth, some Americans have suggested that Kennedy's strong appeal to African Americans might have tamped down race riots in America's cities during the decade's second half and, in a similar vein, some believed that his affinity for youth might have averted the most militant student unrest. However, neither of these arguments ever fully flowered. Since Kennedy was less likely to get a civil rights bill through Congress in 1964, it is possible that black frustrations would have reached a boiling point earlier. Like Johnson, Kennedy probably would have seen American cities burn, because African American anger was fueled by many decades of broken promises and unequal treatment. The economic cost of centuries of prejudice against black Americans simply became too monumental to accept. Student activism began before heavy U.S. involvement in Vietnam and may even have had its roots in Kennedy's call on America's youth to become fully engaged in politics. The student movement addressed issues of free speech, racial and gender equality, environmentalism, and opposition to the arms race, but it is difficult to imagine generational and class conflict becoming so brutal without the volatile issue of Vietnam. Even *if* Kennedy had avoided U.S. involvement in the war, a generation of change-seeking youths likely would have found bountiful reasons for protest on other issues but perhaps without the violent cultural clashes that occurred between those who pleaded for peace and those who proclaimed "my country, right or wrong."

All of this is merely informed speculation. After his death, Kennedy became a lump of clay to be molded by his supporters. His messages carried unlimited malleability in the 1960s and later. As Thomas Brown has argued, people on the left saw him as "evolving into an economic radical (his clash with U.S. Steel), a critic of the cold war (the test ban treaty and promise of a troop pullout from Vietnam), and an egalitarian (his embrace of a sweeping civil rights bill)."[134] Those on the right saw hopeful signs in his push for a tax cut and in his patriotic calls for self-sacrifice. Over time, both Democrats and Republicans found reasons to tie themselves to his memory, as Johnson had done during his presidency.

For better or worse, Johnson was constantly compared to his predecessor in Kennedy's real and imagined forms. To many Americans, Kennedy became a mirage of the 1960s that might have been. And at the same time, the gangly Johnson, with his southern drawl and awkward mannerisms, represented the unhappy reality of human shortcomings at a time when the very texture of the nation seemed to be losing cohesion.

CHAPTER 5

Culture of Conspiracy

> *"The Kennedy assassination is like a thousand-piece jigsaw puzzle for which we have 100,000 pieces."*
>
> Tom Bethell, one-time researcher for Jim Garrison[1]

Confusion and speculation about details of John F. Kennedy's assassination began spreading across America just minutes after gunshots echoed through Dealey Plaza. Officials eager to promote calm and reporters frantic to get the biggest story of their careers unwittingly took the first steps in creating the contested ground that has surrounded Kennedy's death for almost fifty years. What seemed to be true at one moment later shifted to reveal errors and gaps in the narrative. As unsettled citizens waded through a disorderly mix of truth and rumor, their brains filtered data through their own memory banks' concept of violence, which sprang from American legend, television, films, and other forms of popular culture. The spark of conspiracy belief flared and made an almost-instant mark on contemporary American culture, opening the public to the mythos of Oliver Stone and many lesser storytellers.

In 1964, most Americans put aside initial suspicions and accepted the Warren Commission's report that there had been no conspiracy, but days of doubt lay ahead. In the coming years, Vietnam and Watergate deepened the average American's cynicism about hidden plots and dishonest government, making it seem quite logical to distrust official explanations of the assassination. By 1967, the scales already had tipped, with the majority of Americans expressing reservations about the single-gunman theory. Doubts about government's honesty only intensified following two big events in the early 1970s—the 1971 publication of the *Pentagon Papers*, which revealed the Johnson administration's Vietnam secrets; and Richard Nixon's 1974 resignation when evidence revealed that he was, after all, a crook.

With faith in government making a steady decline since the Kennedy years, Stone's 1991 assassination conspiracy film *JFK* met a receptive audience. Even before this landmark work, American popular culture had transformed the slain president's death in many ways that challenged the boundaries of good taste. One example: John F. Kennedy Jr.'s then-girlfriend Daryl Hannah appeared on a 1993 *Spy* magazine cover wearing a sexed-up suit similar to the one Jacqueline Kennedy wore on the day of his father's assassination. And, in 2004, a video game was introduced that allowed players to assume the assassin's role and shoot the president, like a target in a county fair shooting gallery. Somehow, conspiracy belief found a home within this morbid assassination culture.

Fascination with the crime grew. In the wake of hurried and error-riddled government investigations, conspiracy theorists spun often-implausible, thoroughly complex tales. The exploding head of the handsome prince became a single image in a compellingly blood-spattered American whodunit. Over the years, facts became scrambled in countless new assassination theories and, for many, the truth became irretrievable, lost forever—just like JFK.

It all began in the first hurried reports from Dealey Plaza as journalists hustled to report what they thought they knew and law enforcement officials tried to reassure the public that the assassination was an isolated crime. Tom Wicker of the *New York Times* wrote a month later, "I know no reporter who was there who has a clear and orderly picture of that surrealistic afternoon; it is still a matter of bits and pieces thrown hastily into something like a whole."[2] Those bits and pieces left Americans feeling that the truth was elusive as they struggled to comprehend the unwanted sense that random chance, or one slight man with a gun, might be rewriting their history. No hand of God seemed to be guiding that chaotic day's events to form a cohesive narrative. Consequently, shaken Americans began trying to fit the pieces of the puzzle together in their own minds, a process that continues almost fifty years later. In a nation that revels in tales of gangsters and gunmen, the bottom line for many Americans was that Lee Harvey Oswald seemed unfit to be a villainous mastermind.

Americans have a long history of embracing conspiracies to explain events or problems. "Many Americans have been curiously obsessed with the contingency of their experiment in freedom," writes David Brion Davis.[3] And anxieties about restrictions on American freedoms often have manifested themselves in the belief that individuals or groups have joined together in secret operations with evil goals. Conspiracy theorists typically have formed subcultures that existed outside the American mainstream. Many conspiracy believers are motivated by startling events, such as JFK's assassination; others emerge more slowly. Since World War II, far-flung conspiracy theories have alleged that:

- Franklin D. Roosevelt knew about the Japanese assault on Pearl Harbor before it happened, a 1940s rumor with surprising longevity.
- The Holocaust never happened but was invented by Jews seeking public favor.
- The U.S. government had secret contact with extraterrestrials, some of whom may have crashed in Roswell, New Mexico, in 1947.
- Massive Communist subversion contaminated a broad swath of the U.S. population, possibly including one or more American presidents.
- U.S. moon landings were staged on movie lots to deceive the entire world.
- TWA Flight 800, which crashed into the Atlantic shortly after its July 1997 takeoff, was shot down by a terrorist rocket.
- The federal government planned the September 11, 2001 terror attacks that killed thousands, destroyed the World Trade Center, and damaged the Pentagon.
- Barack Obama's lack of American citizenship was hidden from the American public.

Over the years since JFK's assassination, conspiracy theories have mushroomed, sometimes finding a welcome home in popular culture, according to historian Robert Alan Goldberg.[4] Some analysts believe this phenomenon pops up in the United States because of the fluid nature of American culture, which tends to minimize group identity, thus creating fertile soil for feelings of uncertainty and trepidation. While European families may have existed on the same land, within the same ethnic groups and social classes for decades or even centuries, each American generation tends to depart from familiar ground in an effort to find a better life. Leaving behind the experiences of their parents' lives, Americans are less securely tethered to traditional beliefs and more open to new and sometimes frightening ideas.

In *A Culture of Conspiracy: Apocalyptic Visions in Contemporary America*, Michael Barkun argues that a conspiracist worldview "implies a universe governed by design rather than randomness":[5] a place in which a lone gunman does not discover just weeks after taking a new job that the president of the United States will soon ride beneath his workplace windows. This perspective makes life more rational than accidental. Some conspiracy advocates perceive most important events as part of a master plan by virtually infallible clandestine groups. Barkun contends that conspiracy belief "ultimately becomes a matter of faith rather than proof,"[6] and this faith emerges among a group that distrusts information received from the mass media, which are seen as tools of the conspirators.[7] Richard Hofstadter called Americans' tendency to adopt conspiracy beliefs "the paranoid style in American politics," and he described it as a political pathology with a feeling of persecution at its core.[8] A thread of those sentiments has long been sewn into American culture. An unseen "they" have hovered in the darkness, threatening the American way of life since the Salem witch trials and possibly since the first European settlers invaded a land occupied by native populations whose cultures seemed alien.

As Americans have tried to make sense of Kennedy's murder, certain preconceptions have colored their thinking. Beyond an openness to the idea of conspiracies, Americans' views have been affected by an acceptance of gun violence as a part of a national culture in which small children's earliest playthings often include toy guns. Equally powerful in shaping interpretations of the assassination is an often cited and frequently espoused cliché: "Everything happens for a reason," a truism at odds with the conclusion that Oswald alone killed Kennedy without a clear motive. Bearing these cultural traits, most Americans have found it impossible to accept the single-gunman theory. Its simplicity and haphazardness make it difficult to believe.

THE WARREN COMMISSION

Faced with a crime that seemed too huge to grasp, President Johnson created the Warren Commission on November 29, 1963, a week after Kennedy's assassination. His charge was simple: Find out the truth. The seven-member panel consisted of Supreme Court Chief Justice Earl Warren, Senator Richard Russell, Senator John Sherman Cooper, Representative Hale Boggs, Representative (and future President) Gerald Ford, former CIA chief Allen Dulles, and Washington insider John McCloy. A general counsel and fourteen assistants performed most of the work, but gatherings including at least one Commission member and staff personnel questioned ninety-four witnesses over six months. Staff members interviewed 395 more, and sixty-three witnesses provided written accounts of their experiences. And the Secret Service and FBI conducted a re-enactment on May 24, 1964 in Dealey Plaza.

From the start, Commission members felt compelled by an unofficial and largely unvoiced directive to finish their investigation as quickly as

Journalism's Role in the Weekend of Confusion

For many American journalists, John F. Kennedy's assassination was truly the story of the century. As television was making its presence felt, individual newspapers around the nation produced as many as eight extras on the day of the assassination. The *New York Times* set a sales record on November 26, when it sold 1,089,000 newspapers, about 400,000 more than was typical at that time.[9] While the TV networks offered non-stop coverage, newspapers allocated roughly half of their space to the assassination over the long weekend, and much of the coverage consisted of photographs.[10] Many scheduled social events and sporting activities were canceled, and that limited competition for news space.

With an increased audience, reporters raced each other, adding to the chances of errors. "There was a lot of bad information" on the day of the assassination, according to Keith Shelton of the *Dallas Times Herald*. "People said they saw Johnson shot; people said they saw the Secret Service exchanging gunfire with people."[11] It was a day when desperation for information facilitated nationwide dispersion of rumors, such as reports that a Secret Service agent had been killed. Later investigations would argue that Kennedy had been shot from behind and that he and Connally had been struck by the same bullet. But, in the first hours, the Associated Press reported that Kennedy had been wounded "in the front of the head,"[12] and other reports declared that Kennedy had been shot before Connally. Less than an hour after Kennedy was declared dead, the police had a suspect and a rifle, but reporters could not agree on the specifics. Some said the murder weapon was found near a second-floor window or on a staircase inside the Texas School Book Depository instead of in a pile of boxes on the sixth floor; others said it was a .30-caliber Enfield, a 7.65mm Mauser, a Japanese rifle, or an army rifle—none of which was right. In the first hours, there were conflicting accounts of the number of gunshots fired, the wounds seen on Kennedy's body, and the timing of Oswald's escape.[13] Many reporters in Dallas, whether they were in the print or broadcast media, had to call their reports in over the phone quickly, which added another layer of interpretation, making misunderstandings and mistakes more likely.

The Warren Commission's report and other analyses have argued that reporters and police shared the blame for the chaos that ruled at City Hall and allowed Jack Ruby to mix with the crowd in the garage so that he could kill Oswald. Journalists are trained to push for access to information, especially when there is a big story at stake. They generally depend on officials to establish their boundaries, but in Dallas authorities nurtured the chaos and made little effort to quell excesses.[14] Those same officials seemed eager to gratify the national press corps and, as a result, information and rumors flowed freely from the police and district attorney's office to reporters. Police Chief Jesse Curry and District Attorney Henry Wade each made multiple misstatements about the case in their efforts to convey the impression that Dallas authorities had the investigation under control. Despite all of the contradictions and erroneous reports, a study done shortly after the assassination showed that most Americans who were questioned said they were convinced of Oswald's guilt by the end of the day on November 22, 1963.[15]

Some journalists pressured police officers as well as civilian drivers to provide free transportation for them in Dallas so that they would not miss any angle of the story. A few reporters were so eager to get fresh information that they were willing to pay the Oswald family or, at least, cover their expenses. Although *Life* magazine openly housed the Oswalds in hotels for a while, a regional editor for *Life* who wanted to buy Oswald's trunk from the family was not allowed to do so. His supervisor did not want Oswald's family to profit in any way from the president's murder.[16]

"That was the first time I had seen the feeding frenzy," said Pierce Allman of WFAA-TV and Radio in Dallas. "I guess it was the fine balance between trying to make news and to report news. I suspect it's the age-old problem: a lot of folks trying to make a name for themselves ... I thought the conduct of a lot of the reporters that we saw in action was inexcusable." Another local reporter, Bob Huffaker of KRLD-TV, recalled, "I was not particularly proud of the behavior of many of these reporters."[17]

More than once over the weekend, journalists found themselves interviewing each other. A couple had seen the gunman in the sixth-floor window of the Texas School Book Depository, and many witnessed Oswald's murder. What each journalist in the police garage knew to be the objective truth—that Oswald had been gunned down—simply was inadequate to fill the broadcast time or the space on newspaper pages. One of the greatest news stories of the century could not stand alone: It required more detail.

possible and to determine that both Oswald and his killer, Jack Ruby, acted alone. This pressure came from several sources: Johnson, who wanted to finish the investigation before 1964's presidential campaign race became heated; members of the Kennedy family, who had no desire to dwell on the death or the motives behind it; and the FBI, which hoped for a solution that did not lead to further investigation of its operations.[18] If a foreign conspiracy had been found, Johnson would have faced demands for retaliation; if the investigation had been more aggressive, Kennedy's reputation might have been smeared; and if agency errors and misdeeds were found, negligent government agencies, such as the FBI and CIA, might have faced recriminations. Not finding a conspiracy seemed to promise a quick end to the case. The idea of randomness was difficult for the public to accept, but putting forth a mixture of coincidences and accidents seemed likely to make the government's job easier, sparing Johnson from being forced to fight a war and providing a cleaner answer for the FBI, CIA, and Secret Service without marring Kennedy's memory.

Finding a conspiracy would have made Johnson's position more precarious, while reflecting much more negatively on law enforcement agencies that failed to save the president. And a deeper investigation might have raised unsettling questions about Kennedy's policies and his personal life.

Under these circumstances, leads that might ferret out stronger information about the presence or absence of a conspiracy became irritants to be quickly discounted rather than intriguing ideas worthy of exploration. The Commission presented its 296,000-word report to Johnson on September 24, 1964. The report and twenty-six additional volumes contained more than 17,000 pages of information, compiled at a cost of $1.2 million. And yet, the findings were incomplete and provocatively shallow.

The panel found that Oswald fired the shots that killed Kennedy and wounded Connally from the sixth floor of the Texas School Book Depository; that Oswald murdered Dallas Police Officer J.D. Tippit during his attempted escape; that Ruby killed Oswald; and that there was no evidence of a conspiracy. Most controversial among the panel's conclusions was the assertion that a single bullet caused Kennedy's back and neck wounds and passed through John Connally's body, puncturing a lung, shattering a wrist, and lodging in his thigh. This became known as the single-bullet or magic-bullet theory. Using the limited range of technological methods available in 1964, the Commission backed up its contention with carefully measured bullet trajectories tested on the day of the re-enactment in Dallas and with an examination of the bullet holes in the injured men's clothes. This bullet was identified as the almost-whole slug found on the stretcher used to carry Connally into Parkland Hospital. Three Commissioners disagreed with the theory, but, rather than digging deeper into evidence to try to arrive at a consensus, the Commission scurried along. Because its top priority was finishing quickly, there was no concerted effort to sell the Commission's conclusions to the public, and the Commission swiftly disbanded so that the report had no ongoing advocacy group to answer questions and fill in blanks. Ownership of the report's conclusions evaporated almost instantly.

Many of the report's assumptions sprang from the evidence found on the Book Depository's sixth floor, where police collected Oswald's Mannlicher-Carcano rifle and three spent rifle shells. Comparing the ballistic evidence with the Zapruder film, Commission members reasoned that a total of three shots had been fired and that one apparently missed because investigators found no trace of the third bullet in the limousine or in the bodies of Kennedy and Connally. (This theory matched up with Connally's recollections only if the first shot missed, but the Commission took no stand on the missed shot's position in the sequence of bullets fired. For years, Connally rejected the single-bullet argument for two reasons: He remembered hearing the first shot before he was struck, and his wife believed that the first bullet hit the president. In 1992, he conceded to author Gerald Posner that the second bullet may have struck him after hitting JFK, if the first shot failed to hit the limo.)[19] Bystanders' accounts bolstered the belief that only three shots were fired, with more than 88 percent of Warren Commission "ear" witnesses agreeing on exactly that many shots.[20]

In the effort to link Oswald to the murders of both Kennedy and Tippit, the Commission relied heavily on documentation showing that Oswald had bought both the rifle used against Kennedy and the pistol that killed Tippit. Additionally, officers found a photograph showing Oswald holding the rifle, although he claimed that the photo was a fake. Further tying Oswald to the crime, law enforcement officers discovered fibers that seemed to match Oswald's shirt tangled in a crevice of the rifle, and they identified a palm print found on the rifle as being Oswald's. Another Oswald palm print was found on a box in the sniper's nest. Bolstering the case against the suspect was a coworker's report that Oswald had carried something long, wrapped in brown paper, to work that morning. Oswald claimed his package held curtain rods for the room he rented in Dallas, but his landlady later stated that his room already had curtain rods. The assumption that Oswald carried his rifle to work was reinforced by officers' discovery that his rifle was not where his wife said he kept it.

Although the evidence connecting Oswald to the weapons seemed strong, some facts cast doubt on the Commission's findings. Perhaps most damaging were discrepancies between the reports of doctors who treated Kennedy in Dallas and those who performed the autopsy hours later at Bethesda Naval Hospital. The doctors in Dallas believed that Kennedy's neck wound indicated a bullet entry, but the autopsy concluded that it was an exit wound appearing at the same spot where the Dallas doctors had performed a tracheotomy. If the neck wound was an entry wound, that was proof of a second gunman—and a conspiracy. The Warren Commission insisted that this contradiction could be easily explained by the fact that doctors in Dallas never turned Kennedy over to look for possible entry wounds in his back; however, the discrepancy raised public suspicions. Another key issue was the convenience of Oswald's employment in a building along the motorcade route, but the Commission considered this random chance: Oswald got the job before authorities announced JFK's visit or the motorcade route.

The predominant unresolved issue was Oswald's lack of an obvious motive. On July 9, 1964, three psychiatrists met with two Commission members and staffers to discuss possible explanations. The doctors saw Oswald as an angry young man, frustrated by his failure to attract the notoriety he thought he deserved. They asserted that he suffered from a reading disability, such as dyslexia, and surmised that he had adopted his mother's need for public recognition. Even his interest in Communism, the doctors suggested, may have begun because he simply wanted to gain status by being able to demonstrate his superior knowledge on at least one subject. Noting Oswald's attempted suicide when refused Soviet citizenship, the doctors questioned whether he truly wanted to escape from police on November 22 or whether he wanted the public to recognize him as an assassin who had thrown the entire nation off kilter. They thought this theory was strengthened by Oswald's decision to leave money and his wedding ring in his wife's bedroom on the morning of the assassination as if he did not expect to return. Unfortunately for the doctors, the theory made no sense in light of Oswald's repeated claims of innocence while in police custody. Faced with this question, the doctors hypothesized that Oswald planned to reveal his actions and motives during his trial.[21]

The Commission found no indication that Oswald had a grudge against Kennedy and no reason to suspect Soviet or Cuban complicity, especially because both the Soviet Union and Cuba had denied visas to Oswald during his trip to Mexico City just weeks before the assassination. Some witnesses reported possible links among Oswald, Ruby, and Tippit, but the Commission found no credible evidence that any of the men knew one another or that they had ties to anti-Castro Cubans who might have wanted to oust Kennedy from the White House in repayment for his restrictions on U.S. military support to the failed Bay of Pigs invasion.

Evidence against Oswald in Tippit's slaying seemed clear-cut. Two witnesses identified him as the man who shot Tippit and seven additional witnesses saw him fleeing the scene, gun in hand. Moreover, the cartridges ejected by the killer matched the gun in Oswald's possession when he was arrested. In its findings, the Commission also tied Oswald to the unrelated attempted murder of right-wing leader General Edwin A. Walker in Dallas during April 1963.

The Commission described Oswald as a loner who cared little about human companionship. It cast Ruby as an unstable outsider who hungered for the approval of others. At his own request, Ruby had undergone a polygraph exam after being interviewed by Chief Justice Earl Warren. The test showed no deception on Ruby's part when he described his motives and his actions on November 24; nevertheless, because a doctor had categorized him as "psychotic depressive," the results were deemed unreliable. Noting his thirst for attention—a trait he shared with the man he killed—the Commission basically accepted Ruby's own testimony that he killed Oswald in a fit of rage. After killing Oswald, Ruby described himself as a hero. Many believed that Ruby killed Oswald "to seal his lips," but the Commission gave no credence to that theory.

> While the Warren Commission found no conspiracy, the KGB, a Soviet spy agency, believed that a group of wealthy renegade oil producers had joined forces to organize the assassination.

Beyond its determinations of guilt, the Warren Commission recommended steps to improve the protection of the president. It urged Congress to pass legislation making it a federal crime to murder the president, the vice president, or the person next in line for the presidency. (Such a law would have made it far easier to get the president's casket out of the hands of Dallas officials and onto the plane returning to Washington.) More fervently, it called for better coordination between the Secret Service, FBI, and CIA. The Commission felt that the Secret Service should have, at the very least, made arrangements for police and custodians to inspect buildings along the parade route that might provide suitable nests for snipers. The FBI, according to the report, should have made the Secret Service aware of Oswald's history and his presence in Dallas.

As the Commission passed judgment on government agencies, Americans heard critiques of the panel's own work. Undeniable flaws in the Commission's report opened the door to future speculation. The hurried panel's failure to pursue information about possible conspiracies represented an important shortcoming—one that was perpetuated by the FBI after the Commission disbanded. In an effort to act tastefully and to respect the feelings of the Kennedy family, the Commission failed to closely inspect autopsy X-rays and photographs. The Kennedys feared misuse of the images by the media, and Warren accepted their rationale. In its investigation of Ruby, the Commission failed to analyze his telephone contacts with reputed mob figures.[22] Within months of the report's release, other questions began popping up. Amateur detectives put the spotlight on several questions: the authenticity of the "backyard" photos showing Oswald holding the rifle, ties that Oswald or Ruby may have had with mobsters or with Cubans, Ruby's ability to get close to Oswald without police assistance, faulty descriptions of the "Oswald" who visited Mexico City, the nature of Kennedy's wounds, and the single-bullet theory. Gerald Ford, the last surviving Commission member, told an interviewer in 2003, "I think at the time a majority of the members of the Commission thought we had done a thorough job."[23] Obviously, this suggests that some members were unconvinced by the panel's conclusions. The Warren Commission worked quickly and reached straightforward conclusions, but the very simplicity of its verdict accelerated the spread of public doubt.

BACKLASH, NEW PROBES, NEW DISCOVERIES

Soon after the report's release, doubters began to make their voices heard, but in the halls of power there were only whispers of disbelief. Johnson thought an international conspiracy may have engineered Kennedy's slaying. Though he publicly accepted the Warren report, he initially suspected that Soviet Premier Nikita Khrushchev and Cuban leader Fidel Castro had plotted JFK's demise and that discovery of their involvement could lead to nuclear war.[24] Later, he focused all of his suspicion on Cuba. Johnson knew something that the Warren Commission did not: that the CIA had hidden its history of working with mobsters to kill Castro. "President Kennedy tried to get Castro," Johnson told domestic affairs adviser Joseph Califano, "but Castro got Kennedy first."[25] Johnson kept quiet about these thoughts because he believed that adding credibility to conspiracy theories could destabilize international affairs.[26] After leaving the White House, Johnson agreed to a series of interviews with Walter Cronkite of CBS, and during one session he admitted that he doubted Oswald acted alone. He thought Oswald had fired the fatal shots, but he suspected the gunman was just one small wheel in a colossal machine.[27] Arthur Krim, a Johnson friend and Democratic Party power, asked the network to delete that comment for national security reasons and, after a confrontation between Johnson's team and top officials at CBS, the network agreed.[28] Also quietly suspicious was Robert Kennedy. He reportedly told Arthur M. Schlesinger Jr. that he suspected Cubans or organized crime bosses were responsible.[29] Some authors have hypothesized that Robert Kennedy may have felt enormous guilt about the possibility that his own anti-Castro zeal led to his brother's death. RFK led Operation Mongoose, an undercover effort to undermine Castro's leadership. Neither Johnson nor Kennedy ever publicly expressed doubts about the Commission's findings.

Operation Mongoose was a secret operation that focused most of its attention on sabotaging Castro's government and encouraging dissent within the Cuban population.

The first literary attack on the Warren report, a brief book of essays by critics, emerged within months of the report's release. By 1966, book-length attacks on the Warren Commission came in a flurry, beginning with Harold Weisberg's *Whitewash*. Mark Lane's *Rush to Judgment,* which suggests a broad conspiracy, became the first commercial success among Warren Commission critiques, and it has reportedly sold more than a million copies to date. Other assassination-related books in that year included Richard Popkin's *The Second Oswald*, which focuses on the idea that an Oswald imposter was used to implicate the real Oswald; Raymond Marcus's *The Bastard Bullet*, which attacks the single-bullet theory; Penn Jones Jr.'s *Forgive My Grief*, which raises questions about mysterious deaths among potential witnesses; Leo Sauvage's *The Oswald Affair* and Edward Jay Epstein's *Inquest*, both of which question Warren Commission methodology. The *New York Times* joined the debate on November 25, 1966, saying, "There are enough solid doubts of thoughtful citizens, among the shrill attacks on the Warren Commission now to require answers." The *Times* contended that its concerns were not driven by the ever-multiplying conspiracy theories but by "the general confusion in the public mind raised by the publication of allegations and the many puzzling questions that have been raised."[30] The following year, Josiah Thompson offered the first reconstruction of the assassination based on a viewing of the Zapruder film in his book *Six Seconds in Dallas*, and Sylvia Meagher's *Accessories after the Fact* spotlighted any testimony or evidence that seemed to contradict the Commission's final report. During this period, magazines such as *Life* and *Esquire* devoted space to growing questions about the report, although the mainstream media, for the most part, shied away from appearing to promote specific theories. When Johnson signed the Freedom of Information and Privacy Act on July 4, 1967, he opened the door to further investigations in government records, leading to the release of millions of assassination-related documents. Thousands of books have followed, offering a wide array of tales about Oswald imposters, secret surgeries on the president's corpse, and government agencies' far-flung conspiracies to kill their own leader.

Most Americans did not rush out to file a Freedom of Information Act request to open specific assassination records, but many have remained at least a bit open to the possibility of conspiracy without becoming full-fledged advocates of the idea. Dennis Hatchell was a Colorado adolescent when the assassination occurred and has not seriously studied all of the varied conspiracy theories. However, like many of his countrymen, he has wondered. "The only thing that piqued my curiosity was . . . whether one person could have pulled the thing off." Recalling many people's fear of a Kennedy dynasty, he said, "Knowing human nature the way we know it now, you spend a lot of time wondering if somebody wasn't rich enough, good enough and clever enough to pull that off."[31] Whether such questions have generated life-changing obsessions or have represented mere musings, the assassination and its mysteries have never ceased to hold a place in the minds of many Americans.

During the mid-1960s, the CIA quietly collected new testimony on Oswald's experiences in the Soviet Union from former KGB officer Yuri Nosenko, a Soviet defector to the United States. Although the agency

Figure 5.1 Marine photo of Lee Harvey Oswald. National Archives, Item from Record Group 233: Records of the U.S. House of Representatives, 1789–2011.

questioned the authenticity of Nosenko's 1964 defection and kept him under house arrest for more than a year, he passed a polygraph exam and contended that the KGB kept Oswald under surveillance in the Soviet Union and that the spy agency considered Oswald to be mentally unfit. He told the CIA that the KGB never established a connection with Oswald because of doubts that someone in his mental state could be useful. In his interrogation, Nosenko went beyond descriptions of Oswald's life in the Soviet Union to address conspiracy theorists' charges that the Soviet Union expedited Oswald's visa to enter the country in 1959. Nosenko insisted that there was nothing unusual about Oswald getting a visa to enter the Soviet Union from Finland on short notice: The Soviet consul in Helsinki, he argued, had the authority to provide instant visas to any Americans seeking to visit the Communist giant. In 1969, Nosenko was officially recognized as a defector rather than a double agent; despite this new status, his testimony on Oswald faced continuing challenges because of inconsistencies in his statements during long interrogations by the CIA.

In 1967, New Orleans District Attorney Jim Garrison began making public claims that he had uncovered a conspiracy to assassinate Kennedy, and he charged Clay Shaw, the only person ever tried for taking part in

JFK's assassination. Garrison's lack of evidence and simultaneous drive for publicity were reminiscent of the ravings of Joseph McCarthy. As he investigated Oswald's contacts during his 1963 stay in New Orleans, Garrison got an early lead in the case from a report by private detective Jack Martin that David Ferrie, a gay man, had maintained contact with Oswald after his return to Texas. Martin later told the FBI that the whole story had been "a figment of his imagination," but this tip remained central to Garrison's case. Ferrie's trip to Houston on the night of the assassination further raised Garrison's suspicions. Unfortunately for Garrison, Ferrie died of natural causes in early 1967, robbing the district attorney of a potential witness and suspect.

Another key element in Garrison's investigation sprang from the statement of an attorney, Dean Andrews, who claimed that a man named Clay Bertrand had contacted him a day after the assassination to ask whether Andrews would defend Oswald. Andrews gave widely divergent descriptions of Bertrand, but Garrison fully accepted Andrews's account and contended that Shaw and Bertrand were the same man. Gordon Novel, a private detective working for Garrison's office reported wild schemes, such as Garrison's plan to shoot Ferrie with a tranquilizer dart, and Novel claimed that he had seen forged letters that were employed to make Garrison's case. The district attorney even used sodium pentothal and hypnosis to convince his primary witness, Perry Russo, to implicate Shaw and claim that he had heard Ferrie, Shaw, and Oswald plotting JFK's murder in 1963.[32] Shaw, who happened to be gay like Ferrie, was a well-known civic leader. It is reasonable to assume that Garrison's accusations may have emanated, at least in part, from homophobia. Looking for a broad conspiracy, Garrison wrongly concluded that Shaw was connected with the CIA, and he used that belief to build a tangled web of imaginary government ties between men in the Big Easy and Kennedy's assassination. One key element in the construction of Garrison's case was his belief that Oswald's Fair Play for Cuba Committee once operated out of a building that housed the offices of Guy Banister, a former FBI agent then working as a private detective. Oswald's pro-Cuba handouts did list 544 Camp Street as his organization's address, but a Secret Service investigation less than a month after the assassination revealed that none of the tenants recalled seeing Oswald or an office for his organization in the building.[33]

NBC News cast doubt on Garrison's case by talking to Louisiana inmates, who reported that one jailed man had been promised release from prison if he perjured himself by testifying against Shaw. The network asserted that both that inmate and Russo had failed polygraph tests. Soon afterward, Garrison's top investigator resigned, characterizing the case as a sham.[34] Garrison went on to allege that both Johnson and Robert Kennedy had participated in a government cover-up. When Shaw's case finally went to trial in 1969, Garrison's prosecution failed. The jury deliberated just fifty-four minutes before returning a verdict of not guilty of conspiring to kill the president; nevertheless, public interest in Garrison's allegations revealed growing suspicions that government officials may have hatched a plot to assassinate Kennedy. On another front, investigative reporters, such as columnist Drew Pearson, began fleshing out accusations about the Kennedy White House's secret campaign against Castro, including some indications that Robert Kennedy may have endorsed the assassination of Castro, thus providing a new motive for Oswald's action.

Washington re-entered the assassination investigation in 1968 when Attorney General Ramsey Clark appointed a committee of medical experts to review the autopsy photos and X-rays, which the Warren Commission had failed to examine. This committee found "serious discrepancies between its review of the autopsy materials and the autopsy itself."[35] The entry wound in the brain clearly was located incorrectly by the pathologists who performed the autopsy. These findings reinforced concerns that the autopsy may have been compromised in some way. The most innocuous possibility is that doctors showed deference to former First Lady Jacqueline Kennedy by performing the autopsy with undue haste so that the body could be available to return to the White House as soon as possible. However, some have alleged that the autopsy's conclusions may have been affected by pressure from government agencies.

During the 1970s, new investigations shed light on Kennedy's murder and his potential enemies. In the aftermath of Watergate, Americans experienced growing suspicions about government cover-ups and concerns about the CIA's activities. A Senate panel bearing an unwieldy title—the Select Committee to Study Governmental Operations with Respect to Intelligence Activities—was created in January 1975 and soon became known as the Church Committee because it was headed by Idaho Senator Frank Church. Introducing new evidence to support an emerging conspiracy theory, the Committee uncovered information confirming that the CIA had conspired with the Mafia to assassinate Castro during the Kennedy era. CIA officials testified that even CIA Director John McCone was unaware of the assassination plots, so there is no direct evidence that either JFK or RFK knew about the schemes.[36] At the time of JFK's death, another CIA operation was under way to assist a Cuban official who was arranging the murder of Castro to be followed by a coup.[37] The Committee further expanded the imagined landscape of conspiracy advocates by interviewing Judith Campbell Exner, who reportedly was one of Kennedy's mistresses at the same time that she was closely tied to mobster Sam Giancana. Though she was not forced to speak in detail about her relationship with Kennedy, she denied ever acting as a go-between for mobsters seeking to contact the president.[38] (Exner's relationship with Kennedy apparently ended in 1962 after FBI Director J. Edgar Hoover, no fan of JFK, warned Robert Kennedy about her connection with Giancana.)[39] Furthermore, the Church Committee confirmed that U.S. law enforcement agencies failed to apply serious attention to conspiracy leads and revealed that both the CIA and FBI had withheld valuable evidence from the Warren Commission.[40]

In another post-Watergate initiative, President Ford named a Commission headed by Vice President Nelson Rockefeller in 1975 to investigate CIA operations within the United States. In its pursuit of a broad agenda, the panel explored purported connections between the CIA and Kennedy's assassination. Ultimately, the Rockefeller Commission endorsed the Warren Commission's findings that Oswald fired both shots that hit JFK and rejected the possibility of another gunman on the grassy knoll in front of Kennedy. The panel tossed aside accusations that two Watergate figures—E. Howard Hunt and Frank Sturgis—were "hobos" taken into custody near Dealey Plaza on November 22, 1963. The panel found no evidence that either man had been in Dallas on that day. Some critics labeled the Rockefeller Commission's final report as just another government whitewash. The Commission relied heavily on CIA records and the testimony of men like Hunt and Sturgis to draw its conclusions, but the analysis of the gunfire evidence, which involved five previously uninvolved doctors, appeared to be solid. Although the Commission ran out of time before fully investigating, it did find evidence of CIA involvement in the assassination of Generalissimo Rafael Trujillo of the Dominican Republic as well as in failed plots against Castro.[41]

As government investigations moved along, the unofficial quest for new assassination information continued. The Politics of Conspiracy, a three-day conference at Boston University, attracted more than 1,500 people interested in the assassination in January 1975.[42] News outlets, too, offered new insights for the public. A CBS News documentary in 1975 showed that Oswald could have made the three shots more quickly than the Warren Commission had estimated. Using eleven volunteer marksmen, CBS found that Oswald had more than enough time to fire three shots.[43] And, on ABC's *Goodnight America*, Geraldo Rivera showed the Zapruder film on national television for the first time.[44] Until that date, most Americans had seen only the freeze-frame shots published by *Life* magazine. TV executives considered the violence too graphic until Americans had become inured to such scenes by nightly visions of the Vietnam war, race riots, and violent political protests on network news broadcasts.

In 1976, the House of Representatives launched its own investigation of the assassinations of both Kennedy and civil rights leader Martin Luther King Jr. Setting to work in the post-Watergate era, members of the House Select Committee on Assassinations were more openly skeptical of reports from the FBI and CIA than their predecessors on the Warren Commission had been in 1964. After more than two years of work and an investigation that cost $5.4 million, the committee issued a report and twelve volumes of appendices in 1979. Included in the report were several noteworthy pieces of information. A 1977 neutron activation analysis by Vincent P. Guinn showed that it is almost certain that no more than two bullets struck Kennedy and that both were fired from a Mannlicher-Carcano rifle like Oswald's.[45] An expert panel's examination of the autopsy photos and X-rays confirmed that they were genuine images of JFK, matching previous photos and X-rays of the slain president.[46] A wound ballistics expert answered one of the lingering conspiracy questions: If Kennedy was shot from behind, why did his head snap backward? This witness stated that a shot to the head could have caused a neurological reaction in which his back muscles tightened, bringing his head backward.[47] Though some conspiracy theorists believed that the backyard photos of Oswald holding his rifle were composite images, as he claimed during his interrogation, Marina Oswald testified that she clearly remembered taking the photos.[48] A panel of twenty-two photographic experts backed up her statement by verifying the photos' authenticity.[49] Contrary to some people's contentions that an Oswald imposter visited the Cuban and Soviet embassies in September 1963, Alfredo Mirabel Diaz, a Cuban diplomat, testified in Havana that he recalled Oswald's appearance as well as his arrogant attitude, which caused loud arguments during both of his appearances at the Cuban Embassy.[50] The committee's investigation refuted one popular element in assassination theories—reports that Oswald was seen taking a white envelope from an FBI agent in New Orleans just months before the assassination. Adrian Alba, a garage owner who had met Oswald during his many work breaks from a nearby coffee factory, claimed to have witnessed the handoff. He said that he knew the man giving Oswald the envelope was an FBI agent because he had visited the garage earlier to pick up a Secret Service car housed there. Alba did not report this exchange to the Warren Commission and when the House committee investigated, it determined that no FBI agents had signed out any of the Secret Service cars in that garage during the time when Alba claimed he saw the exchange.[51] In its investigation of Jack Ruby's connection to the case, the committee interviewed Harry Haler, an associate of Ruby. Haler described Ruby's affinity for the Kennedy family: "He was very, very fond of the whole Kennedy family, to a fanatical . . . He just loved them like a kid would like Babe Ruth or Joe DiMaggio. He absolutely adored them. You couldn't say anything about the Kennedys."[52]

Within the report, the committee criticized the FBI, the CIA, and the Warren Commission for failing to adequately pursue the possibility of a conspiracy and for covering up their own mistakes. (One example: An infuriated J. Edgar Hoover had reprimanded seventeen agents for lax treatment of Oswald and inattention to his behavior prior to the assassination; at the same time, Hoover had hidden his actions from the Warren Commission to protect the FBI's reputation.)[53] Interestingly, the committee found that the Justice Department, under the leadership of Robert Kennedy, failed to carry out its investigative responsibilities, especially in the days immediately following the assassination.[54] In addition, the committee reported a "significant link between Ruby and organized crime" and asserted that Ruby had help from members of the Dallas Police Department when he entered the garage through an alleyway and gunned down Oswald.[55] While significantly veering away from the Warren Commission's findings on some issues, the committee agreed that Oswald fired the shots that killed JFK and found that the single-bullet theory was apparently true.

> If Ruby entered the garage by walking down a ramp, he definitely passed police officers without being challenged; if he entered through an alleyway door, as the House Select Committee concluded, he needed the aid of a police officer to unlock the door.

Trying to fill a gap left by the Warren Commission, the committee argued that Oswald was motivated by his preoccupation with "political ideology."[56]

In sharp contrast to the Warren Commission and the Rockefeller Commission, the House Select Committee declared that a group of conspirators probably planned and carried out JFK's murder. At the same time, the committee ruled out almost all of the usual suspects—the Soviet Union, Cuba, anti-Castro Cuban groups, organized crime, the Secret Service, the FBI, and the CIA. And the committee offered no conjecture about the conspiracy's source. (The only frequently mentioned conspiracy prospect not specifically cleared by the committee report was a right-wing/military cabal.) To determine that a conspiracy almost certainly existed, the committee relied heavily on acoustical analysis of noise recorded on a dictabelt from a police motorcycle operator's open microphone at the time of the assassination. Although the recording registered no sound of gunshots, experts told the panel that it virtually guaranteed that four shots had been fired. These witnesses reported in the last week of committee hearings that the recording showed "impulse patterns" that represented four shots, thus necessitating the belief that a second gunman fired on Kennedy, since Oswald left only three shells in the sniper's nest. And an additional gunman almost certainly proved the existence of a conspiracy, the committee believed. Its members placed their faith in this report despite the Warren Commission's finding that only 5 percent of witnesses reported hearing more than three shots.[57] In 1982, a committee appointed by the National Academy of Sciences determined that the acoustical interpretation provided to the committee was misleading and that "reliable acoustic data do not support a conclusion that there was a second gunman." This panel concluded that the dictabelt recording had been made a minute after the assassination.[58]

The long parade of government investigations ended with a 1988 Department of Justice report that found no viable evidence of a conspiracy to kill President Kennedy. Many Americans felt that these probes brought them no closer to the truth about JFK's assassination, and they found no "closure," in the words of author Barbie Zelizer.[59] One new theory arose in 1988 when James Reston Jr. speculated that Connally, not Kennedy, was Oswald's target. In a *Time* article and later book, Reston tied Oswald to Connally, noting that Oswald had mistakenly believed that Connally was secretary of the Navy when he found out that he had received an undesirable discharge after defecting to the Soviet Union. Oswald had written to Connally in January 1962. Connally responded with a letter saying that he was no longer secretary of the Navy and that he would pass on Oswald's complaint to his successor—not the response Oswald had hoped to receive.[60] However, Reston's theory gained little acceptance.

The flood of conspiracy books continued. In 1989, Jim Marrs pursued Jones' earlier point in his new book, *Crossfire*, which asserted that there had been 103 mysterious deaths among people tied to the assassination and its investigation. Other books, including Mark North's *Act of Treason: The Role of J. Edgar Hoover in the Assassination of President Kennedy* and Lane's *Plausible Denial: Was the CIA Involved in the Assassination of President Kennedy?*, were published close to the December 1991 release date of Oliver Stone's *JFK*, and by February 1992, just two months after the film's release, four assassination books were on the *New York Times* bestseller lists.[61]

Just as there are and were independent conspiracy advocates, some of the many Americans who have devoted considerable time to investigating the assassination have concluded that Oswald acted alone. Gerald Posner's 1993 book *Case Closed* became a Pulitzer Prize finalist by making a convincing case against Oswald. Through painstaking research, Posner

Conspiracy Theories

A wide variety of conspiracy theories have been hatched since 1963. Here is a rundown of the most frequently mentioned suspicions, each of which has been advocated with a large number of variations:

- *The right wing did it*: Mark Lane contended that, with the help of Ruby and Tippit, a right-wing conspiracy killed Kennedy and turned Oswald into a fall guy. Additional combinations of conspirators have been proposed by other authors, who believe right-wing extremists thought Kennedy was "soft on Communism."
- *Pro-Castro Cubans or left-wing allies did it*: After release of information about CIA attempts to assassinate the Cuban leader, many speculated that Castro supporters, Soviet spies, or their Communist allies in the United States ordered Kennedy's execution.
- *Anti-Castro Cubans did it*: Jim Garrison claimed that anti-Castro Cubans in New Orleans and their associates set up an ambush of Kennedy. Perhaps as many as sixteen gunmen targeted the president in Garrison's scenario. He alleged that the leading non-Cuban plotters were homosexuals. Others have imagined different alliances of anti-Castro forces in the assassination.
- *The military industrial complex did it*: Oliver Stone argued that a right-wing conspiracy driven by the military industrial complex killed Kennedy so that he would not withdraw U.S. troops from Vietnam and weaken the CIA. (In Stone's version, anti-Castro Cubans joined with the government conspirators.)
- *The mob did it*: G. Robert Blakey, who was chief counsel for the House Select Committee on Assassinations, later coauthored a book that pinned the blame on Mafia members. This theory drew on information about CIA-sponsored mob attempts to kill Castro. Beyond the attempts to kill Castro, some believers in this theory have given credence to rumors that the Kennedys were indebted to the mob for JFK's 1960 election victory or that mobsters were angry about Attorney General Robert Kennedy's aggressive attempts to stifle organized crime.
- *The Secret Service did it*: David Lifton suggested that Kennedy's body was altered between its departure from Parkland Hospital and its arrival in Washington. He believed this represented the perfect way to cover up a Secret Service conspiracy. Another believer, Howard Donahue, alleged that a Secret Service agent accidentally killed Kennedy with his rifle. Donahue's quest to legitimize his theory is chronicled in *Mortal Error* by Bonar Menninger.[62]
- *The CIA did it*: Frustrated by Kennedy's failure to offer additional support to the Bay of Pigs invasion and by his efforts to reduce the agency's power, agents, either under orders or acting as part of a rogue conspiracy, carried out a veiled coup d'état, according to some theories.

- *The FBI did it*: Because J. Edgar Hoover made little effort to hide his disdain for the Kennedys, and because the feeling was mutual, his agency has been accused of planning and mobilizing the assassination, perhaps through its contacts with Oswald. Under this theory, Ruby, who was briefly courted to be an FBI informant, is sometimes pictured as a government-paid assassin.
- *The Soviet KGB did it*: As the United States' political adversary, the Soviet Union fell under suspicion, especially in the days immediately after the assassination. Some have seen Oswald's defection to the Soviet Union as an ideal opportunity to set the plan in motion.

examined the many well-known conspiracy storylines and the details on which they are built. For instance, instead of just reporting the results of paraffin tests on Oswald's face and hands, he explained that a positive paraffin test on Oswald's hands may be meaningless because paraffin reacts to many substances besides gunpowder, and that the negative paraffin test on his cheek may be equally inconsequential because FBI tests showed that someone could fire a rifle without having a positive paraffin test on his cheek.[63] To counter conspiracy theorist Marrs's alarm about mystery deaths among those connected to the investigation, Posner followed the House Select Committee's research and accounted for each of the 103 deaths, drawn from a list of more than 10,000 people loosely tied to the various assassination investigations. He found that most died of natural causes and that, statistically, even if 103 had died in other ways, that would not be unusual when considered as a subgroup of 10,000 subjects.[64] In most cases, Posner's work was thorough and convincing, but on some issues he was quick to reject assertions that interfered with his desired conclusion. Sometimes, he discounted testimony because the witness suffered from alcoholism or emotional problems, but the witnesses he supported did not face the same level of psychological scrutiny. And he dismissed some testimony as lacking corroboration, but at others times he was swayed by one individual's recollections. Based on Ruby's testimony, the Warren Commission had rejected journalist Seth Kantor's assertion that he had seen Ruby at Parkland Hospital on the afternoon of the assassination, but Posner accepted Kantor's uncorroborated statement as true.[65]

Into the twenty-first century, new books are still emerging. The heftiest among them is Vincent Bugliosi's book *Reclaiming History: The Assassination of President John F. Kennedy*, which fills more than 1,600 pages and includes a CD to house his endnotes and bibliographic material. This 2007 tome agrees with Posner's book on the big issues, but the two authors disagree on many individual details. Bugliosi demeans Posner's work almost as much as he criticizes the more outrageous conspiracy theories, which he addresses in great depth. Describing his own investigation largely in first person, Bugliosi accuses Posner of taking credit for other people's findings and casts scorn on his effort for lack of thoroughness. (Posner's book is 608 pages long.) A portion of Bugliosi's huge study was published as a smaller book, *Four Days in November: The Assassination of President John F. Kennedy*, which provides a useful account of the events of that weekend without digging into the subsequent investigations and conspiracy theories. This book informs an old timeline by integrating newly discovered evidence.

Over the last three decades, technological improvements have provided new insights on the assassination. Enhanced versions of the Zapruder film have shown that the shots were fired over the course of 8.4 seconds, a much longer time span than had been originally estimated. Working with the Zapruder film and other clips shot by amateur photographers, computer animator Dale K. Myers has produced and refined a reconstruction of the crime. Myers has been able to reproduce the shooting from a number of angles. His findings reinforce the difficult-to-believe single-bullet theory and affirm the guilt of Oswald by indicating that the bullets could have come from nowhere except the Texas School Book Depository's sixth floor.[66]

THE ASSASSINATION IN THE AMERICAN PSYCHE AND IN POPULAR CULTURE

JFK's assassination was not the kind of news story that makes headlines for a few days and then slips out of the American consciousness. Instead, it became embedded in America's cultural DNA, not as a momentary event, but as a cultural phenomenon ingrained in American identity, both for those who remembered it and for those who did not. Whether driven by sadness, a sense of loss, shock, curiosity, doubt, or suspicion, many of the nation's citizens have been unwilling to let this event fade into the past. Journalists have continued to draw Americans' attention to anniversaries, memorials, new pieces of brain-teasing evidence, and sadly ironic details. The nation watched Kennedy's toddler children grow into adulthood—and, still, Americans talked about where they were when they heard the news, what they thought really happened, and how the assassination may have changed history. Through it all, questions remained. By 2003, a Gallup Poll showed that only 19 percent of Americans believed Oswald acted alone.[67] With the continuing flood of information, the absence of a readily accepted solution remains unsettling. A 2004 poll showed that most Americans believe in a government cover-up, and yet the majority do not support another government investigation.[68] In the Space Age, sophisticated thinking and information were supposed to lead to unquestionable solutions; in the twenty-first century, Americans know better.

Across the decades, the assassination has found a place in both history and popular culture. Of course, Kennedy was a pop culture figure even when he was alive. Just like Elizabeth Taylor and Cary Grant, he and his wife were frequently featured on the covers of the "movie magazines"—like *Photoplay, Motion Picture,* and *Modern Screen*—that covered the celebrity news of that era. People flocked to see the Kennedys just as current-day fans maneuver to catch a glimpse of Brad Pitt or Angelina Jolie. In one memorable news photo, President Kennedy is shown wearing only a bathing suit on a crowded beach. He is wet, smiling, well muscled, and he is surrounded by female beachgoers, whom we might call groupies today. It is difficult to imagine any president since 1963 fitting into that scene, which almost looks like an outtake from the Frankie Avalon–Annette Funicello beach movies of the 1960s. Nevertheless, Kennedy's status as a "star" of sorts is one element in the question of why his assassination has remained a hot topic in pop culture.

Death is difficult to face, even when it comes quietly in the night to the ill and aging. People cope with it in different ways. Some cry, but others laugh to break the tension. They whisper funny memories about the decedent or the circumstances of his death. Others hide from death, staying away from funerals, looking the other way when death strikes nearby. With constant media coverage, it was impossible to avoid awareness of JFK's death, and in the early years, when his passing carried an almost sacred aura, there was little room for humor of any kind. Americans quickly absorbed the gory view of the widow's bloody clothes, and within weeks *Life* published frames from Abraham Zapruder's film: not the kill shot, but the dying president's foot hanging limply over the car door as his body, barely alive, filled the back seat. They were unforgettable images for anyone old enough to see them. And, over time, like the storytellers at Irish wakes, some began to see bits of humor in it all, something absurd about the lovely couple wearing blood and brain matter instead of white tie and tails. For those who were not old enough to remember, or were born later, the photos took on a new meaning. They were scenes of a famous crime—nothing personal. And so, while some remain passionate about JFK and his worth, others have begun to see the killing as nothing more than an alluring mystery. To them, its human quality has faded while zeal about possible conspiracies has survived. The tragedy has been deconstructed into a series of clichéd and too-often-replicated stock scenes, iconic images separated from their emotional context.

Just as film and television shaped public memories of the assassination, they also provided a context for interpreting the crime. Pervasive violence on screen, whether on television or in the movies, programmed Americans to get beyond the initial shock and mourning by accepting violence as a part of life. In *Shooting Kennedy: JFK and the Culture of Images*, David Lubin writes that, after immersion in the American consciousness, assassination images became almost invisible to Americans. Lubin describes Zapruder's twenty-six-second film as "a modernist text," saying that it provides the opportunity for "infinitely variable subjective interpretations."[69] Rather than producing clear-cut evidence, continued study of the 8mm camera film has opened it up to more widely divergent assignments of meaning. Lubin contends that Americans of the 1960s viewed the images through eyes that had been conditioned by fictional representations found in the mysterious films of Alfred Hitchcock and other masters of horror/mystery films. Specifically, he notes that in two Hitchcock classics, 1954's *Rear Window* and 1960's *Psycho*, men are perched above their targets. Because the American public never saw Oswald in his sniper's nest, Lubin argues that we see him in our minds through Hitchcock's classic scenes. When Americans of that era pictured an unseen man in a window, they envisioned Jeff focusing his camera lens on unsuspecting neighbors in *Rear Window* and Norman Bates dressed as his mother, staring out of the Bates Hotel at all of the potential victims just outside his reach in *Psycho*. Lubin finds commonalities between the well-dressed Cary Grant in 1959's *North by Northwest* as he runs through a field trying to avoid a villainous crop-duster and Kennedy in Dallas: Both handsome leading men were dressed to kill as they became victims of shocking assaults by a mysterious attacker from above.[70] Kennedy was, after all, the Cary Grant of presidents.

Lubin argues that the assassination reached into the future, too, and shaped the way later films portrayed death. In 1967's *Bonnie and Clyde*, director Arthur Penn modeled the blood-spattered deaths of the lead characters after what he saw in the Zapruder film. He even included a split second when part of Clyde's brain is blown away, just like JFK's. Penn argues that violence is "a part of the character of America. It began with the Western, the 'frontier.' America is a country where people realize their ideas in violent ways."[71]

Television violence, which existed in the form of quick and clean deaths in the early 1960s, has advanced to a level of blood and gore that would have been considered bad taste in 1963. Today, millions of Americans dine in front of TVs as they watch procedural police shows with splayed-open, autopsied corpses lying in the foreground while the characters casually converse. A 2002 scientific study estimated that three to five acts of violence were depicted in a typical primetime hour of television.[72] Historian James W. Hilty sees television violence as providing a perspective through which Americans viewed the assassination once the paralyzing trauma had passed. "It's the New York, Philadelphia, Chicago police shows that . . . permeated television and sort of perforated the culture down deep and conveyed the notion that shoot 'em up is just good, healthy, clean American fun, and the president got in the way of a bullet." Hilty found that attitude to be "very reflective of what Americans are like."[73]

America's interest in antiheroic figures on film and on TV may have affected perceptions of the assassination as well. The nation has a strange fascination with bad guys in popular entertainment. One manifestation of this is avid interest in mobsters. Just a few examples include 1930s gangster movies featuring James Cagney and Edward G. Robinson, *The Godfather* trilogy of 1972, 1974, and 1990, the popular gangsta rap of the late 1980s and early 1990s, and *The Sopranos* TV series, which captivated many Americans during its run from 1999 to 2007. Oswald, like Kennedy, has become an iconic image. And, as Lubin suggests in his book, the backyard photo of Oswald holding his rifle is reminiscent of the *Minuteman* sculpture erected in Concord, Massachusetts in 1875: "legs apart, bare-armed but bearing arms, he epitomizes rugged self-reliance, taking a stand on matters of civic importance."[74] This image mirrors the pose of a Western drifter and gunslinger, too. Oswald attracted no public fan club, but many Americans developed an interest in this alienated young man who, like Kennedy, has become a lasting image open to interpretation: Is he a lost boy, a cold-blooded killer, a patsy, a sociopath, or an assassin who succeeded with the help of random chance? Since Kennedy's slaying, those interested in the assassination have had an opportunity to buy a wide array of murder memorabilia, including T-shirts, mugs, and posters featuring either JFK or Oswald. One manufacturer sold a JFK T-shirt that says, "Government Lies," and can be paired with an Oswald T-shirt that proclaims, "Trust Government." Another T-shirt shows an internet image of Ruby shooting Oswald, although this collage pictures Ruby bearing a guitar rather than a gun and instead of clenching his fist as he feels the pain of a gunshot, Oswald is clasping a microphone and belting out a rock song. The image manipulated by George E. Mahlberg from a photo by Bob Jackson is entitled "You ain't nothing but a hound dog!" In the 1990s, the gun Jack Ruby used to kill Oswald drew $200,000 at auction, and the coroner's toe tag that was attached to Oswald's body sold for $6,000.[75] At a 2008 auction in Las Vegas, an eager buyer got the toe tag for $66,000. The gun was up for sale again, but the owner rejected the highest bid of

$750,000, which he considered to be about one third of its value.[76] Because his time in the public eye began less than two days before it ended, Oswald holds a morbid spot in popular culture. His short life in the spotlight began and ended with murder.

Another lens that clarifies the nation's attitudes toward the assassination is America's gun culture, which has proliferated since the Civil War, when guns first became more affordable. A 2007 article in the (London) *Observer* noted that the number of Americans who have died from gun violence in the United States since JFK's assassination exceeds the number of Americans who died in all of the nation's twentieth-century wars. The same article reported that about half of all American households contained guns.[77] Kennedy's assassination is a dividing line in the history of American gun violence. His death and Oswald's subsequent murder made some people stop and think about violence's role in American culture, and in the city of Dallas, in particular.

> It was an event that painted Dallas as a place where maybe two-thirds of the citizenry went armed and where there was extraordinarily easy access to firearms, Hitty says, I mean the realization that Oswald purchased the rifle for this absurd sum of $19.95, and that he also owned a pistol. Now here was a guy who could not afford regular lunches, but he owned two firearms. And he had a record that one would suspect would disqualify him from ever purchasing a firearm, but there was no control over firearms. Simply said, America is a very violent society.[78]

Political scientist Sheldon Appleton says statistics show almost a hundred attempts were made to kill American public officials in the twentieth century.[79] Some observers argue that the Kennedy administration itself operated within a culture of violence, as its acceleration of the arms race and its relentless pursuit of Castro suggest. Viewed from this perspective, Kennedy's death seems to fit neatly into that culture.[80] Revelations about U.S. plots against Castro have led some conspiracy theorists to view the assassination as "a public suicide," in the words of Hilty.[81]

When Kennedy died, it would have been impossible to anticipate the many popular culture incarnations that his death would prompt. Of all of these efforts, conspiracy believer Oliver Stone's *JFK* stands out as a product skillfully engineered to connect Americans with what the director sees as an assassination cover-up. Stone did not set out to illuminate the facts of the case—and his carelessness with the truth caused immediate outrage in the academic community, but from Stone's perspective the film's emotional impact proved its success as more than a commercial venture. Mixing news footage with the make-believe of movies, Stone's film delivers a memorable, evocative message that has stayed with many Americans longer than the details of government investigations. Overlapping dialogue and rapidly changing images create a hectic pace and make viewers feel the confusion of trying to digest too much information without truly understanding—a condition Stone identifies with Americans' battle to make sense of the assassination itself. Over the two decades since its release, the film has drawn new generations into the assassination narrative, now a mystery for the ages.

Among *JFK*'s striking scenes is one in which a shadowy figure visits Oswald's corpse and places the murder weapon in his hand to provide an incriminating palm print; there is, of course, no evidence that such an event occurred. To make his overall point, Stone inserts many events that never happened; historian Michael L. Kurtz has counted at least eight significant false incidents as well as several fictional characters.[82] There are many noteworthy flaws in Stone's version of the assassination and its aftermath. He overestimates Oswald's distance from Kennedy—just 88 feet. He wrongly suggests that the single-bullet theory requires the bullet to hang suspended in the air and zigzag back and forth; he incorrectly cites where Connally was sitting in relation to Kennedy by ignoring the reality that Connally's jump seat placed him lower and to the left of the president; he erroneously claims that the "magic bullet" was "pristine" rather than obviously misshapen by its travels; and he repeatedly asserts that the head of a man shot from behind and to the right could not possibly fly back and to the left. Ironically, in making the film, Stone inadvertently disproved part of his own theory. Many of the witnesses who had claimed to see gunmen on the grassy knoll also recalled seeing a puff of smoke from the rifle fire; however, Stone was unable to duplicate the smoke without using special effects. (Experts say smoke from a rifle would disappear almost instantly after the shot was fired.)[83] Over and over again, Stone returns to the question of whether one man could fire the shots in 5.6 seconds, but he ignores the fact that the clock need not start with setting up the first shot; instead, the time frame only covers the period from the moment the first shot was heard to the moment when the last shot struck Kennedy. In his writings, Stone goes even further, contending that Oswald was not in the sixth-floor window at the Texas School Book Depository.[84] Despite all of the holes that historians have poked in Stone's theories, a 1992 article in the *American Historical Review* by Robert A. Rosenstone argues that "if it is part of the burden of the historical work to make us rethink how we got to where we are, and to make us question values that we and our leaders and our nation live by, then, whatever its flaws, *JFK* has to be among the most important works of American history ever to appear on the screen."[85] In the same journal issue, historian Marcus Raskin writes that "*JFK* is meant to use the assassination to force an audience to decide whether it wants to ground the American political process in the post-Cold War era with the same structures and habits of mind that governed it during the Cold War."[86]

Stone claims that he was not seeking to portray the truth but instead to offer a "counter-myth" to the "official myth" of the Warren Commission report, and he certainly cannot be accused of staying too close to the documented truth. "We are all victims of counterfeit history," he argues in his own defense.[87] Through the film, he charges that the military industrial complex formed a conspiracy to kill JFK and that the conspirators enjoyed the support of government officials. He implicates Johnson in the post-assassination cover-up and the strategic placement of his image during a discussion of the conspiracy blatantly suggests that he may have acted as part of a conspiracy to kill Kennedy. (A 2003 Gallup Poll showed that 18 percent of Americans believed that Johnson played a role in the assassination.)[88] A Vietnam veteran, Stone turns Kennedy's death into a war story. If Kennedy had lived, Stone insists, he would not have committed American soldiers to fight in Vietnam. "Kennedy in 1963, like Alexander the Great before him, was increasingly calling for radical change on several fronts," Stone claims.[89] In fact, Kennedy's civil rights legislation and his American University speech both demonstrated that he was developing a greater willingness to promote changes that were quite unpopular among some constituents, but the term "radical" hardly fits the real man, who was an extremely cautious, pragmatic, and generally moderate politician.

The biggest problem with Stone's film probably is his choice of a hero. New Orleans District Attorney Jim Garrison stands out as someone who refused to accept the official explanation of the assassination, but he is well known for making wide-ranging charges with reckless disregard for the truth. Stone admits that his Garrison is more heroic than the real man, but he believes that centering the film on Garrison is an essential storytelling device. As the backdrop for his story, he uses Garrison's trial of Clay Shaw, but the details of Garrison's case against Shaw, which were sketchy at best, do not receive as much emphasis as Stone's central argument that a conspiracy existed. Like a rickety house, Garrison's case was built by imaginatively hammering together stray innuendos rather than by building on a solid foundation of facts. Consequently, venerating Garrison undercuts Stone's message.

And yet, his persistent argument sways the emotions of many who see the film. Large numbers of moviegoers and, later, TV viewers have watched the film and accepted its narrative as essentially accurate. Although most audience members failed to adopt Stone's specific conspiracy theory, the majority seemed more certain of a conspiracy and more confident about their own suspicions.[90] "Nothing is as difficult as turning one's eyes from the screen to the audience during such a hypnotic film as *JFK*," wrote film maven Amos Vogel. "But when we do look at the audience—at its total absorption, its rapt silence, its awed submission to the electrifying images and sound—we see profound evidence of the power and the danger of the cinema."[91] During the film's theatrical run, one psychological survey attempted to gauge the film's emotional punch by comparing the feelings of moviegoers waiting to see it and those emerging after viewing the film. The study found that those who had viewed the film were about twice as likely to be angry as those waiting to watch it.[92]

In the face of widespread criticism from historians, politicians, and journalists, Stone says that his work merely urges Americans to "consider the possibility" that a coup d'état removed Kennedy from office.[93] He encourages Americans to look beyond government reports. In 1995, when John F. Kennedy Jr. was publisher of the new magazine *George*, his staff encouraged him to interview Stone as a sales gimmick. A reluctant Kennedy and an associate met Stone over dinner in Santa Monica. During the meal, Stone tried to convince Kennedy that a conspiracy had killed his father. Kennedy left the table, later returning to quickly finish the meal. Kennedy's biographer, Richard Blow, wrote that Stone "made John feel like Captain Kirk being stalked by the world's looniest Trekkie."[94]

Though Stone says he never intended to retell history, he managed to make history by motivating change in the real world. In retrospect, some have compared *JFK*'s impact to the effects of Harriet Beecher Stowe's *Uncle Tom's Cabin*, which generated anti-slavery feelings in the North during the years leading up to the Civil War. After the film's release, a popular outcry for release of assassination documents led to the John F. Kennedy Assassination Records Collection Act of 1992, which accelerated processing and release of documents related to Kennedy's slaying by establishing the Assassination Records Review Board. Many previously secret FBI and CIA documents are now available for public review at National Archives II in College Park, Maryland. More than 20,000 cubic feet of records, including more than four million documents, are in the collection and, although the Assassination Records Review Board no longer exists, documents are still being processed by agencies and opened to the public. The legislation required that all documents except those specifically excluded by the incumbent president must be opened by 2017. Thus far, opening the records has not produced a deluge of information that contradicts the conclusions of the Warren Commission. Release of documentation actually has countered some conspiracy theories. (The most memorable revelation was evidence that Commission member Gerald Ford altered details of the Warren report before its release. In a late revision, the future president changed the reported location of JFK's first entry wound, arbitrarily relocating it two to three inches higher on Kennedy's back. When researchers drew attention to the change, Ford said he acted to clarify, not to deceive.)[95]

Over the decades, JFK's assassination has found a home in the American imagination through popular culture art forms that go far beyond Oliver Stone's vision. In 1974, Director David Miller's *Executive Action*, a less-heralded conspiracy-theory film, offered moviegoers another scenario involving a right-wing plot. And TV's *The X-Files* dedicated one episode to a character known only as "Cigarette-Smoking Man," who follows military orders and kills Kennedy. In *Quantum Leap*, another TV science-fiction series, the time-traveling hero finds himself inhabiting Lee Harvey Oswald's body shortly before the assassination.

Writers of fiction also have taken creative approaches to the assassination. The most prominent novel, Don DeLillo's 1988 *Libra*, describes JFK's slaying as a harmless plot gone awry when a CIA faction tries to prod the United States into invading Cuba by staging a failed attempt to kill Kennedy. Norman Mailer's "non-fiction novel," *Oswald's Tale*, uses the memories of a large number of people who knew Oswald and Ruby to construct a detailed story that identifies Oswald as a protagonist capable of acting alone, although certainly not a hero. Other assassination-related works of fiction feature Kennedy speaking from heaven, recovering from gunshot wounds to be a better man, being saved by a time traveler, and being slain in 1960 when he was president-elect. Some explore his life as a sexual being and sex object. One short story, "JFK Secretly Attends Jackie's Auction," offers the reader a President Kennedy whose injuries have made it impossible for him to keep secrets. The CIA jails him in a secret compound until he is given one day of freedom to attend an auction of his late wife's possessions. And the flood of assassination-related works of fiction is apparently nowhere near its end. Two 2009 novels addressed the assassination. Diane and David Munson's *The Camelot Conspiracy* endorses the idea of a second gunman in Dealey Plaza, while E. Duke Vincent's *The Camelot Conspiracy: The Kennedys, Castro and the CIA: A Novel* presents a mobster as the narrator who tries to stop his compatriots in organized crime who plan to kill the president.

For more serious art connoisseurs, Andy Warhol used assassination imagery and color to create a variety of silk-screen pieces, often featuring repetition and different photographic processes. Among them were *Jackie "The Week That Was"* in 1963; *Sixteen Jackies, Nine Jackies, Three Jackies,*

Gold Jackie, and two versions of *Round Jackie*, all in 1964; three pieces entitled simply *Jackie* and another piece, *Jacqueline Kennedy No. 3*, in 1965; *Silver Jackie* and *Two Jackies* in 1966; and *Flash—November 22, 1963* in 1968.[96] As Art Simon writes in *Dangerous Knowledge: The JFK Assassination in Art and Film*, the works of Warhol and others "challenged the solemnity, even the sacredness, that had developed around the murder, its image, and the ensuing years of inquiry."[97] Among the other pop art images of note is Ed Patschke's *Purple Ritual*, which represents the famous backyard photo of Oswald without background and frames it with patriotic symbols.

Bruce Conner's film *Report*, released in ten different versions beginning in 1964, uses repetitive film images from the weekend of the assassination with the intent of raising viewers' consciousness about violence, but years later it unexpectedly became a source of amusement for some, further extending the separation between the solemn event of Kennedy's death and reflexive views of it. "No one really laughed watching *Report* until around 1976," Conner told an interviewer.[98] At that time, people began to see the film as camp. The mid-1970s was a period open to both assassination investigations and disrespectful approaches to the event in popular culture. During those years, the video group known as Ant Farm/T.R. Uthco produced a comical assassination re-enactment in Dealey Plaza called *Eternal Frame*, and a *National Lampoon* parody used frames from that film to imitate *Life*'s packaging of the Zapruder film. Around this time, people began joking about Jacqueline Kennedy's brief crawl onto the back of the limousine after the final shot struck her husband. From a distance, some viewed her actions as a sign of cowardice, something that elicited sneers and snickering. In the late 1970s and early 1980s, a punk rock band named Dead Kennedys garnered success. Laughing at JFK's death apparently reached its heyday during the years of Jimmy Carter's and Ronald Reagan's presidencies. This came in sharp contrast to the somber atmosphere that surrounded his memory in the years immediately following his death. In one part of American culture, Kennedy's once-sacred memory had become profane.

Whether Americans laugh, cry, or argue, JFK and his assassination clearly have not faded into obscurity. He is still a vivid figure in American popular culture. When he was alive, rivals belittled his successes by emphasizing his focus on "image," and for nearly fifty years after his own death he has survived as an image open to interpretation. His achievements and his speeches are not forgotten by students of history, but for many people the image is what holds sway: His good looks, his fashionable wife, his adorable children, his sexy secrets all are part of the package, a package that is all the more compelling because of the unceasing mystery surrounding his death.

CONCLUSION

Historians and biographers have primarily taken a hands-off approach to Kennedy's assassination, leaving the analysis to journalists, lawyers, and amateur detectives. However, the conspiracy theory phenomenon is too big to be ignored. Author and biographer William Manchester, who penned *The Death of a President*, believed Americans increasingly accepted conspiracy theories because the idea of a single gunman did not match up with the hugeness of the crime. "To employ what may seem an odd metaphor," he wrote in a 1992 *New York Times* letter to the editor, "there is an esthetic principle here. If you put six million dead Jews on one side of a scale and on the other side put the Nazi regime—the greatest gang of criminals ever to seize control of a modern state—you have a rough balance: greatest crime, greatest criminals. But if you put the murdered president of the United States on one side of a scale and that wretched waif Oswald on the other side, it doesn't balance. You want to add something weightier to Oswald. It would invest the president's death with meaning, endowing him with martyrdom. He would have died for something."[99] Historian Robert Dallek expressed similar sentiments in an ABC News documentary in 2004. "I know that millions and millions of people in this country believe there was a conspiracy," he said. "People want to believe that the world is not that random, that things are not that chaotic, that something larger, bigger was at stake here because I think it's very difficult for them to accept the idea that someone as inconsequential as Oswald could have killed someone as consequential as Kennedy."[100]

Hilty sees another quite logical cause for many Americans' adoption of conspiracy theories. He contends that Americans' "unwillingness to live with the shame associated with the assassination led them to espouse these beliefs. I mean we couldn't blame ourselves and the people in Texas couldn't blame themselves for allowing this to happen so we had to shift the blame to Italian Mafioso or to CIA rogue elements or to the military industrial complex or . . . to despised figures and international espionage of one kind or another." He remains struck by "the notion of the violent act itself and how easily it was done—that no amount of protection afforded the president could really guarantee his safety if an assassin really wanted to get through. And the reality that someone with very little planning could accomplish it was, I think, a shock." Because he's taken interest in the blossoming of conspiracy theories, he has spoken to many people who refuse to believe that Oswald acted alone.

> There's this love/hate relationship the country has with the Kennedys. Feelings emerged later on that perhaps he wasn't

really such a wonderful person after all, that Camelot was a huge myth and that perhaps he deserved it because of covert activities and because of his philandering. I think I've heard almost every conspiracy theory, including the one that maybe Mrs. Kennedy shot him. Doubts about the assassination have spawned an unbelievable disconnect between reality and the myth. [101]

Since 1963, conspiracy theorists have produced each scenario based on a crazy-quilt merging of facts, assumptions, rumors, and enlightened guesses. Insisting that each piece of misinformation represents a predetermined action, they leave little room for innocent errors or chaotic communications. Disproving each assertion is like trying to turn an Alpine avalanche into a neat stack of snowballs: The task is unending. It cannot be done.

Rather than clearing the air, the Warren Commission contributed to doubts about the facts of the assassination. If that panel had taken more time and been more careful, there would be fewer doubters today and less reason to doubt. Commission members' understandable feelings that the investigation should tread lightly around the Kennedys inadvertently prolonged the time that the family has spent entrenched in assassination culture. In the long run, if the members of the Warren Commission had taken a more legalistic and objective approach to their role in the investigation, it probably would have benefited the slain president's family and the nation as a whole.

Despite the flaws in the initial investigation, I believe that enough evidence has been confirmed to conclude that Oswald fired the bullets that killed President Kennedy. To date, I do not think that any of the conspiracy theorists have proven their case. I am not totally closed-minded about the possibility of a conspiracy, just as I am open to the possibility that mankind might one day learn that intelligent life exists somewhere else in the vast universe. Nevertheless, almost fifty years after the assassination, I have trouble imagining that conspiracy secrets have remained under cover for so long. Given human nature, it seems likely that at least one participant in a conspiracy would have revealed his secret to intimates or on his deathbed. If there was a conspiracy, I doubt that opening classified documents is going to reveal the truth, because any undeniable paper trail would have gone up in smoke years ago. At the time of the assassination, the late president's body probably represented the most under-examined piece of evidence and, someday, it might be politically correct and scientifically meaningful to disinter the corpse. Zachary Taylor was exhumed in 1991—141 years after his death—to determine whether he had been poisoned. (He had not.) And Lee Harvey Oswald's body was disinterred in 1981 just to confirm that Oswald was buried in Oswald's grave. (He was.)

Without further evidence, I am inclined to believe that both Oswald and Ruby acted alone. As a loner who never worked well with others, Oswald was a highly unlikely conspirator. Throughout his life, he had few friends. In the Marines and in a long series of unsatisfying jobs, he demonstrated an aversion to being part of a team and accepting priorities set by others. The only close relationship of his life was his marriage, and he abused his wife.

Ruby was more interested in pleasing people. He bought sandwiches for journalists and police officers and tried to cultivate relationships in which he received respect. People who knew Ruby saw him as a highly unlikely member of the mob or of any stealth operation. By all accounts, he was mentally unstable and prone toward impulsive violence. He sometimes engaged in fistfights at his strip clubs, and he often carried a gun. According to Tony Zoppi, who was an entertainment writer for the *Dallas Morning News* in 1963, "You have to be crazy to think anybody would have trusted Ruby to be part of the mob. He couldn't keep a secret for five minutes. He was just a hanger-on, somebody who would have liked some of the action but was never going to get any."[102] Another *Dallas Morning News* reporter during the 1960s, Hugh Aynesworth, concurred in 2004. "Jack Ruby was a wannabe, never was, but it's really a joke if you think Jack Ruby could be involved in a conspiracy," he said. "This is a man, if he knew anything, I guarantee you he'd tell somebody within one block. He wanted to be important."[103] With little chance of freedom, Ruby lived for four years after killing Oswald and never revealed ties to the mob or to any conspiracy, even when he was dying of cancer.

In some ways, Oswald and Ruby are a matched set. Both had difficult childhoods. Oswald's father died before he was born; Ruby was one of eight children, with an alcoholic father and a mentally disturbed mother. Each spent part of his youth outside the home—Oswald in an orphanage and a truancy center, and Ruby in foster care. Growing up this way, both developed a need for attention, the kind of appetite that could lead to monumental actions intended to achieve public notoriety. Indeed, as Lubin has observed, "Lee Harvey Oswald went into the Texas Theater [where he was arrested] a nobody and came out a star."[104] His murder brought his stardom to a quick end, but Ruby lived to see that he may have viewed himself as a hero, but a jury of his peers thought otherwise.

In my view, conspiracy theories represent an emotional reaction to the events of November 22, 1963. Instinctively, Americans are disinclined to accept an explanation that suggests randomness or the capacity of relatively insignificant individuals to alter history. Moreover, I believe that many individuals dealt with their initial shame and guilt about the assassination by casting suspicious eyes toward the dark corners of the American landscape where large, ominous forces might flourish deep in the shadows. A culture of violence opened many American minds to imaginative and lurid theories about the assassination. Accepting that Americans could conspire to kill their president and concentrating on the gruesome details of his death required much less introspection than taking a hard look at the culture that made his assassination so easy. The paranoia that provides the underpinning for many Americans' need to own firearms represents the same impulse that has made Americans particularly susceptible to conspiracy theories over the course of the nation's history.

As far as the players in this montage are concerned, I am not among those who chuckle at Jacqueline Kennedy's retreat from the back seat of the limousine. If she had been rational enough to be cowardly, she would have realized that climbing onto the back of the car made her an easy target. I do not believe that she was trying to get away from her dying husband: I think she was looking for the life she had enjoyed twenty seconds earlier. Just as fervently, I refuse to fault her for creating the Kennedy myth. She was a young widow who experienced a shocking loss. It is understandable that she wanted people to think good things about her dead husband. Members of the press did not have to perpetuate the Camelot idea if they found it inappropriate, and members of the public could have rejected it immediately, but in a way they needed it, too, as a way of coping with the loss.

Lee Harvey Oswald essentially got what he wanted. Although he may not have consciously chosen to die at 24, his decision to leave cash and his wedding ring for his wife suggests that he was prepared to die in the process of capturing fame. In my view, Ruby was propelled by emotions that he could not control. Dying of cancer in prison was punishment enough for a little man who wanted to be a hero.

An often-overlooked tragic figure in this whole tableau is Johnson. He was never able to escape Kennedy's shadow, and in a way I think his presidency was doomed because of the way it began. Sure, he won a landslide victory in his bid for re-election, but many Democrats could have trounced Goldwater in 1964, just as many Republicans could have thrashed George McGovern eight years later. Johnson was a well-intentioned man in an impossible situation. He enjoyed early triumphs, but he suffered greatly during his presidency. After his civil rights and anti-poverty initiatives, he saw the urban race riots as a betrayal; instead, they were the product of economic stagnation and social frustration among African Americans and had little to do with anything Johnson could have done or failed to do. Without question, Johnson made errors in Vietnam that overshadowed his successes. Perhaps, he would have made the same choices if he had handpicked the team advising him, but since he felt obliged to keep Kennedy's advisers, he never got that opportunity. When Robert McNamara was forced out of his position as secretary of defense, Johnson's friend Clark Clifford achieved in a few months what it had taken McNamara four years to do: recognizing that the war was a lost cause and telling the president how he felt.[105] Without proven foreign policy credentials, Johnson probably trusted himself less than Kennedy would have, and that made him less likely to raise questions or change course. And when things started to go badly, the mercurial Johnson wrapped himself in his fears, jealousy, paranoia, and self-pity—another victim of the gunshots in Dallas.

Kennedy wanted to be remembered well by history, and the assassination may have helped to achieve that goal. Forever young and graceful, he never had to face the tough choices that lay ahead on Vietnam and social violence. I think that he was a good president, who was getting better and probably would have skirted deeper involvement Vietnam. While dodging war, he might have trimmed the budget even more by working out a joint moon mission with the Soviet Union. However, I strongly reject the idea that his survival would have averted all of the problems of the late 1960s. I doubt that any American president could have made the coming years less volatile in the Middle East or eased U.S. dependence on foreign oil—both of which were huge problems on the American horizon. On the streets of the United States, Kennedy likely would have faced the same social unrest that Johnson found so difficult to resolve, but if he had survived JFK would have had the luxury of watching his children grow up.

In life and death, President Kennedy has demonstrated a rare gift for inspiring people, something none of his successors has duplicated. And I believe his appeal goes beyond his handsome face and his tragic death. He offered something special, something even his equally handsome brothers could not duplicate. He was a flawed man and a fallible politician far removed from the lofty idealism of Camelot, but he touched many Americans in a unique way. For this reason, I believe that his disappearance from the national stage had a critical impact on history. Because of what he represented in the minds of many Americans, his abrupt absence affected the way the American people approached the future. Whether he would have been more successful than Johnson, we will never know, just as we probably will never get an absolutely indisputable account of his assassination. Instead of resting comfortably in the pages of history, he remains an object of speculation—the one that got away and the best might-have-been story of the twentieth-century American presidency.

Documents

John F. Kennedy's Inaugural Address

John F. Kennedy's inaugural address set the stage for his presidency. Its content showed that his greatest emphasis as president would be on foreign affairs, and its eloquence suggested that Kennedy was raising the tenor of American political discourse. Considered one of the best inaugural addresses in U.S. history, this speech served as an introduction of sorts between Kennedy and the American people. Long after his death, it reflects an enduring document that represents Kennedy's quest for excellence.

Vice President Johnson, Mr. Speaker, Mr. Chief Justice, President Eisenhower, Vice President Nixon, President Truman, Reverend Clergy, fellow citizens:

We observe today not a victory of party but a celebration of freedom—symbolizing an end as well as a beginning—signifying renewal as well as change. For I have sworn before you and Almighty God the same solemn oath our forebears prescribed nearly a century and three quarters ago.

The world is very different now. For man holds in his mortal hands the power to abolish all forms of human poverty and all forms of human life. And yet the same revolutionary beliefs for which our forebears fought are still at issue around the globe—the belief that the rights of man come not from the generosity of the state but from the hand of God.

We dare not forget today that we are the heirs of that first revolution. Let the word go forth from this time and place, to friend and foe alike, that the torch has been passed to a new generation of Americans—born in this century, tempered by war, disciplined by a hard and bitter peace, proud of our ancient heritage—and unwilling to witness or permit the slow undoing of those human rights to which this nation has always been committed, and to which we are committed today at home and around the world.

Let every nation know, whether it wishes us well or ill, that we shall pay any price, bear any burden, meet any hardship, support any friend, oppose any foe to assure the survival and the success of liberty.

This much we pledge—and more.

To those old allies whose cultural and spiritual origins we share, we pledge the loyalty of faithful friends. United, there is little we cannot do in a host of cooperative ventures. Divided, there is little we can do—for we dare not meet a powerful challenge at odds and split asunder. To those new states whom we welcome to the ranks of the free, we pledge our word that one form of colonial control shall not have passed away merely to be replaced by a far more iron tyranny. We shall not always expect to find them supporting our view. But we shall always hope to find them strongly supporting their own freedom and to remember that, in the past, those who foolishly sought power by riding the back of the tiger ended up inside.

To those peoples in the huts and villages of half the globe struggling to break the bonds of mass misery, we pledge our best efforts to help them help themselves, for whatever period is required—not because the communists may be doing it, not because we seek their votes, but because it is right. If a free society cannot help the many who are poor, it cannot save the few who are rich.

To our sister republics south of our border, we offer a special pledge—to convert our good words into good deeds—in a new alliance for progress—to assist free men and free governments in casting off the chains of poverty. But this peaceful revolution of hope cannot become the prey of hostile powers. Let all our neighbors know that we shall join with them to oppose aggression or subversion anywhere in the Americas. And let every other power know that this Hemisphere intends to remain the master of its own house.

To that world assembly of sovereign states, the United Nations, our last best hope in an age where the instruments of war have far outpaced the instruments of peace, we renew our pledge of support—to prevent it from becoming merely a forum for invective—to strengthen its shield of the new and the weak—and to enlarge the area in which its writ may run. Finally, to those nations who would make themselves our adversary, we offer not a pledge but a request: that both sides begin anew the quest for peace, before the dark powers of destruction unleashed by science engulf all humanity in planned or accidental self-destruction.

We dare not tempt them with weakness. For only when our arms are sufficient, beyond doubt can we be certain beyond doubt that they will never be employed.

But neither can two great and powerful groups of nations take comfort from our present course—both sides overburdened by the cost of modern weapons, both rightly alarmed by the steady spread of the deadly atom, yet both racing to alter that uncertain balance of terror that stays the hand of mankind's final war.

So let us begin anew—remembering on both sides that civility is not a sign of weakness, and sincerity is always subject to proof. Let us never negotiate out of fear. But let us never fear to negotiate.

Let both sides explore what problems unite us instead of belaboring those problems which divide us.

Let both sides, for the first time, formulate serious and precise proposals for the inspection and control of arms—and bring the absolute power to destroy other nations under the absolute control of all nations.

Let both sides seek to invoke the wonders of science instead of its terrors. Together let us explore the stars, conquer the deserts, eradicate disease, tap the ocean depths and encourage the arts and commerce.

Let both sides unite to heed in all corners of the earth the command of Isaiah—to "undo the heavy burdens . . . [and] let the oppressed go free."

And if a beach-head of cooperation may push back the jungle of suspicion, let both sides join in creating a new endeavor, not a new balance of power, but a new world of law, where the strong are just and the weak secure and the peace preserved.

All this will not be finished in the first one hundred days. Nor will it be finished in the first one thousand days, nor in the life of this Administration, nor even perhaps in our lifetime on this planet. But let us begin.

In your hands, my fellow citizens, more than mine, will rest the final success or failure of our course. Since this country was founded, each generation of Americans has been summoned to give testimony to its national loyalty. The graves of young Americans who answered the call to service surround the globe.

Now the trumpet summons us again—not as a call to bear arms, though arms we need—not as a call to battle, though embattled we are—but a call to bear the burden of a long twilight struggle, year in and year out, "rejoicing in hope, patient in tribulation"—a struggle against the common enemies of man: tyranny, poverty, disease and war itself.

Can we forge against these enemies a grand and global alliance, North and South, East and West, that can assure a more fruitful life for all mankind? Will you join that historic effort?

In the long history of the world, only a few generations have been granted the role of defending freedom in its hour of maximum danger. I do not shrink from this responsibility—I welcome it. I do not believe that any of us would exchange places with any other people or any other generation. The energy, the faith, the devotion we bring to this endeavor will light our country and all who serve it—and the glow from that fire will truly light the world.

And so my fellow Americans: ask not what your country can do for you—ask what you can do for your country.

My fellow citizens of the world: ask not what America will do for you, but what together we can do for the freedom of man.

Finally, whether you are citizens of America or citizens of the world, ask of us here the same high standards of strength and sacrifice which we ask of you. With a good conscience our only sure reward, with history the final judge of our deeds, let us go forth to lead the land we love, asking His blessing and His help, but knowing that here on earth God's work must truly be our own.[1]

Excerpt from John F. Kennedy News Conference May 9, 1962

*B*ecause of the style differences between John F. Kennedy and Lyndon B. *Johnson, many people assumed that their relationship was less than a cordial partnership. These assumptions were incorrect; the two men worked together as colleagues, if not best friends. Nevertheless, a feud between Johnson and the president's brother, Robert, made LBJ fear that RFK would try to push him off the Democratic ticket in 1964. Members of the press and other politicians had begun speculating about that prospect by mid-1962. In a press conference, President Kennedy attempts to put these questions to rest.*

Q: Mr. President, there have been rumors in print and out of Texas that Vice President Johnson might be dropped from the Democratic ticket in 1964. I'd like to ask you if you have any reason whatever to believe that either end of the Democratic ticket will be different in 1964.

THE PRESIDENT: Well, I don't know about what they will do with me, but I am sure that the vice president will be on the ticket if he chooses to run. We were fortunate to have him before—and would again— and I don't know where such a rumor would start. He's invaluable. He fulfills a great many responsibilities as vice president. He participates in all of the major deliberations. He's been in the Congress for years. He is invaluable. So of course he will be, if he chooses to be, part of the ticket."[2]

DOCUMENT 3

Excerpts, Secret Service Agent Clint Hill, March 9, 1964

*C*lint Hill was the Secret Service agent who bounded onto the presidential limousine after shots struck JFK in Dallas. Assigned to protect the first lady, Hill moved quickly to alight from a Secret Service car and climb onto the injured president's car, pushing the First Lady down and positioning his body to protect the gravely injured president. Below, he is questioned by the Warren Commission.

MR. [ARLEN] SPECTER: Did you have any occasion to notice the Texas School Book Depository Building as you proceeded in a generally northerly direction on Houston Street?

MR. HILL: Yes, sir. It was immediately in front of us and to our left.

MR. SPECTER: Did you notice anything unusual about it?

MR. HILL: Nothing more unusual than any other building along the way . . . We scan the buildings and look specifically for open windows, for people hanging out, and there had been, on almost every building along the way, people hanging out, windows open.

MR. SPECTER: And did you observe, as you recollect at this moment, any open windows in the Texas School Depository Building?

MR. HILL: Yes, sir; there were.

MR. SPECTER: Now, what is your best estimate of the speed of the president's automobile as it turned left off of Houston onto Elm Street?

MR. HILL: We were running still 12 to 15 miles per hour, but in the curve I believe we slowed down maybe to 10, maybe to 9 . . . Well, as we came out of the curve, and began to straighten up, I was viewing the area which looked to be a park. There were people scattered throughout the entire park. And I heard a noise from my right rear, which to me seemed to be a firecracker. I immediately looked to my right and, in so doing, my eyes had to cross the presidential limousine and I saw President Kennedy grab at himself and lurch forward and to the left . . . I jumped from the car, realizing that something was wrong, ran to the presidential limousine. Just about as I reached it, there was another sound, which was different than the first sound. I think I described it in my statement as though someone was shooting a revolver into a hard object—it seemed to have some type of an echo.

I put my right foot, I believe it was, on the left rear step of the automobile, and I had a hold of the handgrip with my hand, when the car lurched forward. I lost my footing and I had to run about three or four more steps before I could get back up in the car. Between the time I originally grabbed the handhold and until I was up on the car, Mrs. Kennedy—the second noise that I heard had removed a portion of the president's head, and he had slumped noticeably to his left. Mrs. Kennedy had jumped up from the seat and was, it appeared to me, reaching for something coming off the right rear bumper of the car, the right rear tail, when she noticed that I was trying to climb on the car. She turned toward me and I grabbed her and put her back in the back seat, crawled up on top of the back seat and lay there . . . We were running between 12 to 15 miles per hour, but no faster than 15 miles per hour.

MR. SPECTER: How many shots have you described that you heard?

MR. HILL: Two.

MR. SPECTER: Did you hear any more than two shots?

MR. HILL: No, sir . . . at the time that I jumped on the car, the car had surged forward. The president at that time had been shot in the head.

MR. SPECTER: Would you tell us with more particularity in what way he grabbed at himself?

MR. HILL: He grabbed in this general area.

MR. SPECTER: You are indicating that your right hand is coming up to your to the throat?

MR. HILL: Yes, sir.

MR. SPECTER: And the left hand crosses right under the right hand.

MR. HILL: To the chest area.

MR. SPECTER: To the chest area. Was there any movement of the president's head or shoulders immediately after the first shot, that you recollect?

MR. HILL: Yes, sir. Immediately when I saw him, he was like this, and going left and forward.

MR. SPECTER: Indicating a little fall to the left front.

MR. HILL: Yes, sir; this was the first shot.

MR. SPECTER: Now, what is your best estimate on the time span between the first firecracker-type noise you heard and the second shot which you have described?

MR. HILL: Approximately five seconds.

REPRESENTATIVE FORD: It was five seconds from the firecracker noise that you think you got to the automobile?

MR. HILL: Until I reached the handhold, had placed my foot on the left rear step.

MR. SPECTER: You say that it appeared that she was reaching as if something was coming over to the rear portion of the car, back in the area where you were coming to?

MR. HILL: Yes, sir.

MR. SPECTER: Was there anything back there that you observed, that she might have been reaching for?

MR. HILL: I thought I saw something come off the back, too, but I cannot say that there was. I do know that the next day we found the portion of the president's head.

MR. SPECTER: Where did you find that portion of the president's head?

MR. HILL: It was found in the street. It was turned in, I believe, by a medical student or somebody in Dallas . . . I simply just pushed and she moved—somewhat voluntarily—right back into the same seat she was in. The president—when she had attempted to get out onto the trunk of the car, his body apparently did not move too much, because when she got back into the car he was at that time, when I got on top of the car, face up in her lap . . . At the time of the shooting, when I got into the rear of the car, she said, "My God, they have shot his head off." Between there and the hospital she just said, "Jack, Jack, what have they done to you," and sobbed . . . I heard Special Agent Kellerman say on the radio, "To the nearest hospital, quick" . . . He said, "We have been hit". . . . I had my legs—I had my body above the rear seat, and my legs hooked down into the rear seat, one foot outside the car . . .

The right rear portion of his head was missing. It was lying in the rear seat of the car. His brain was exposed. There was blood and bits of brain all over the entire rear portion of the car. Mrs. Kennedy was completely covered with blood. There was so much blood you could not tell if there had been any other wound or not, except for the one large gaping wound in the right rear portion of the head . . .

I went into the emergency room with the president, but it was so small, and there were so many people in there that I decided I had better leave and let the doctors take care of the situation. So I walked outside; asked for the nearest telephone; walked to the nearest telephone. About that time Special Agent in Charge Kellerman came outside and said, "Get the White House." I asked Special Agent Lawson for the local number in Dallas of the White House switchboard, which he gave to me. I called the switchboard in Dallas; asked for the line to be open to Washington, and remain open continuously. And then I asked for Special Agent in Charge Behn's office. Mr. Kellerman came out of the emergency room about that time, took the telephone and called Special Agent in Charge Behn that we had had a double tragedy; that both Governor Connally and President Kennedy had been shot. And that was about as much as he said. I then took the telephone and shortly thereafter Mr. Kellerman came out of the emergency room and said, "Clint, tell Jerry this is unofficial and not for release, but the man is dead." Which I did. During the two calls, I talked to the Attorney General [Robert Kennedy], who attempted to reach me, and told him that his brother had been seriously wounded; that we would keep him advised as to his condition . . .

I remained with Mrs. Kennedy except for one time when I was requested to come to the morgue [at Bethesda Naval Hospital] to view the president's body . . . I saw an opening in the back, about 6 inches below the neckline to the right-hand side of the spinal column.

MR. SPECTER: And did you have a reaction or impression as to the source of point of origin of the second shot that you described?

MR. HILL: It was right, but I cannot say for sure that it was rear, because when I mounted the car it was—it had a different sound, first of all, than the first sound that I heard. The second one had almost a double sound—as though you were standing against something metal and firing into it, and you hear both the sound of a gun going off and the sound of the cartridge hitting the metal place, which could have been caused probably by the hard surface of the head. But I am not sure that that is what caused it.

MR. SPECTER: Now, do you now or have you ever had the impression or reaction that there was a shot which originated from the front of the presidential car?

MR. HILL: No.[3]

DOCUMENT 4

Excerpt from Speech to be Given at Dallas's Trade Mart, Nov. 22, 1963

John F. Kennedy never delivered the speech written for his appearance at the Trade Mart in Dallas. The section excerpted below can be seen as an indictment of the kind of political fervor that feeds hatred and makes assassinations a part of American political history.

In a world of complex and continuing problems, in a world full of frustrations and irritations, America's leadership must be guided by the lights of learning and reason—or else those who confuse rhetoric with reality and the plausible with the possible will gain the popular ascendancy with their seemingly swift and simple solutions to every world problem.

There will always be dissident voices heard in the land, expressing opposition without alternatives, finding fault but never favor, perceiving gloom on every side and seeking influence without responsibility. Those voices are inevitable.

But today other voices are heard in the land—voices preaching doctrines wholly unsuited to the sixties, doctrines which apparently assume that words will suffice without weapons, that vituperation is as good as victory and that peace is a sign of weakness. At a time when the national debt is being steadily reduced in terms of its burden on our economy, they see that debt as the greatest single threat to our security. At a time when we are steadily reducing the number of federal employees serving every thousand citizens, they fear those supposed hordes of civil servants far more than the actual hordes of opposing armies.

We cannot expect that everyone, to use the phrase of a decade ago, will "talk sense to the American people." But we can hope that fewer people will listen to nonsense.[4]

Vice President Lyndon B. Johnson Daily Diary Worksheet for Evening of November 22, 1963

When Lyndon Johnson returned from Dallas to Washington, he was the president of the United States, but he was functioning out of the vice president's office. This list of his meetings and phone calls on that night offers a hint of the swift pace that Johnson will maintain in the early days of his presidency.

6:45		McGeorge Bundy in EOB (Executive Office Building)
6:50		White House Naval Aide Tazewell Shepard
6:55		Secretary [Averill] Harriman and Sen. J. William Fulbright
7:05	Telephone	President [Harry S.] Truman
7:10	Telephone	General [Dwight D.] Eisenhower
7:29	Telephone	Sargent Shriver
7:35		Mac Kilduff
7:36		Eating dinner in 274 EOB
7:40		Congressional delegation: [Speaker of the House John] McCormack, [Rep.] Hale Boggs, [Rep. Charles] Halleck, [Rep. Carl] Albert, [Sen. Mike] Mansfield, [Sen. Everett] Dirksen, [Sen.Hubert] Humphrey, [Sen. George] Smathers, [Sen. Tom] Kuchel, [Sen. Thurston] Morton
8:06		Mac Kilduff, George Reedy, Bill Moyers
8:25	Telephone	Ted Sorensen
8:31	Telephone	Speaker McCormack

8:45		Kilduff
9:00	Telephone	Sen. [Richard] Russell
9:06	Telephone	Justice Arthur Goldberg
9:10	Telephone	[Democratic Party insider] Dick Maguire
9:25		Depart EOB[5]

National Day of Mourning Proclaimed by President Johnson, November 23, 1963

*T*he first order of business for the new president was to help the nation through the period of shock following Kennedy's assassination and to allow Americans to grieve for their lost president. The proclamation declaring Monday, November 25, 1963, as a national day of mourning was Johnson's first.

A PROCLAMATION
To the People of the United States:

John Fitzgerald Kennedy, 35th President of the United States, has been taken from us by an act which outrages decent men everywhere.

He upheld the faith of our fathers, which is freedom for all men. He broadened the frontiers of that faith, and backed it with energy and the courage which are the mark of the nation he led.

A man of wisdom, strength, and peace, he moulded and moved the power of our nation in the service of a world of growing liberty and order. All who love freedom will mourn his death.

As he did not shrink from his responsibilities, but welcomed them, so he would not have us shrink from carrying on his work beyond this hour of national tragedy.

He said himself: "The energy, the faith, the devotion which we bring to this endeavor will light our country and all who serve it—and the glow from that fire can truly light the world." Now, THEREFORE, I, LYNDON B. JOHNSON, president of the United States of America, do appoint Monday next, November 25, the day of the funeral service of President Kennedy, to be a national day of mourning throughout the United States. I earnestly recommend the people to assemble on that day in their respective places of divine worship, there to bow down in submission to the will of Almighty God, and to pay their homage of love and reverence to the memory of a great and good man. I invite the people of the world to share our grief and to join us in this day of mourning and rededication.

Lyndon B. Johnson[6]

Eulogy of John F. Kennedy by Senator Mike Mansfield, Delivered in Capitol Rotunda, November 24, 1963

*S*enate Majority Leader Mike Mansfield was one of three speakers delivering *S* eulogies in the Capitol Rotunda on the day that thousands of Americans stood in long lines for the opportunity to walk past the president's casket. Mansfield's speech was the most poetic of those delivered and was Jacqueline Kennedy's favorite.

There was a sound of laughter; in a moment, it was no more. And so she took a ring from her finger and placed it in his hands.

There was a wit in a man neither young nor old, but a wit full of an old man's wisdom and of a child's wisdom, and then, in a moment, it was no more. And so she took a ring from her finger and placed it in his hands.

There was a man marked with the scars of his love of country, a body active with the surge of a life far, far from spent and, in a moment, it was no more. And so she took a ring from her finger and placed it in his hands.

There was a father with a little boy, a little girl and a joy of each in the other. In a moment, it was no more, and so she took a ring from her finger and placed it in his hands.

There was a husband who asked much and gave much, and out of the giving and the asking wove with a woman what could not be broken in life, and in a moment it was no more. And so she took a ring from her finger and placed it in his hands, and kissed him and closed the lid of a coffin.

A piece of each of us died at that moment. Yet, in death he gave of himself to us. He gave us of a good heart from which the laughter came. He gave us of a profound wit, from which a great leadership emerged. He gave us of a kindness and a strength fused into a human courage to seek peace without fear.

He gave us of his love that we, too, in turn, might give. He gave that we might give of ourselves, what we might give to one another until there would be no room, no room at all, for the bigotry, the hatred, prejudice and the arrogance which converged in that moment of horror to strike him down.

In leaving us—these gifts, John Fitzgerald Kennedy, president of the United States, leaves with us. Will we take them, Mr. President? Will we have, now, the sense and the responsibility and the courage to take them?[7]

DOCUMENT 8

Eulogy of John F. Kennedy by Earl Warren, Delivered in Capitol Rotunda, November 24, 1963

Chief Justice Earl Warren was a jurist, not a politician, so his eulogy bears a slightly different tone. In retrospect, his speech holds extra meaning because of his work leading the commission assigned to uncover the truth about the assassination.

There are few moments in our national life that unite Americans and so touch the heart as the passing of a president of the United States.

There is nothing that adds shock to our sadness as the assassination of our leader, chosen as he is to embody the ideals of our people, the faith we have in our institutions and our belief in the fatherhood of God and the brotherhood of man.

Such misfortunes have befallen the nation on other occasions, but never more shockingly than two days ago.

We are saddened; we are stunned; we are perplexed.

John Fitzgerald Kennedy, a great and good president, the friend of men of goodwill, a believer in the dignity and equality of all human beings, a fighter for justice and apostle of peace, has been snatched from our midst by the bullet of an assassin.

What moved some misguided wretch to do this horrible deed may never be known to us, but we do know that such acts are commonly stimulated by forces of hatred and malevolence, such as today are eating their way into the bloodstream of American life.

What a price we pay for this fanaticism!

It has been said that the only thing we learn from history is that we do not learn. But surely we can learn if we have the will to do so. Surely there is a lesson to be learned from this tragic event.

If we really love this country, if we truly love justice and mercy, if we fervently want to make this nation better for those who are to follow us, we can at least abjure the hatred that consumes people, the false accusations that divide us and the bitterness that begets violence.

Is it too much to hope that the martyrdom of our beloved president might even soften the hearts of those who would themselves recoil from assassination, but who do not shrink from spreading the venom which kindles thoughts of it in others?

Our nation is bereaved. The whole world is poorer because of his loss. But we can all be better Americans because John Fitzgerald Kennedy has passed our way, because he has been our chosen leader at a time in history when his character, his vision and his quiet courage have enabled him to chart for us a safe course through the shoals of treacherous seas that encompass the world.

And now that he is relieved of the almost superhuman burdens imposed on him, may he rest in peace.[8]

Excerpt from Lyndon Johnson Telephone Conversation with Paul Miller, Chairman of Associated Press Board, Monday, March 9, 1964 at 4:02 p.m.

Working with the media was a struggle for Lyndon Johnson. He felt that in a battle with JFK's memory, he would always lose. Johnson and other more objective observers thought that some journalists so missed Kennedy that they could not accept Johnson in the White House. This conversation provides insight into his frustration.

JOHNSON: At news conferences, when I went down, they said I ought to stand up. When I stood up, they said I ought to sit down. When I had it in the State Department, [journalist] Mary McGrory said the room was too dark. When I had it in the East Room, they said it was too light. And I don't give a damn. Just so it is comfortable for them. [Press handler] Arthur Sylvester, who works at Defense—his boy got up and said, "Why do you have us in this uncomfortable room where we're so crowded?" There were ten seats that weren't occupied . . . When they tape them and play every bit of it without our correcting a word, they say that's not live. So you've got to give them four hours live. By that time, your news is out of date . . . I counted up and I've been on television fourteen times in a hundred days. Kennedy had been on six. Eisenhower was on three. And I had about a dozen columns giving me hell for not being on television enough![9]

EYES ONLY

Memorandum from John P. Roche
to Lyndon Johnson

The flap over William Manchester's The Death of a President *lowered public opinion of the Kennedy family and painted Lyndon Johnson in a bad light. Jacqueline Kennedy went to court to stop its publication, but she eventually negotiated an agreement with Manchester. In this memo, a Johnson aide analyzes the likely political effects of the controversy.*

Dec. 23, 1966

EYES ONLY
MEMORANDUM FOR The President

The ultimate political sin is to bore the sovereign people and I believe "The Kennedys" (a body corporate, like General Motors, I gather) have just about hit the boredom threshold with their shenanigans about the Manchester book [*The Death of a President*].

While no one can enjoy the spectacle, it is possible to draw some hopeful conclusions from it.

First, the Kennedy "corporation" is in fantastic disarray. My spies tell me that Jacqueline is already blaming Bobby for her troubles (she abruptly changed her vacation plans, shunning Sun Valley for the Caribbean). And if I know Bobby, he won't suffer in silence; indeed, a "Kennedy spokesman" already tried to tie the can to little Arthur's tail saying that Schlesinger wrote the telegram [in July saying the Kennedy family would not interfere with publication of the book] and persuaded Bobby to sign it. [Jacqueline Kennedy subsequently decided to sue Manchester to block publication of some personal details and unflattering descriptions of Lyndon Johnson.]

As more and more of the deleted passages are leaked to the press, this squabbling will increase. Most of the charges will simply make Mrs. Kennedy look like a silly fool; for example, today we learned that one of the deletions referred to her discovery of a "line in her face."

I don't mean to sound cold-blooded about this mess. I held President Kennedy in extremely high regard and worked with him from 1956 to 1962—when he cut me dead because I refused to support Teddy [Edward Kennedy in Massachusetts' Democratic primary for JFK's vacated U.S. Senate seat] against my close personal friend Eddie McCormack. Even this did not alter my admiration for him: politics is, after all, a body-contact sport and I could hardly expect him to give me a medal.

The point of these autobiographical musings is that my remarks here indicate no disrespect for John Kennedy. But my respect for him is non-transferable and irrelevant to the fact that his martyrdom has been ruthlessly manipulated by the "corporation."

I thus feel it is legitimate to be cold-blooded about the political impact of the Kennedy myth. And from that point of view, I am interested to see Mrs. Kennedy—the Keeper of the Sacred Flame—acting like an arrogant French seventeenth-century queen.

I might add that my wife—whose gut political instincts are far better than mine—is convinced that after a couple of months of argument over the Manchester deletions a hundred million Americans are going to wake up one morning and say "to hell with the Kennedys."

In short, they will erode if not destroy their greatest political asset: the myth of JFK.

Second, the Manchester caper should have as an accidental benefit the overshadowing of the nasty attacks on the Warren Commission.

Although it still may be useful to follow up the suggestion I made of a narrow, expert investigation (under congressional auspices) of the medical data not available to the Warren Commission, my hunch is that we should sit tight for a month or so and then see how the wind lies.

Third, given the state of chaos created by the Manchester dispute, I think that you will not be hurt by anything in the book.

The press will be after you (and all of us) to keep the fires burning. I would urge you to issue absolute orders that the Administration is *silence*. Let the Kennedy stockholders fight this one out among themselves.

Besides, if I know Teddy White, he will surface with his version of Jacqueline's remarks. (He has already taken up the cudgels in the *Times* on the propriety of the book.) This will keep things moving.

To conclude, the whole episode is further evidence of the validity of Murphy's Second Law, "If you play with anything too hard, it will break."

John P. Roche [Political Adviser to President Johnson][10]

DOCUMENT 11

Church Committee, Excerpt from the Investigation of the Assassination of President John F. Kennedy

A subgroup of the Church Committee investigated the Warren Commission's findings and found fault with the CIA and FBI for failing to cooperate fully with those investigating the assassination. This document cites the agencies' failures.

Performance of Intelligence Agencies

The committee emphasizes that it has not uncovered any evidence sufficient to justify a conclusion that there was a conspiracy to assassinate President Kennedy.

The committee has, however, developed evidence which impeaches the process by which the intelligence agencies arrived at their own conclusions about the assassination, and by which they provided information to the Warren Commission. This evidence indicates that the investigation of the assassination was deficient and that facts which might have substantially affected the course of the investigation were not provided the Warren Commission or those individuals within the FBI and the CIA, as well as other agencies of government, who were charged with investigating the assassination.

The Committee has found that the FBI, the agency with primary responsibility in the matter, was ordered by Director [J. Edgar] Hoover and pressured by higher government officials to conclude its investigation quickly. The FBI conducted its investigation in an atmosphere of concern among senior bureau officials that it would be criticized and its reputation tarnished. Rather than addressing its investigation to all significant circumstances, including all possibilities of conspiracy, the FBI investigation focused narrowly on Lee Harvey Oswald.

The committee has found that even with this narrow focus, the FBI investigation, as well as the CIA inquiry, was deficient on the specific question of the significance of Oswald's contacts with pro-Castro and anti-Castro groups for the many months before the assassination. Those individuals directly responsible for the investigations were not fully conversant with the fluctuations in American policy toward those who opposed Castro, and they lacked a working knowledge of pro-Castro and anti-Castro activity. They did not know the full extent of U.S. operations against Cuba including the CIA efforts to assassinate Castro. The committee further found that these investigative deficiencies are probably the reason that significant leads received by intelligence agencies were not pursued.

Senior bureau officials should have realized the FBI efforts were focused too narrowly to allow for a full investigation. They should have realized the significance of Oswald's Cuban contacts could not be fully analyzed without the direct involvement of FBI personnel who had expertise in such matters. Yet these senior officials permitted the investigation to take this course and viewed the Warren Commission investigation in an adversarial light.

Senior CIA officials also should have realized that their agency was not utilizing its full capability to investigate Oswald's pro-Castro and anti-Castro connections. They should have realized the CIA operations against Cuba, particularly operations involving the assassination of Castro, needed to be considered in the investigation. Yet, they directed their subordinates to conduct the investigation without telling them of these vital facts. These officials, whom the Warren Commission relied upon for expertise, advised the Warren Commission that the CIA had no evidence of foreign conspiracy.

Why senior officials of the FBI and the CIA permitted the investigation to go forward, in light of these deficiencies, and why they permitted the Warren Commission to reach its conclusion without all relevant information is still unclear. Certainly, concern with public reputation, failure and embarrassment, and the extreme compartmentation of knowledge of sensitive operations may have contributed to these shortcomings. But the possibility exists that senior officials in both agencies made conscious decisions not to disclose potentially important information.

Because the Select Committee to Study Governmental Operations With Respect to Intelligence Activities ended on May 31, 1976, a final resolution of these questions was impossible. Nevertheless, the committee decided to make its findings public, because the people have a right to know how these special agencies of the government fulfill their responsibilities.

The Committee recommends that its successor, the Senate Select Committee on Intelligence, the permanent Senate Committee overseeing intelligence operations, continue the investigation in an attempt to resolve these questions. To assist its successor, this committee has forwarded all files pertaining to this investigation.

This phase of the committee's work will undoubtedly stir controversy. Few events in recent memory have aroused the emotions of this nation and the world, as those in Dallas, in November 1963. Conspiracy theories and theorists abound, and the public remains unsatisfied. Regrettably, this report will not put the matter to rest. Even after additional investigative work, no additional evidence may come to light on the ultimate question of why President Kennedy was assassinated.[11]

DOCUMENT 12

Authentication of John F. Kennedy Autopsy Radiographs and Photographs

Many elements of the assassination investigation became the subject of controversy. Among the questioned items were the autopsy photos and x-rays. Some conspiracy believers claimed that someone had tampered with JFK's body or that he was not the person autopsied. This concluding section in a longer report was delivered to the House Select Committee on Assassinations.

Conclusion

March 9, 1979

By Clyde C. Snow and Ellis R. Kerley

Based on our examination of the autopsy x-rays and photographs and comparison of these with known ante-mortem x-rays and photographs of John F. Kennedy, we conclude as follows:

1. The individual shown in the autopsy x-rays is John F. Kennedy.
2. The individual shown in the autopsy photographs is John F. Kennedy.
3. The brain shown in autopsy photographs #46–#53 cannot be positively identified as that of John F. Kennedy. However, this brain displays trauma consistent to the known pattern of injury sustained by President Kennedy and, in the absence of any positive evidence to the contrary, there is no reason to believe that it is not the brain of the late president.[12]

DOCUMENT 13

John F. Kennedy's Inquest

*T*he *official document representing John F. Kennedy's inquest demonstrates both his position as leader of a nation and his designation as just another human being who died an untimely death.*[13]

Notes

Abbreviations in Notes

House Select Committee on Assassinations – HSCA
John F. Kennedy Library – JFKL
John F. Kennedy Assassination Records at Archives II – JFK-NA
Lyndon B. Johnson Library – LBJL
National Security Archive – NSA

1 Unforgettable

1 Newseum with Cathy Trost and Susan Bennett, *President Kennedy Has Been Shot* (Naperville, IL: Sourcebooks Mediafusion, 2003), 85.

2 Colin McEnroe, "Sole-Gunman Theory in Kennedy Assassination Gains Ground," *Hartford Courant*, Nov. 22, 1993, A1.

3 Martin Waldron, "Critics Still Doubt Slayer Was Alone," *New York Times*, Nov. 22, 1973, 46.

4 McEnroe, A1.

5 Lydia Saad, "Americans: Kennedy Assassination a Conspiracy," Gallup News Service, Nov. 21, 2003, http://www.gallup.com/poll/9751/americans-kennedy-assassination-conspiracy.aspx; accessed Dec. 15, 2010.

6 Dana Blanton, "Poll: Most Believe 'Cover-Up' of JFK Assassination Facts," Fox News, June 18, 2004, http://www.foxnews.com/story/0,2933,102511,00.html; accessed Dec. 15, 2010.

7 Vincent Bugliosi, *Reclaiming History: The Assassination of President John F. Kennedy* (New York: W.W. Norton & Co., 2007), 1505.

8 Arlington National Cemetery Web Page, http://www.arlingtoncemetery.mil/visitor_information/index.htm; accessed March 29, 1973.

9 Bugliosi, 1504.

10 "Frequently Asked Questions/The Sixth Floor Museum" Website, http://www.jfk.org/about/faqs; accessed April 2, 2011.

11 Theodore H. White, *The Making of the President 1964* (New York: Signet, 1966), 16.

12 William Manchester, *The Death of a President* (New York: Galahad Books, 1996), 627.

13 Arthur G. Neal, *National Trauma and Collective Memory*, 2nd ed. (Armonk, NY: M.E. Sharpe, 2005), 4.

14 Lance Morrow, "J.F.K.: After 20 Years, the Question: How Good a President?" *Time*, Nov. 14, 1983, 67.

15 Tom Brokaw, *Boom! Talking about the Sixties* (New York: Random House Trade Paperback, 2008), 11.

16 Frederic Jameson, "Periodizing the Sixties," in *The '60s Without Apology*, ed. Sohnya Sayers et al. (Minneapolis: University of Minnesota Press, 1985), 182–3.

17 See Harold Orlansky, "Reactions to the Death of President Roosevelt," *Journal of Social Psychology*, 26 (1947): 235–65.

18 Jane Howard, "The Day JFK Died," *Ladies Home Journal*, Nov. 1983, 170.

19 James Reston, "What was Killed was not Only the President but the Promise," *New York Times Magazine*, Nov. 15, 1965, 127.

20 Jay Mulvaney and Paul De Angelis, *Dear Mrs. Kennedy* (New York: St. Martin's Press, 2010), 219.

21 Tom Wicker, *JFK and LBJ: The Influence of Personality upon Politics* (Chicago: Ivan R. Dee Publishers, 1968), 159.

22 "Foreign Countries, Too, Mourn 'First Citizen of the World,'" *U.S. News & World Report*, Dec. 7, 1963, 48–9.

23 Pete Hamill, "JFK: The Real Thing," *New York*, Nov. 28, 1988, 50.

24 William E. Leuchtenburg, "John F. Kennedy Twenty Years Later," *American Heritage*, Dec. 1983, 58.

25 Susan Page, "50 Years after Win, JFK's Legacy Endures," *USA Today*, Oct. 4, 2010, http://www.usatoday.com/news/washington/2010-09-26-jfk-kennedy-mystique_N.htm; accessed Dec. 15, 2010.

26 Jack Nelson, "Lincoln, FDR Ranked 1–2 in Leadership Poll," *Los Angeles Times*, Feb. 21, 2000, A17.

27 Richard Slotkin, *Gunfighter Nation* (Norman, OK: University of Oklahoma Press, 1998), 498.

28 Walter Cronkite, "An Ambition for America," *Newsweek*, Nov. 28, 1983, 66.

29 *The Gallup Poll*, "Presidential Job Approval Center: Key Statistics," http://www.gallup.com/poll/124922/Presidential-Approval-Center.aspx; accessed March 6, 2011.

30 Alan Brinkley, *Liberalism and its Discontents* (Cambridge, Harvard University Press, 1998), 213.

31 Charles M. Bonjean, Richard J. Hill, and Harry W. Martin, "Reactions to the Assassination in Dallas," in *The Kennedy Assassination and the American Public*, ed. Bradley S. Greenberg and Edwin B. Parker (Stanford: Stanford University Press, 1965), 194.

32 "Kennedy Remembered: Kennedy Has Become America's Favorite President," *Newsweek*, Nov. 28, 1983, 64.

33 Marjorie Connelly, "Americans Are Still Voting for J.F.K.," *New York Times*, Aug. 16, 1996, http://www.nytimes.com/1996/08/16/national/19960816_KENNEDY.html; accessed Dec. 18, 2010.

34 Henry Allen, "JFK: The Man and the Maybes," *Washington Post*, Nov. 22, 1988, E2.

35 Jacqueline Kennedy, *Jacqueline Kennedy: Historic Conversations on Life with John F. Kennedy* (New York: Hyperion, 2011), 62.

36 Associated Press, "Poll: Americans Rate Limbaugh Most Influential Conservative, Choose JFK for Mount Rushmore," http://www.cbsnews.com/stories/2009/11/29/ap/entertainment/main5827316.shtml; accessed March 23, 2011.

37 Page.

38 Saad, "Kennedy Still Highest Rated Modern President," Gallup News Service, Dec. 6, 2010, http://www.gallup.com/poll/145064/kennedy-highest-rated-modern-president-nixon-lowest.aspx; accessed May 24, 2011.

39 John Kifner, "Once More, with Feeling: Recycling the Kennedys," *New York Times*, Nov. 16, 1997, Section 4, Page 4.

40 Associated Press, "Reagan Moves up on 'Greatest' Poll," *New York Times*, Feb. 20, 2001, 19A.

41 Lydia Saad, "Best President? Lincoln on Par with Reagan, Kennedy," Gallup Poll, Feb. 11, 2009, http://www.gallup.com/poll/114292/best-president-lincoln-par-reagan-kennedy.aspx; accessed Feb. 4, 2011.

42 John F. Kennedy, "The Next 25 Years," *Look*, Jan. 16, 1962, 17.

43 Saad, "Best President? Lincoln on Par with Reagan and Kennedy."

44 There were a total of 129 articles about Eisenhower and 196 about Johnson. In all, 613 focused on Kennedy.

45 Searches for the three men without the title of "president" bring an even more lopsided result because so many locations in the United States carry John F. Kennedy's name.

46 "Kennedy Remembered: Kennedy Has Become America's Favorite President," 64.

47 Emile Durkheim, *The Elementary Forms of the Religious Life* (New York: Free Press, 1965), 263.

48 Amy Adamczyk, "On Thanksgiving and Collective Memory: Constructing the American Tradition," *Journal of Historic Sociology*, 15 (Sept. 2002): 359.

49 Jeffrey K. Olick, Vered Vinitzky-Seroussi, and Daniel Levy, "Introduction," in *The Collective Memory Reader* (New York: Oxford University Press, 2011), 16–18.

50 Svetlana Boym, "From 'Nostalgia and Its Discontents'," in *The Collective Memory Reader*, 452.

51 See Joy Hakim, *A History of US: Terrible War, 1855–1865*, 3rd ed. (New York: Oxford University Press, 2005),145–7; Hakim, *A History of US: Age of Extremes, 1880–1917*, 3rd ed. (New York, Oxford University Press, 2005), 52–3, 55; Hakim, *A History of US: All the People, Since 1945*, 4th ed. (New York: Oxford University Press, 2010), 106–8.

52 Allen R. Vogt, "The Kennedy Assassination and the History Teacher," *History Teacher* 20 (Nov. 1986): 8–9.

53 Neal, 12.

54 Barbie Zelizer, *Covering the Body: The Kennedy Assassination, the Media, and the Shaping of Collective Memory* (Chicago: University of Chicago Press, 1992), 3.

55 Claude Lévi-Strauss, *The Savage Mind* (Chicago: University of Chicago Press, 1966), 259.

56 Howard Schuman and Jacqueline Scott, "Generations and Collective Memories," *American Sociological Review* 54 (Jan. 1989): 362–7.

57 Sheldon Appleton, "Assassinations," *Public Opinion Quarterly* 64 (Winter 2000): 500.

58 Michael Frisch, *A Shared Authority: Essays on the Craft and Meaning of Oral and Public History* (Albany: State University of New York Press, 1990), 16.

59 Ibid., 29–54.

60 John A. DeFrancisco, Letter to the Rev. Graham R. Hodges, June 23, 1999, Graham R. Hodges Papers, Box 1, Originals of the 100 Letters Folder, JFKL.

61 Roger Brown and James Kulik, "Flashbulb Memories," in *Memory Observed: Remember in Natural Contexts,* ed. Ulrich Neisser (San Francisco: W.H. Freeman and Co., 1982), 23–40.

62 Appleton, 500.

63 F.W. Colegrove, "The Day They Heard about Lincoln," in *Memory Observed: Remember in Natural Contexts,* 41–2.

64 Ulric Neisser, "Snapshots or Benchmarks?" in *Memory Observed: Remember in Natural Contexts,* 45.

65 Mary Augusta Rodgers, "An American Family, November 1963," *Redbook,* Nov. 1964, 70.

66 Jérôme Bourdon, "Some Sense of Time: Remembering Television," *History and Memory,* 15 (Fall/Winter 2003): 24.

67 Fred Bruning, "Part II: The Kennedy Complex," *Newsday,* Nov. 22, 1993, 44.

68 Elmer W. Lower, "A Television Network Gathers News," in *The Kennedy Assassination and the American Public,* 72.

69 William H. Chafe, *The Unfinished Journey* (New York: Oxford University Press, 2010), 199.

70 Martin Luther King Jr., "It's a Difficult Thing to Teach a President," *Look,* Nov. 17, 1964, 64.

71 John Weisman, "Remembering JFK . . . Our First TV President," *TV Guide,* Nov. 19, 1988, 3.

72 Walter Cronkite and Don Carleton, *Conversations with Cronkite* (Austin: Dolph Briscoe Center for American History, 2010), 203.

73 Press release, "The Death of President Kennedy," CBS News, Nov. 26, 1963, Columbia University Bureau of Applied Social Science Records, Box 4, Network Information Folder, JFKL.

74 Press release, "The NBC Network Service: November 22–26, 1963," NBC News, Columbia University of Applied Social Science Records, Box 4, Network Information Folder, JFKL.

75 "As 175 Million Americans Watched . . .," *Newsweek,* Dec. 9, 1963, 90.

76 Jack Gould, "Millions of Viewers See Oswald Killing on 2 TV Networks," *New York Times,* Nov. 23, 1963, in *Four Days in November: The Original Coverage of the John F. Kennedy Assassination by the Staff of the* New York Times, ed. Robert B. Semple Jr. (New York: St. Martin's Press, 2003), 321.

77 Wilbur Schramm, "Communication in Crisis," in *The Kennedy Assassination and the American Public,* 14.

78 Ibid., 4.

79 Paul B. Sheatsley and Jacob J. Feldman, "A National Survey on Public Reactions and Behavior," in *The Kennedy Assassination and the American Public,* 159.

80 Schramm, 24.

81 Norma Feshbach and Seymour Feshbach, "Personality and Political Values: A Study of Reactions to Two Accused Assassinations," in *The Kennedy Assassination and the American Public,* 295.

82 Bonjean, Hill, and Martin, 197.

83 Chet Huntley, Oral history interview by H. Gans, Dec. 17, 1963, 1–2, Columbia University Bureau of Applied Social Research Records, Box 1, Chet Huntley Folder, John F. Kennedy Library, Boston.

84 Ruth Leeds Love, "Television and the Kennedy Assassination," *New Society*, Oct. 13, 1966, 569.

85 Huntley, 3.

86 David Brinkley, Oral history interview by Herbert J. Gans, Dec. 13, 1963, 2–4, Columbia University Bureau of Applied Social Research Records, Box 1, David Brinkley Folder, JFKL.

87 Ibid., 6.

88 Howard K. Smith, Oral history interview by Herbert J. Gans, Dec. 13, 1963, 20. Columbia University Bureau of Applied Social Research Records, Box 1, David Brinkley Folder, JFKL.

89 Weisman, 7.

90 Newseum with Cathy Trost and Susan Bennett, 268.

91 Ibid., 270.

92 Ibid., 270–1.

93 "As 175 Million Americans Watched . . .," 88.

94 Art Simon, *Dangerous Knowledge: The JFK Assassination in Art and Film* (Philadelphia: Temple University Press, 1996), 106.

95 William A. Mindak and Gerald D. Hursh, "Television's Functions on the Assassination Weekend," in *The Kennedy Assassination and the American Public*, 136.

96 Alan Levy, "The Day JFK Died: What People Remember," *Good Housekeeping*, Nov. 1965, 225.

97 Mindak and Hursh, 139.

98 Love, 567–71.

99 Smith, 6.

100 James W. Hilty, *Robert Kennedy Brother Protector* (Philadelphia: Temple University Press, 1997), 161–63.

101 George Reedy, *Lyndon Johnson: A Memoir* (New York: Andrews and McMeel Inc., 1971), 126.

102 Roy Wilkins, Oral history interview I by Thomas H. Baker, April 1, 1969, 3, LBJL.

103 Harry McPherson, Oral history interview I by T.H. Baker, Dec. 5, 1968, 7, LBJL.

104 Morris Abram, Oral history interview I by Michael L. Gillette, March 20, 9, LBJL.

105 In 1977, Walter Mondale became the first vice president to have a White House office.

106 Robert Dallek, *Flawed Giant: Lyndon Johnson and his Times, 1961–1973* (New York: Oxford University Press, 1998), 9–10.

107 Gerald S. Strober and Deborah H. Strober, eds., *"Let Us Begin Anew:" An Oral History of the Kennedy Presidency* (New York: HarperCollins Publishers, 1993), 194.

108 Theodore C. Sorensen, *Kennedy* (New York: Harper & Row, 1965), 265–6.

109 Abe Fortas, Oral history interview by Joe B. Frantz, Aug. 14, 1969, 11, LBJL.

110 Merle Miller. *Lyndon: An Oral Biography* (New York: G.P. Putnam's Sons, 1980), 279.

111 Lawrence F. O'Brien, Oral history interview I by Michael L. Gillette, Sept. 18, 1985, 13.

112 Leonard Baker, *The Johnson Eclipse* (New York: The MacMillan Company, 1966), 167.
113 Lynda Bird Johnson Robb, interview by author, Sept. 28, 2005.
114 Walter Cronkite, "LBJ: Tragedy and Transition," CBS News, May 2, 1970, Transcript, 32, CBS Interview "Tragedy and Transition," Box 1, CBS Transcript—Transcribed Copy 1–123 with Reel and Markings Folder, LBJL.
115 Harris Wofford, Interview by author, Feb. 26, 2005.
116 John Siegenthaler, Interview by author, March 2, 2005.
117 Doris Kearns Goodwin, *Lyndon Johnson and the American Dream* (New York: St. Martin's Griffin, 1991), 41–2.
118 Hugh Sidey, Oral history interview I by Paige Mulhollan, July 22, 1971, 15, LBJL.
119 Nicholas Katzenbach, Interview by author, March 6, 2005.
120 Kennedy took eighty-three trips in 1963 alone. *Report of the Select Committee on Assassinations of the U.S. House of Representatives* (Ipswich, MA: Mary Ferrell Foundation Press, 2007), 35.
121 Manchester, 44.
122 Charles Bartlett, Oral history interview by Fred Holborn, Jan. 6, 1965, 152, JFKL.
123 Manchester, 10.

2 Texas Tragedy

1 Newseum with Trost and Bennett, 16.
2 James Ewell, "Detailed Security Net Spread for Kennedy," *Dallas Morning News*, Nov. 21, 1963, Section 4, Page 1.
3 Warren Commission, *The Warren Commission Report* (New York: St. Martin's Press, 1964), 48.
4 Gerald Blaine with Lisa McCubbin, *The Kennedy Detail* (New York: Gallery Books, 2010), 214.
5 Special to the *New York Times*, "Boy Describes Shooting," *New York Times,* Nov. 23, 1963, in *Four Days in Novemb*er (New York: St. Martin's Press, 2003), 48–9.
6 Vincent Bugliosi, *Four Days in November: The Assassination of President John F. Kennedy* (New York: W.W. Norton & Co., 2007), 65.
7 Blaine, 387–9.
8 Ibid., 216.
9 Ibid., 219.
10 Bugliosi, *Four Days in November*, 71.
11 Manchester, 168.
12 Steven M. Gillon, *The Kennedy Assassination—24 Hours after* (New York: Basic Books, 2009), 56.
13 Warren Commission, 55.
14 Bugliosi, *Four Days in November*, 97.
15 Lady Bird Johnson, Transcript from tapes, Nov. 22, 1963, 2, LBJL Records, Special File on Assassination of John F. Kennedy, Box 18, Manchester File folder, JFK-NA.
16 Blaine, 232.
17 Jimmy Breslin, "The Breslin Report: Death in the Emergency Room—JFK 25 Years Later," *Newsday*, Nov. 22, 1988, 10.

18 Bugliosi, *Four Days in November*, 114.
19 Newseum with Trost and Bennett, 79.
20 Stevenson, who provided information to reporters, actually was assistant deputy chief. At the time of the shooting, he was at the Trade Mart awaiting the president's arrival.
21 David S. Broder Papers, Box 10, Folder 2, JFKL.
22 Manchester, 220.
23 Ibid., 303.
24 Gillon, 125.
25 Godfrey McHugh, Oral history interview by Sheldon Stern, May 19, 1978, 47, JFKL.
26 Lady Bird Johnson, 4.
27 Kenneth P. O'Donnell, Oral history interview I, 7/23/69, by Paige E. Mulhollan, 43–44, LBJL.
28 Newseum with Trost and Bennett, 118.
29 Manchester, 326.
30 Ibid., 339.
31 Bugliosi, *Four Days in November*, 223.
32 Manchester, 388.
33 Bugliosi, *Four Days in November*, 224.
34 Ibid., 382.
35 Manchester, 406.
36 Bugliosi, *Four Days in November*, 237.
37 Mulvaney and De Angelis, 18.
38 Manchester, 516–17.
39 John McCormack, "Eulogies Given by Leaders," *New York Times*, Nov. 25, 1963 in *Four Days in November*, 396
40 Manchester, 590.
41 Bugliosi, *Four Days in November*, 166.
42 Newseum with Trost and Bennett, 129.
43 Ruth Paine, Testimony, March 20, 1964, Warren Commission Hearings, III, 83–4.
44 Bugliosi, *Four Days in November*, 210.
45 Warren Commission, 16.
46 Warren Commission, 789.
47 Doug J. Swanson, "The Trial of Jack Ruby: Circus in the Courtroom," *Dallas Morning News*, Nov. 20, 1983, Twenty Years Later Special Section, 49.
48 Bugliosi, *Four Days in November*, 256.
49 Newseum with Trost and Bennett, 159–60.
50 Bugliosi, *Four Days in November*, 319.
51 "Measuring Worth," http://www.measuringworth.com/ppowerus/result.php; accessed May 22, 2011.
52 Thomas J. Kelley, "Reports of Inspector Thomas J. Kelley, U.S. Secret Service," in Appendix XI of Warren Commission, 627.
53 Tom Pettit, "The Television Story in Dallas," in *The Kennedy Assassination and the American Public*, 63.
54 Warren Commission, 216.
55 Newseum with Trost and Bennett, 209.

56   John Herbers, "Slain Policeman is Honored by Dallas," *New York Times,* Nov. 26, 1963, in *Four Days in November,* 563.

57   Bugliosi, *Four Days in November,* 509–10.

58   Marie Tippit, a mother of three, received more than $600,000 in contributions from fellow Americans. Americans gave Marina Oswald more than $70,000 in donations. She immediately hired an agent to handle the lucrative sale of many of her husband's possessions. See Manchester, 635.

59   Lyndon B. Johnson, Letters to Caroline Kennedy and John F. Kennedy Jr.. Records of the Lyndon B. Johnson Library, Special File on the Assassination of John F. Kennedy, Box 18, Manchester File folder, JFK-NA.

3 Mourning in the Shadows

1   Walt Whitman, "Oh Captain, My Captain," Stanza 3.

2   Bradley S. Greenberg, "Diffusion of News about the Kennedy Assassination," in *The Kennedy Assassination and the American Public,* 102.

3   Special to the *New York Times,* "Chicago," *New York Times,* Nov. 23, 1963, in *Four Days in November,* 83.

4   Greenberg, "Diffusion of News about the Kennedy Assassination," 96.

5   George Barrett, "First 'Is it True?' Then Anger and Anguish among New Yorkers and Visitors," *New York Times,* Nov. 23, 1963, 5.

6   Greenberg, "Diffusion of News of the Kennedy Assassination," *Public Opinion Quarterly* 28, no. 2 (Summer 1964), 226–7.

7   Ibid., 231.

8   Ibid., 227.

9   Thomas J. Banta, "The Kennedy Assassination: Early Thoughts and Emotions, *Public Opinion Quarterly* 28, no. 2 (Summer 1964): 218–19.

10   Roy E. Carter Jr., "Public Response to the Assassination: The First Twenty-Four Hours," Proceedings of the 19th Annual Conference on Public Opinion Research, *Public Opinion Quarterly* 28, no. 4 (1964): 652–3.

11   Gillon, 99.

12   Bonjean, Hill, and Martin, 181.

13   Keith Crain, "When President was Slain, no News was Bad News," *Crain's Detroit Business,* Nov. 29, 1993, 6.

14   Harry McPherson, *A Political Education* (Austin: University of Texas Press, 1995), 213.

15   Greenberg, "Diffusion of News of the Kennedy Assassination," 225.

16   Manchester, 440.

17   White, *The Making of the President 1964,* 28.

18   Nan Robertson, "Thousands Expected to Pay Respects at Grave," *New York Times,* Nov. 22, 1964, 74.

19   "Spiral of Hate," Editorial, *New York Times,* Nov. 25, 1963, in *Four Days in November,* 446.

20   Bugliosi, *Four Days in November,* 340.

21   Sheatsley and Feldman, "A National Survey on Public Reactions and Behavior," 154.

22   Sheatsley and Feldman, "The Assassination of the President: A Preliminary Report on Public Reactions and Behavior," *Public Opinion Quarterly* 28, no. 2 (Summer 1964): 196.

23 Ibid., 199.

24 Fred I. Greenstein, "College Students' Reactions to the Assassination," in *The Kennedy Assassination and the American Public*, 239.

25 Neal, *National Trauma and Collective Memory: Major Events in the American Experience* (Armonk, NY: M.E. Sharpe, 1996), 116, accessed via EBSCO Publishing—Net Library on Nov. 5, 2010.

26 Ibid., 210.

27 Miki Mahoney, "Women, Men Weep in Streets," *Philadelphia Inquirer*, Nov. 23, 1963, 1.

28 Alan Levy, "The Day JFK Died: What People Remember Now," *Good Housekeeping*, Nov. 1965, 87.

29 Special to the *New York Times*, "Los Angeles," *New York Times*, Nov. 23, 1963, in *Four Days in November*, 84.

30 Sheldon Appleton, "The Mystery of the Kennedy Assassination: What the American Public Believes," *Public Perspective*, Oct. 1998, 13.

31 Sheatsley and Feldman, "The Assassination of the President," 207.

32 "Wallace Voices Deep Sympathy," *Montgomery Advertiser*, Nov. 23, 1963, in Kenneth W. Munden Papers, Box 1, Alabama Folder, JFKL.

33 Marty Trillhaase, "Question: Where Were You? Thirty Years after JFK's Death, Longtime I.F. Residents Remember," *Idaho Falls Post Register*, Nov. 21, 1993, A1.

34 Greenstein, "Young Men and the Death of a Young President," in *Children and the Death of a President* ed. Martha Wolfenstein and Gilbert Kliman (Garden City, NY: Doubleday & Co., 1965), 190.

35 Feshbach and Feshbach, "Personality and Political Values," 292–3.

36 Joseph Alsop, as quoted in memorandum attached to oral history interview by Elspeth Rostow, June 23, 1964, 1, JFKL.

37 Joseph Alsop, "The Legacy of John F. Kennedy," *Saturday Evening Post*, Nov. 21, 1964, 18.

38 Mulvaney and De Angelis, 104.

39 Simeon Booker, "How JFK Surpassed Abraham Lincoln," *Ebony*, Feb. 1964, 27.

40 Norman M. Bradburn and Jacob J. Feldman, "Public Apathy and Public Grief," in *The Kennedy Assassination and the American Public*, 274.

41 Mulvaney and De Angelis, 115.

42 "J.F.K., 1917–1963," *National Review*, Dec. 10, 1963, 1.

43 Mary August Rodgers, "An American Family, November 1963," *Redbook*, Nov. 1964, 69.

44 Theodore Sorensen, "They Underestimated J.F.K.," *New York Times*, Nov. 22, 1988, 27A.

45 Henry R. Luce, Oral history interview by John L. Steele, Nov. 11, 1965, 41–2, JFKL.

46 Manchester, 506.

47 Joseph S. Nye Jr., Philip D. Zelikow, and David C. King, *Why People Don't Trust Government* (Cambridge: Harvard University Press, 1997), 81.

48 Liz Halloran, "Pew Poll: Trust in Government Hits Near-Historic Low," National Public Radio, April 18. 2010, http://www.npr.org/templates/story/story.php?storyId'126047343; accessed Jan. 30, 2011.

49 James Reston, "Why America Weeps," *New York Times*, Nov. 23, 1963, 1.

50 Sheatsley and Feldman, "The Assassination of President Kennedy," 196.

51 Roberta S. Sigel, "Television and the Reactions of Schoolchildren to the Assassination," in *Kennedy Assassination and the American Public*, 206.

52 The Reverend William A. Holmes, "One Thing Worse than This," Nov. 24, 1963, reprinted in *A Man Called John F. Kennedy: Sermons on his Assassination,* ed. Charles J. Stewart and Bruce Kendall (Glen Rock, NJ: Paulist Press, 1964) 37.

53 Dear Abby, *Where Were You When President Kennedy was Shot?* (Kansas City: Andrews and McMeel, 1993), 89.

54 The Reverend Thomas Parry Jones, "An American Tragedy," Nov. 24, 1963, reprinted in *A Man Called John F. Kennedy: Sermons on his Assassination,* 90.

55 Dear Abby, *Where Were You When President Kennedy Was Shot?*, 83.

56 Claude Sitton, "Racial Hostility Ignored by South," *New York Times*, Nov. 23, 1963, in *Four Days in November*, 93.

57 Michael Ensley, Interview by author, Nov. 22, 2001.

58 Wayne King, "Dallas Still Wondering: Did it Help Pull Trigger?" *New York Times*, Nov. 22, 1983, A24.

59 "Memories of Day in Dallas Remain Vivid 20 Years Later," *Washington Post*, Nov. 22, 1983, A12.

60 Newseum with Trost and Bennett, 232.

61 Oct. 26, 1999 letter, Graham R. Hodges Papers, Box 1, Originals of the 100 Letters Folder, JFKL.

62 James W. Hilty, Interview by author, July 19, 2001.

63 Unsigned essay, John F. Kennedy Condolence Mail, Box 57, Children's Letters Folder #2, JFKL.

64 Ira D. Gruber, "Inflaming the Ignorant," Letter to the editor, *New York Times*, Nov. 26, 1963, 36.

65 Samuel L. Tucker Jr., "Violence in our Civilization," Letter to the editor, *New York Times*, Nov. 26, 1963, 36.

66 Celinda Casas, "John F. Kennedy," in *Children Write about John F. Kennedy*, ed. William B. Walsh (Brownsville, TX: Springman-King Publishing Co., 1964), 16.

67 Arthur M. Schlesinger Jr., *A Thousand Days* (Boston: Houghton Mifflin Co., 1965), 1026.

68 The Reverend Robert Cromey, Interview by author, Nov. 20, 2001.

69 Margaret Glose, Interview by author, Nov. 18, 2001.

70 Janet Fishburn, Interview by author, Nov. 11, 2001.

71 The Reverend Karel Ramsey, Interview by author, Nov. 19, 2001.

72 The Reverend Adrianne Carr, Interview by author, Nov. 25, 2001.

73 The Reverend Richard McGowan, Interview by author, Nov. 19, 2001.

74 The Reverend George A. Buchanan, "An Ironical Whirlwind of Violence," Nov. 24, 1963, Charles Stewart Papers, Box 4, Presbyterian 2 of 6 Folder, JFKL.

75 Dr. Seymour J. Cohen, "John Fitzgerald Kennedy," *Anshe Emet Bulletin*, Dec. 6, 1963, 1.

76 H.H. Hobbs, "November 22, 1963," Nov. 24, 1963, Charles Stewart Papers, Box 1, Baptists 2 of 4 Folder, JFKL.

77 O.J. Closter, "The New Heaven and the New Earth," Nov. 24, 1963, Charles Stewart Papers, Box 3, Lutheran 1 of 4 Folder, JFKL.

78 John Herbers, "Dallas is Groping for a Reason Why," *New York Times,* Nov. 25, 1963, in *Four Days in November*, 346.

79 "Dallas Asks Why It Happened; Worry Over 'Image' Is Voiced," *New York Times*, Nov. 24, 1963, in *Four Days in November*, 282—3.

80 Robert Pierpoint, Oral history interview by Sheldon Stern, Nov. 18, 1982, 25, JFKL.

81 Bicknell Eubanks, "Dallas Tries to Regain Equilibrium," *Christian Science Monitor*, Nov. 25, 1963, 1.

82 Wayne King, A24.

83 Herbers, "Slain Policeman is Honored by Dallas," *New York Times*, Nov. 26, 1963, in *Four Days in November*, 564—5.

84 Herbers, 347.

85 Ibid., 348.

86 "*Dallas Times Herald* Asks Prayer to End Bitterness and Hate," *New York Times*, Nov. 24, 1963, in *Four Days in November*, 284.

87 Manchester, 330.

88 Herbers, "Dallas is Groping for a Reason Why," 347.

89 James W. Pennebaker and Becky L. Banasik, "On the Creation and Maintenance of Collective Memories: History as Social Psychology," in *Collective Memory of Political Events* (Hove, East Sussex: Psychology Press, 2008), 10.

90 Bonjean, Hill, and Martin, 184.

91 Newman R. McLarry, "My Dear Caroline," *Dallas Times Herald*, Nov. 24, 1963, 2A.

92 Bugliosi, *Four Days in November*, 402.

93 Newseum with Trost and Bennett, 264.

94 Manchester, 633.

95 Ibid., 637.

96 Pennebaker and Banasik, 10.

97 The Reverend Barry M. Carter, "Where is Your Brother?" Nov. 24, 1963, reprinted in *A Man Called John F. Kennedy: Sermons on his Assassination*, 80.

98 The Reverend Loring D. Chase, "Whosoever Hateth his Brother," Nov. 24, 1963, Charles Stewart Papers, Box 4, UCC Congregational 1 of 6 Folder, JFKL.

99 Chet Huntley, Statement, Nov. 22, 1963, National Broadcasting Company, reprinted in *Southern Cross*, Nov. 25, 1963, Chet Huntley papers, Box 1, Nov. 24–25 Folder, John F. Kennedy Library.

100 Henry Steele Commager, "How Explain Our Illness?" *Washington Post*, Dec. 1, 1963, E1.

101 Norman Cousins, "The Legacy of John F. Kennedy," *Saturday Review*, Dec. 7, 1963, 26.

102 Editorial, "Spiral of Hate," *New York Times*, Nov. 25, 1963, 18.

103 "Opinion of the Week: At Home and Abroad," *New York Times*, Nov. 24, 1963, E9.

104 Richard Starnes, "Wanted: Moral Rebirth of People," *Philadelphia Daily News*, Nov. 29, 1963, 44.

105 "A Legacy of Courage," *Christian Science Monitor*, Nov. 25, 1963, 18.

106 "The American Condition," *Nation*, Dec. 21, 1963, 2.

107 Associated Press, "Shock Disbelief Unite Nation in Agony of Sorrow," *Philadelphia Inquirer*, Nov. 23, 1963, 4.

108 Hale Boggs, "Statement of Representative Hale Boggs on the Assassination of President John F. Kennedy," Nov. 22, 1963, attached to oral history interview by Charles T. Morrissey, May 10, 1964, JFKL.

109 Monroe Miller and Roger Zimmerman, "Immediate and Subsequent Reactions in Manhattan," in *The Kennedy Assassination and the American Public*, 272.

110 "Philadelphians Weep at President's Death," *Evening Bulletin*, Nov. 22, 1963, 1–3.

111 Sheatsley and Feldman, "A National Survey on Public Reactions and Behavior," 154.

112 Bonjean, Hill, and Martin, 183.

113 Manchester, 567.

114 Bugliosi, *Four Days in November*, 500.

115 James Reston, "A Portion of Guilt for All," *New York Times*, Nov. 25, 1963, in *Four Days in November*, 448.

116 Maxwell Taylor, Oral history interview by Elspeth Rostow, Jun. 23, 1964, 25–6, JFKL.

117 Special to the *New York Times*, "A Flame Went out," *New York Times*, Nov. 23, 1963, in *Four Days in November*, 103.

118 "Sorrow All Over World," *New York Times*, Nov. 25, 1963, in *Four Days in November*, 419.

119 "Sorrow Rings a World," *Life: John F. Kennedy Memorial Edition* (Winter 1988).

120 Newseum with Trost and Bennett, xiii.

121 Connelly, Interview by author, Jan. 6, 2002.

122 Robert D. Hess and Judith V. Torney, *The Development of Political Attitudes in Children* (Garden City, NY: Anchor Books, 1967), 102.

123 Greenstein, "The Benevolent Leader: Children's Images of Political Authority," *American Political Science Review* 54 (Dec. 1960): 940.

124 Ibid., 936.

125 Ibid., 937.

126 Greenstein, *Children and Politics* (New Haven: Yale University Press, 1965), 42.

127 Sigel, "An Exploration into Some Aspects of Political Socialization: School Children's Reactions to the Death of a President," in *Children and the Death of a President*, 36.

128 Greenstein, "The Benevolent Leader Revisited: Children's Images of Political Leaders in Three Democracies," *American Political Science Review* 69 (Dec. 1975): 1373.

129 Karen Orren and Paul Peterson, "Presidential Assassination: A Case Study in the Dynamics of Political Socialization," *Journal of Politics* 29 (May 1967): 398.

130 Ibid., 399.

131 Ibid., 401.

132 Sigel, "An Exploration into Some Aspects of Political Socialization: School Children's Reactions to the Death of a President," 51.

133 Ibid., 44–5.

134 Ibid., 43.

135 Ibid., 46.

136 Ibid., 54.

137 Joanne Lannin, "Where We Were–and What We Became–When Kennedy Died: 35-Year Anniversary," *Portland Press Herald*, Nov. 22, 1998, 1G.

138 Jeff Rivers, "Aftershocks Go on and on, 30 Years after JFK's Death," *Hartford Courant*, Nov. 18, 1993, A2.

139 Sigel, "Television and the Reactions of Schoolchildren to the Assassination," 215.

140 Sigel, "An Exploration into Some Aspects of Political Socialization: School Children's Reactions to the Death of a President," 49.

141 Dec. 1, 1963 Letter, John F. Kennedy Condolence Mail, Box 67, Children's Letters Folder #76, JFKL.

142 Nov. 23, 1963 Letter, John F. Kennedy Condolence Mail, Box 67, Children's Letters Folder #75, JFKL.

143 Undated letter, John F. Kennedy Condolence Mail, Box 58, Children's Letters Folder #9, JFKL.

144 Glose, Interview by author, Nov. 18, 2001.

145 Hector de la Rosa, "The Photo on the Walls," *Newsweek*, Nov. 28, 1983, 72.

146 Theodore H. White, "Original Delivered to Mrs. Kennedy," Theodore White Papers, Box 59, Camelot Papers—Item II-A—Reference Copy, JFKL.

147 Ramsey, Interview by author, Nov. 19, 2001.

148 Connelly, Interview by author, Jan. 6, 2002.

149 Mulvaney and De Angelis, 207.

150 Christopher J. Hurn and Mark Messer, "Grief and Rededication," in *The Kennedy Assassination and the American Public*, 346.

151 Lannin, 1G.

152 Lyndon Johnson, Interview by Walter Cronkite, Transcript, 3, "LBJ: 'Tragedy and Transition,'" CBS, May 2, 1970, "LBJ: 'Tragedy and Transition'" Box 1, Transcript—Transcribed Copy 1–123 (with reel marking) Folder, LBJL.

153 David Burner and Thomas R. West, *The Torch is Passed: The Kennedy Brothers and American Liberalism* (St. James, NY: Brandywine Press, 1992), 158.

4 Life After Death

1   Thucydides, *The History of the Peloponnesian War*, Book II, trans. Benjamin Jowett, 2nd ed. (Oxford: Clarendon Press, 1900), 43.

2   Dean Rusk, Oral history interview by Richard Geary Rusk and Thomas J. Schoenbaum, RUSK JJJ JJJ, April 1986, 7, Richard B. Russell Memorial Library, University of Georgia.

3   "The Bandwagon Number," *Newsweek*, July 4, 1960, 20.

4   Orville Freeman, Oral history interview by Russell Fridley, Jan. 29, 1996, 33, Papers of Orville Freeman, Box 40, Interview of Orville Freeman, Conducted by Russell Fridley Jan. 29, 1996 Folder, Minnesota Historical Society.

5   Freeman, Typed transcripts of diary, Nov. 20, 1963 entry, Microfilm roll M17, Minnesota Historical Society.

6   Nigel Hamilton, *JFK: Reckless Youth* (New York: Random House, 1991), 42.

7   "The New President, Lyndon B. Johnson," CBS News, Nov. 23, 1963, Paley Center for Media, New York.

8   Senator Allen J. Ellender, Oral history interview by Larry Hackman, Aug. 29, 1967, 12, JFKL.

9   Robert A. Wallace, Oral history interview II by Larry J. Hackman, Jan. 4, 1972, 100, JFKL.

10 Dallek, 14.

11 "Facts and Information about President Kennedy," Undated, Papers of Lyndon B. Johnson, President, EX FG2/Kennedy John F., Box 42, FG2, Kennedy, John F., Dec. 28, 1965 [2 of 2] Folder, LBJL.

12 "LBJ's Favorites," LBJL Website, http://www.lbjlib.utexas.edu/johnson/archives.hom/FAQs/Favorites/lbjtable.asp; accessed July 19, 2006.

13 Lyndon Baines Johnson, *The Vantage Point: Perspectives of the Presidency 1963–1969* (New York: Holt, Rinehart and Winston, 1971), 10.

14 Charles Roberts, Oral history interview by Joe B. Frantz, Jan. 14, 1970, 30, LBJL.

15 Johnson, *The Vantage Point*, 10.

16 Ibid., 19.

17 National Geographic Channel, "The Lost JFK Tapes: The Assassination" (Universal City, CA: Vivendi Entertainment, 2009).

18 Telephone conversation between Lyndon Johnson and Supreme Court Justice Arthur Goldberg, Nov. 22, 1963, Transcript, 1, http://maryferrell.org/mffweb/archive/viewer/showDoc.do?absPageID=69788&imageOnly=true; accessed Feb. 27, 2011.

19 Miller, 324.

20 Jack Valenti, "The Unforgettable Afternoon," *New York Times*, Nov. 22, 1998, 17.

21 Jeff Shesol, *Mutual Contempt* (New York: W.W. Norton & Company, 1997), 119.

22 Manchester, 543.

23 Ibid., 225.

24 White, *The Making of the President 1964*, 59.

25 Gillon, 219.

26 Marshall Green, Memorandum, Nov. 23, 1963, James C. Thomson Papers, Box 4, Briefing President, 11/64 Folder, JFKL.

27 John Chancellor, Oral history interview by Dorothy Pierce McSweeny, April 25, 1969, 8-9, LBJL.

28 Manchester, 639.

29 Tom Wicker, *JFK and LBJ*, 205.

30 Doris Kearns Goodwin, *Lyndon Johnson and the American Dream* (New York: St. Martin's Griffin, 1991), 170.

31 Charles Roberts, Oral history interview by Charles Morrissey, April 11, 1966, 19, JFKL.

32 Manchester, 582–3.

33 Ibid., 538.

34 Johnson, "Address Before a Joint Session of Congress," *Public Papers of the Presidents of the United States: Lyndon B. Johnson 1963–64*, Book I (Washington: U.S. Government Printing Office, 1965), 8–10.

35 Lyndon B. Johnson, "Address to the Nation on Thanksgiving Day," Nov. 28, 1963, in *Public Papers of the Presidents of the United States: Lyndon B. Johnson*, Book I (Washington: U.S. Government Printing Office, 1965), 12.

36 Maurice Isserman and Michael Kazin, *America Divided* (New York: Oxford University Press, 2000), 103.

37 Joseph Alsop, "President Johnson," Nov. 27, 1963, New York Herald Tribune Inc.

38 Editorial, "The President's First Week," *Wall Street Journal*, Nov. 29, 1963, 10.

39 Theodore White, "When Did Politics Resume?" Feb. 28, 1964, Theodore H. White Papers, Box 108, TMOP '64 Notes and Interviews Chapter 6 Folder, Harvard University Archives.

40 Dallek, 4.

41 Chafe, 219.

42 Ibid., 215.

43 Isserman and Kazin, 108.

44 Ibid., 109.

45 Randall B. Woods, *LBJ: Architect of American Ambition* (New York: Free Press, 2006), 444.

46 David Burner and Thomas R. West, *The Torch is Passed* (New York: Brandywine Press, 1984), 181.

47 Kearns Goodwin, 200.

48 Max Holland, *The Kennedy Assassination Tapes* (New York: Alfred A. Knopf, 2004), 237.

49 Kenneth O'Donnell, Oral history interview by Paige E. Mulhollan, July 23, 1969, 63, LBJL.

50 Edwin O. Guthman and Jeffrey Shulman, *Robert F. Kennedy in his Own Words* (New York: Bantam Books, 1988, 417.

51 Stewart Alsop, Oral history interview by Paige E. Mulhollan, July 15, 1969, 9, LBJL.

52 Clark Clifford, Oral history interview II by Paige E. Mulhollan, July 2, 1969, 4, LBJL.

53 Clark Clifford, Oral history interview IV by Joe B. Frantz, Aug. 7, 1969, 7, LBJL.

54 Kenneth P. O'Donnell, Oral history interview I by Paige E. Mulhollan, July 23, 1969, 52, LBJL.

55 Gillon, 233.

56 Dallek, 183-4.

57 Bruce Schulman, *Lyndon B. Johnson and American Liberalism* (New York: Bedford/ St. Martin's, 2007) 96.

58 The twenty-fourth amendment to the Constitution outlawed poll taxes in federal elections in 1964, but black voters in some southern states were unable to vote in state elections without paying a poll tax until a 1966 Supreme Court ruling outlawed poll taxes in state elections as well as federal elections. By 1968, black voter registration in the eleven former Confederate states averaged 62 percent. For more on black voter participation, see Dallek, 220.

59 Burner and West, 209.

60 Frederick E. Nolting Jr., Telegram to Secretary of State, May 15, 1961, Papers of Lyndon B. Johnson, Vice Presidential Security Files, Vice Presidential Travel, Box 1, Summaries of Vice President Johnson's Trips 1961–63 (1) Folder, LBJL.

61 Lyndon B. Johnson, "Mission to Southeast Asia, Indian and Pakistan," Memorandum to the President, May 23, 1961, Papers of John F. Kennedy, Presidential Office Files, Box 30, Special Correspondence Johnson, Lyndon B. January 1961–May 1961 Folder, JFKL.

62 Lyndon B. Johnson, "Press Conference of the Vice President of the United States," May 24, 1961, Papers of Pierre Salinger, Box 9, Johnson, Vice President Lyndon B., Press conference, 5/24/61 Folder, JFKL.

63 Lyndon B. Johnson, Letter to Jacqueline Kennedy, Dec. 16, 1966, LBJL Records, Special File on the Assassination of John F. Kennedy, Box 1, Manchester File folder, JFK-NA.

64 Jacqueline Kennedy, Letter to Lyndon B. Johnson, December 1966, LBJL Records, White House Famous Names, Box 36, Kennedy, Mrs. John F.—1966 folder, JFK-NA.

65 Steel, 135.

66 Henggeler, 205.

67 Holland, 353.

68 Jacqueline Kennedy Onassis, Oral history interview by Joe B. Frantz, Jan. 11, 1974, 17, LBJL.

69 Holland, 361–2.

70 John P. Roche, Memorandum to Lyndon B. Johnson, Dec. 23, 1966, LBJL Records, Special File on the Assassination of John F. Kennedy, Box 18, Manchester File folder, JFK-NA.

71 Lyndon B. Johnson, "Statement before House Foreign Affairs Committee," June 5, 1961, 7, 12, Papers of Lyndon B. Johnson, Vice Presidential Security File, Box 11, Proposed Statement of Vice President before House Foreign Affairs Committee Folder, LBJL.

72 Moya Ann Ball, "The Phantom of the Oval Office: The John F. Kennedy Assassination's Symbolic Impact on Lyndon B. Johnson, His Key Advisers, and the Vietnam Decision-Making Process," *President Studies Quarterly* 4 (Winter 1994): 112.

73 Alexander Bloom and Wini Breines, eds., *"Takin' it to the streets": A Sixties Reader* (New York: Oxford University Press, 2003), 162–3.

74 "U.S. Military Casualties in Southeast Asia—Deaths by Calendar Year," The Vietnam Veterans Memorial: The Wall—USA, http://thewall-usa.com/summary.asp; accessed Feb. 25, 2011.

75 George Gallup, *The Gallup Poll: Public Opinion, 1935–71*, vol. 3 (New York: Random House, 1972), 1945.

76 Ibid., 2027.

77 Telephone Conversation Between President Johnson and Postmaster General Lawrence O'Brien, March 30, 1967, 9:23 a.m., *Foreign Relations of the United States, 1964–68, V* (Washington: U.S. Government Printing Office, 2002), Item 124, 297.

78 Robert S. McNamara, *In Retrospect: The Tragedy and Lessons of Vietnam* (New York: Vintage Books, 1995), 61.

79 Office of the White House Press Secretary, "Interview of the President by Mr. David Brinkley and Mr. Chet Huntley for the Huntley–Brinkley Report," The President's Office, Washington, D.C., September 9, 1963," Sept. 9, 1963, National Security Files, Box 316, Meetings on Vietnam, 9/1/63-9/10/63 Folder, JFKL.

80 Chafe, 256–7.

81 Hugh Sidey, "'He Asked Me to Listen to the Debate," *Time*, Nov. 14, 1983, 69.

82 Harry McPherson, Oral history interview IV by T.H. Baker, March 24, 1969, 7, LBJL.

83 Paul Henggeler, *In his Steps: Lyndon Johnson and the Kennedy Mystique* (Chicago, Ivan R. Dee, 1991), 201.

84 Holland, 342.

85 McPherson, Oral history interview IV, 4.

86 Kearns Goodwin, 336.

87 Ibid., 343.

88 Arthur M. Schlesinger Jr., *Robert Kennedy and his Times* (Boston: Houghton Mifflin Co., 1978), 846.

89 Chafe, 343.

90 McCarthy had a strong liberal voting record in the Senate, but did not appeal strongly to black voters.

91 Schlesinger, *Robert Kennedy and his Times*, 875.

92 Joseph A. Califano Jr., *The Triumph and Tragedy of Lyndon B. Johnson* (New York: Simon and Schuster, 1991), 297.

93 "Chicago Examined: Anatomy of a Police Riot," *Time*, Dec. 6, 1968, http://www.time.com/time/magazine/article/0,9171,844633,00.html; accessed May 30, 2011.

94 Tom Wicker, "In the Nation: The Question of Chicago," *New York Times*, Sept. 1, 1968, E10.

95 Rowland Evans and Robert Novak, *Lyndon B. Johnson: The Exercise of Power* (New York: New American Library, 1966), 312.

96 Schlesinger, *Robert Kennedy and his Times*, 665–6.

97 Alan Brinkley, 255–6.

98 Henggeler, 4.

99 Manchester, 626.

100 Richard Goodwin, *Remembering America* (Boston: Little, Brown and Co., 1988), 248.

101 Unsigned Election Memo, Undated, Presidential Papers of Lyndon B. Johnson, Ex FG2/Kennedy, John F., Box 41, FG2, Kennedy, John F. 12/28/65 (1 of 2) Folder, LBJL.

102 Bob Faiss, Memorandum to Jim Jones, Dec. 10, 1968, Presidential Papers of Lyndon B. Johnson, Ex FG2/Kennedy, John F., Box 41, FG2, Kennedy, John F. 12/28/65 (1 of 2) Folder, LBJL.

103 Robert E. Kintner, Memorandum to President Lyndon Johnson, Dec. 12, 1966, Presidential Papers of Lyndon B. Johnson, Ex FG2/Kennedy, John F., Box 41, FG2, Kennedy, John F. 12/28/65 (1 of 2) Folder, LBJL.

104 James W. Symington, Memorandum to President Lyndon Johnson, April 14, 1966, Presidential Papers of Lyndon B. Johnson, Ex FG2/Kennedy, John F., Box 41, FG2, Kennedy, John F. 12/28/65 (1 of 2) Folder, LBJL.

105 Fred Panzer, Memorandum for Hayes Redmon, "Summary of Press Criticisms of President Kennedy in general," June 18, 1966, Office Files of Frederick Panzer, Box 10, Criticism—John F. Kennedy Folder, LBJL and Fred Panzer, Memorandum to Hayes Redman, "Summary of Criticisms of President Kennedy's Press Relations," Office Files of Frederick Panzer, Box 10, Criticism—John F. Kennedy Folder, LBJL.

106 Recording of telephone conversation between President Lyndon B. Johnson and Senator Edward Kennedy, March 8, 1965, 9:10 p.m., Recordings of telephone conversations –White House Series, Recordings and Transcripts of Conversations and Meetings, WH6503.04 PNO5, LBJL.

107 Lawrence F. O'Brien, Oral history interview VII by Michael L. Gillette, Feb. 12, 1986, 8, LBJL.

108 William S. White, Oral history interview with Dorothy Pierce McSweeny, March 10, 1969, 2, LBJL.

109 Stewart Alsop, 9.
110 McPherson, *A Political Education*, 177.
111 Ibid., 248.
112 Henggeler, 5–6.
113 Arthur Krim, Oral history interview II by Michael L. Gillette, May 17, 1982, 9, LBJL.
114 James Marlow, "The World Today," Associated Press, Nov. 22, 1965.
115 Zelizer, 103.
116 Pete Hamill, "JFK: The Real Thing," *New York Magazine*, Nov. 28, 1988, 46.
117 The Gallup Poll, "Presidential Job Approval Center: Key Statistics," http://www.gallup.com/poll/124922/Presidential-Approval-Center.aspx; accessed March 6, 2011.
118 Walter Cronkite, "LBJ: Tragedy and Transition," Transcript, 10–11, CBS Interview "Tragedy and Transition," Box 1, CBS Transcript—As Aired Folder, LBJL.
119 Henggeler, 134.
120 Ibid., 145.
121 United Press International, "O'Donnell," Feb. 17, 1966.
122 Ronald Steel, *In Love with the Night* (New York: Touchstone, 2000), 132.
123 McNamara, 96.
124 Ed Guthman, Interview by author, Feb. 22, 2005.
125 Lawrence O'Brien, Oral history interview VI by Michael L. Gillette, Feb. 11, 1986, 41, LBJL.
126 Ralph G. Martin, *JFK: A Hero for Our Time* (New York: MacMillan Publishing Company, 1983), 500.
127 Ted Sorensen, *Counselor: A Life at the Edge of History* (New York: HarperCollins Publishers, 2008), 359.
128 James G. Blight, janet M. Lang, and David A. Welch, *Vietnam if Kennedy Had Lived: Virtual JFK* (New York: Rowman & Littlefield Publishers, Inc., 2009), 273.
129 Koji Masutani, *Virtual JFK: Vietnam if JFK Had Lived,* DVD, New York: Docurama Films, 2009.
130 McPherson, Oral history interview IV, 23.
131 Clifford, Oral history interview II, 10.
132 Dean Rusk, Oral history interview II by Paige E. Mulhollan, Sept. 26, 1969, 4, LBJL.
133 Jay Lindsay, "JFK Moon Mission Tape Reveals Inner Doubts about Space Program," *Huffington Post*, May 25, 2011, http://www.huffingtonpost.com/2011/05/25/jfk-moon-mission_n_866715.html; accessed May 25, 2011,
134 Thomas Brown, *JFK: History of an Image* (Ann Arbor: UMI Books on Demand, 2002), 23.

5 Culture of Conspiracy

1 David M. Frank, *Missing Evidence: The JFK Assassination*, DVD (New York: History Channel, 1998.)
2 Tom Wicker, "That Day in Dallas," in *The Kennedy Assassination and the American Public* (Stanford: Stanford University Press, 1965), 29.

3 David Brion Davis, "Introduction," in *The Fear of Conspiracy: Images of Un-American Subversion from the Revolution to the Present*, ed. David Brion Davis (Ithaca: Cornell University Press, 1971), xiii.

4 Robert Alan Goldberg, *Enemies Within: The Culture of Conspiracy in Modern America* (New Haven: Yale University Press, 2001), xi.

5 Michael Barkun, *A Culture of Conspiracy: Apocalyptic Visions in Contemporary America* (Berkeley: University of California Press, 2003), 3.

6 Ibid., 7.

7 Ibid., 13.

8 Richard Hofstadter, "The Paranoid Style in American Politics," in *The Fear of Conspiracy: Images of Un-American Subversion from the Revolution to the Present*, 2–3.

9 Zelizer, 76.

10 Edwin B. Parker and Bradley S. Greenberg, "Newspaper Content on the Assassination Weekend," in *The Kennedy Assassination and the American Public* (Stanford: Stanford University Press, 1965), 47–9.

11 Newseum with Trost and Bennett, 87.

12 Manchester, *The Death of a President*, 354.

13 William L. Rivers, "The Press and the Assassination," in *The Kennedy Assassination and the American Public* (Stanford: Stanford University Press, 1965), 56–7.

14 Schramm, 12–13.

15 Lewis Lipsitz and J. David Colfax, "The Fate of Due Process in a Time of Crisis," in *The Kennedy Assassination and the American Public*, 328.

16 Newseum with Trost and Bennett, 190.

17 Ibid., 267.

18 Isserman and Kazin, 101.

19 Gerald Posner, *Case Closed: Lee Harvey Oswald and the Assassination of JFK* (New York: Anchor Books, 1993), 333.

20 Ibid., 235.

21 "Report of Meeting of Members of Staff," President's Commission on the Assassination of the President, July 9, 1964, HSCA Numbered Files, Box 138, 007233 Folder, JFK-NA.

22 Posner, 364.

23 Gerald R. Ford, Oral history interview by Vicki Daitch, July 8, 2003, 11, JFKL.

24 Earl Warren, Oral history interview I by Joe B. Frantz, Sept. 21, 1971, 11, LBJL.

25 Califano, 295.

26 Dallek, 51–3.

27 Mildred Stegall, Memorandum to Dorothy(?), CBS Interview "Tragedy and Transition" Papers, Box 1, Transcript—Hardesty memo folder, LBJL.

28 Arthur Krim, Oral history interview VI by Michael L. Gillette, Oct. 13, 1983, 35, LBJL.

29 Gillon, 116.

30 Editorial, "Unanswered Questions," *New York Times*, Nov. 25, 1966, 36.

31 Dennis Hatchell, Interview by author, Aug. 2, 2001.

32 Bugliosi, *Reclaiming History*, 1374.

33 Anthony K. Gerrets and Roger D. Counts, Warren Commission Exhibit No. 1414, Warren Commission Hearings, vol. 22, Dec. 9, 1963, History Matters Archive, http://www.history-matters.com/archive/jfk/wc/wcvols/wh22/html/WH_Vol22_0429b.htm; accessed April 29, 2011.

34 Posner, 437–9.

35 Zelizer, 109.

36 Arthur M. Schlesinger Jr., "JFK Revisited," Cigar Aficionado, Dec. 1998, 170.

37 Senate Select Committee to Study Governmental Operations with Respect to Intelligence Activities, The Investigation of the Assassination of President John F. Kennedy: Performance of the Intelligence Agencies, Book V (Washington: Government Printing Office, 1976), 3–6.

38 Judith Campbell Exner, testimony, Sept. 22, 1975, Senate Select Committee on Governmental Operations with Respect to Intelligence Activities Records, Box 6, Folder 5, JFK-NA.

39 Schlesinger, Robert Kennedy and his Times, 494–5.

40 Brent Scowcroft, Memorandum to President Gerald R. Ford, June 24, 1976, 1, Gerald R. Ford Library Records, Scowcroft/Kissinger West Wing Files, 1974–77, Box 1, 7602957 (9) Folder, JFK-NA.

41 These specific findings were omitted from the commission's final report. See David Belin, "Investigation of CIA Involvement in Plans to Assassinate Foreign Leaders–DRAFT," May 29, 1975, 1, Gerald R. Ford Library Records, Jeanne Davis National Security Council Convenience File, Box 1, Rockefeller Commission Report—Assassination of Foreign Leaders (2) Folder, JFK-NA.

42 Simon, 17.

43 Bugliosi, Reclaiming History, 495–6.

44 Goldberg, 127.

45 Vincent P. Guinn, "1977 Neutron Activation Analysis Measurements on Bullet-Lead Specimens Involved in the 1963 Assassination of President John F. Kennedy," Sept. 1978, HSCA Numbered Files, Box 207, 011438 Folder, JFK-NA.

46 Clyde C. Snow and Ellis R. Kerley, "Authentication of John F. Kennedy Autopsy Radiographs and Photographs," March 9, 1979, HSCA Numbered Files, Box 289, 015055 Folder, JFK-NA.

47 Select Committee on Assassinations of the U.S. House of Representatives, Report of the Select Committee on Assassinations of the U.S. House of Representatives (Ipswich, MA: Mary Ferrell Foundation Press, 2007), 43–4.

48 Marina Oswald, testimony, Sept. 20, 1977, 33, HSCA Numbered Files, Box 260, 014562 Folder, JFK-NA.

49 Select Committee on Assassinations of the U.S. House of Representatives, 56.

50 Alfredo Mirabal Diaz, Aug. 26, 1978, 10–16, HSCA Numbered Files, Box 258, 014446 Folder, JFK-NA.

51 Select Committee on Assassinations of the U.S. House of Representatives, 194.

52 Harry Haler, testimony, March 16, 1978, 60, HSCA Numbered Files, Box 273, 014671 Folder, JFK-NA.

53 Senate Select Committee to Study Governmental Operations with Respect to Intelligence Activities, 4.

54 Select Committee on Assassinations of the U.S. House of Representatives, 238.

55 Rex Bradford, "Introduction," *Report of the Select Committee on Assassinations of the U.S. House of Representatives*, viii–ix.

56 *Report of the Select Committee on Assassinations of the U.S. House of Representatives*, 61.

57 Posner, 235.

58 Committee on Ballistic Acoustics, National Research Council, "Reexamination of Acoustic Evidence in Kennedy Assassination," *Science* 218 (Oct. 1982): 133.

59 Zelizer, 119.

60 James Reston Jr., "Was Connally the Real Target?" *Time*, Nov. 28, 1988, 30–41.

61 Stephen E. Ambrose, "Writers on the Grassy Knoll: A Reader's Guide," *New York Times*, Feb. 2, 1992, http://www.nytimes.com/books/98/11/22/specials/ambrose-knoll.html; accessed April 3, 2011.

62 Bugliosi, *Reclaiming History*, 925–8.

63 Posner, 348–9.

64 Ibid., 481–504.

65 Ibid., 372.

66 *ABC News Presents the Kennedy Assassination: Beyond Conspiracy*, ed. Peter Jennings, DVD (Port Washington, NY: Koch Vision, 2004).

67 Saad, "Americans: Kennedy Assassination a Conspiracy."

68 Blanton.

69 David Lubin, *Shooting Kennedy: JFK and the Culture of Images* (Berkeley: University of California Press), 173–4.

70 Ibid., 18–21.

71 Ibid., 29–30.

72 Jeffrey Johnson, Patricia Cohen, Elizabeth M. Smailes, Stephanie Kasen, and Judith S. Brook, "Television Viewing and Aggressive Behavior During Adolescence and Adulthood," *Science* 295 (March 29, 2002), 2468.

73 James W. Hilty, Interview by author, July 19, 2001.

74 Lubin, 233.

75 Posner, 468.

76 Scott Wyland, "Pop Culture at a Hefty Price," *Las Vegas Review-Journal*, May 17, 2008, http://www.lvrj.com/news/16741621.html; accessed May 5, 2011.

77 Paul Harris, "Guns Take Pride of Place in U.S. Family Values," (London) *Observer*, Oct. 14, 2007, http://www.guardian.co.uk/world/2007/oct/14/usa.usgunviolence; accessed May 4, 2011.

78 Hilty, Interview by author.

79 Appleton, "Assassinations," 495.

80 Marcus Raskin, "JFK and the Culture of Violence," *American Historical Review* 97 (April 1992): 494–9.

81 Hilty, Interview by author.

82 Michael L. Kurtz, "Oliver Stone, JFK, and History," in *Oliver Stone's USA: Film, History, and Controversy*, ed. Robert Brent Toplin (Lawrence: University of Kansas Press, 2000), 169.

83 Bugliosi, *Reclaiming History*, 895.

84 Oliver Stone, "On Nixon and JFK," in *Oliver Stone's USA*, 285.

85 Robert A. Rosenstone, "JFK: Historical Fact/Historical Film," *American Historical Review* 97 (April 1992): 511.

86 Raskin, 490.

87 Oliver Stone, "Stone on Stone's Image," in *Oliver Stone's USA*, 58.
88 Saad, "Americans: Kennedy Assassination a Conspiracy."
89 Stone, "Stone on Stone's Image," 61.
90 Lisa D. Butler, Cheryl Koopman, and Philip G. Zimbardo. "The Psychological Impact of Viewing the Film JFK: Emotions, Beliefs, and Political Behavioral Intentions, *Political Psychology* 16 (June 1995): 245–6.
91 Amos Vogel, "JFK: The Question of Propaganda," *Antioch Review* 50 (Summer 1992): 585.
92 Butler et al., 244.
93 Bugliosi, *Reclaiming History*, 1357.
94 Richard Blow, *American Son: A Portrait of John F. Kennedy Jr.* (New York: Henry Holt and Co., 2002), 66–7.
95 Mike Feinsilber, "Gerald Ford Forced to Admit the Warren Report Fictionalized," Associated Press, July 2, 1997.
96 Simon, 101–2.
97 Ibid., 99.
98 Ibid., 137.
99 William Manchester, "No Evidence for a Conspiracy to Kill Kennedy," *New York Times*, Feb. 5, 1992, www.nytimes.com/1992/02/05/opinion/-no-evidence-for-a-conspiracy-to-kill-kennedy-809692.html; accessed April 27, 2011.
100 *ABC News Presents the Kennedy Assassination: Beyond Conspiracy.*
101 Hilty, Interview by author.
102 Posner, 361.
103 *ABC News Presents the Kennedy Assassination: Beyond Conspiracy.*
104 Lubin, 227.
105 Dallek, 511.

Documents

1 John F. Kennedy, Inaugural Address, Jan. 20, 1961, in *Public Papers of the Presidents of the United States 1961: John F. Kennedy* (Washington: United States Government Printing Office, 1962), 1–3.
2 John F. Kennedy, News Conference, May 9, 1962, *Public Papers of the Presidents: John F. Kennedy 1962* (United States Government Printing Office, 1963), 380.
3 Clinton J. Hill, Testimony, *Warren Commission Report*, vol. 2, Hearings before the President's Commission on the Assassination of President Kennedy, 132–44.
4 John F. Kennedy, "Remarks Prepared for Delivery at the Trade Mart in Dallas," Nov. 22, 1963, in *Public Papers of the Presidents of the United States 1963: John F. Kennedy* (Washington: United States Government Printing Office, 1964), 895.
5 "Vice President Lyndon B. Johnson Daily Diary (worksheet)," Lyndon B. Johnson Library Website, http://www.lbjlibrary.org/collections/daily-diary.html; accessed Feb. 27, 2011.
6 Lyndon B. Johnson, "National Day of Mourning Proclaimed by President Johnson," Nov. 23, 1963, in *Public Papers of the Presidents of the United States 1963: John F. Kennedy,* 899.
7 Mike Mansfield, Eulogy, Nov. 24, 1963, in *Four Days in November*, 396–7.
8 Earl Warren, Eulogy, Nov. 24, 1963, in *Four Days in November*, 397–8.

9   Telephone conversation between Lyndon B. Johnson and Paul Miller, March 9,
    1964, 4:02 p.m., in *Taking Charge: The Johnson White House Tapes, 1963–64*, ed.
    Michael R. Beschloss (New York: Simon & Schuster, 1997), 274.
10 John P Roche, Eyes Only Memorandum for the President, Dec. 23, 1966, Special
    File on the Assassination of President John F. Kennedy, Box 1, Manchester File
    Folder, LBJL.
11 Senate Select Committee to Study Governmental Operations with Respect to
    Intelligence Activities, *The Investigation of the Assassination of President John F.
    Kennedy: Performance of the Intelligence Agencies, Book V* (Washington: Government
    Printing Office, 1976), 6-7.
12 Clyde C. Snow and Ellis R. Kerley, "Authentication of John F. Kennedy Autopsy
    Radiographs and Photographs," March 9, 1979, 12, HSCA Numbered Files, Box
    289, 015055 Folder, JFK-NA.
13 Theron Ward, John F. Kennedy Inquest, HSCA Numbered Files, Box 16, 000640,
    Folder, JFK-NA.

Selected Bibliography

Archives

John F. Kennedy Library, Boston, MA
Lyndon B. Johnson Library, Austin, TX
National Archives II, College Park, MD
Harvard University Archives, Cambridge, MA
The Paley Center for Media, New York

Books and Videos

ABC News. *The Assassination of President Kennedy*. DVD. New York: ABC News Productions, 2007.

Baker, Leonard. *The Johnson Eclipse*. New York: Macmillan, 1966.

Barkun, Michael. *A Culture of Conspiracy: Apocalyptic Visions in Contemporary America*. Berkeley: University of California Press, 2003.

Beschloss, Michael R. *Taking Charge: The Johnson White House Tapes, 1963–64*. New York: Simon & Schuster, 1997.

Blaine, Gerald with Lisa McCubbin, *The Kennedy Detail*. New York: Gallery Books, 2010.

Blight, James G., janet M. Lang, and David A. Welch. *Vietnam if Kennedy Had Lived: Virtual JFK*. New York: Rowman & Littlefield Publishers, Inc., 2009.

Bloom, Alexander and Wini Breines, eds. *"Takin' it to the Streets."* New York: Oxford University Press, 2003.

Blow, Richard. *American Son: A Portrait of John F. Kennedy Jr*. New York: Henry Holt and Co., 2002.

Brinkley, Alan. *Liberalism and its Discontents*. Cambridge: Harvard University Press, 1998.

Broder, David S. *Changing of the Guard*. New York: Simon and Schuster, 1980.

Brokaw, Tom. *Boom! Talking about the Sixties*. New York: Random House, 2008.

Brown, Thomas. *JFK: History of an Image*. Ann Arbor: UMI Books on Demand, 2002.

Bugliosi, Vincent. *Four Days in November: The Assassination of President John F. Kennedy.* New York: W.W. Norton & Co., 2007.

Bugliosi, Vincent. *Reclaiming History: The Assassination of President John F. Kennedy.* New York: W.W. Norton & Co., 2007.

Burner, David and Thomas R. West. *The Torch is Passed: The Kennedy Brothers and American Liberalism.* New York: Brandywine Press, 1984.

Califano, Joseph A. Jr. *The Triumph and Tragedy of Lyndon Johnson.* New York: Simon & Schuster, 1991.

Chafe, William H. *The Unfinished Journey.* New York: Oxford University Press, 2010.

Clark, Thurston. *Ask Not: The Inauguration of John F. Kennedy and the Speech that Changed America.* New York: Penguin Books, 2011.

Cronkite, Walter and Don Carleton. *Conversations with Cronkite.* Austin, TX: Dolph Briscoe Center for American History, 2010.

Dallek, Robert. *Flawed Giant: Lyndon Johnson and his Times, 1961–1973.* New York: Oxford University Press, 1998.

Dallek, Robert. *An Unfinished Life: John F. Kennedy, 1917–1963.* New York: Little, Brown and Co., 2003.

Davis, David Brion, ed. *The Fear of Conspiracy: Images of Un-American Subversion from the Revolution to the Present.* Ithaca: Cornell University Press, 1971.

Dear Abby. *Where Were You when President Kennedy was Shot?* Kansas City: Andrews and McMeel, 1993.

DeLillo, Don. *Libra.* New York: Penguin Books, 1991.

Durkheim, Emile. *The Elementary Forms of the Religious Life.* New York: Free Press, 1965.

Evans, Rowland and Robert Novak. *Lyndon B. Johnson: The Exercise of Power.* New York: New American Library, 1966.

Foreign Relations of the United States, 1964–68, vol. 5. Washington: U.S. Government Printing Office, 2002.

Frank, David M. *Missing Evidence: The JFK Assassination, DVD.* New York: History Channel, 1998.

Frisch, Michael. *A Shared Authority: Essays on the Craft and Meaning of Oral and Public History.* Albany: State University of New York Press, 1990.

Fursenko, Aleksandr and Timothy Naftali. *"One Hell of a Gamble": Khrushchev, Castro, and Kennedy 1958–1964.* New York: W.W. Norton & Co., 1997.

Giglio, James N. *The Presidency of John F. Kennedy.* Lawrence: University Press of Kansas, 1991.

Gillon, Steven M. *The Kennedy Assassination—24 Hours after.* New York: Basic Books, 2009.

Goodwin, Richard. *Remembering America.* Boston: Little, Brown and Co., 1988.

Greenberg, Bradley S. and Edwin B. Parker, eds. *The Kennedy Assassination and the American Public: Social Communication in Crisis.* Stanford: Stanford University Press, 1965.

Greenstein, Fred I. *Children and Politics.* New Haven: Yale University Press, 1965.

Guthman, Edwin O. and Jeffrey Shulman, eds. *Robert F. Kennedy in his Own Words*. New York: Bantam Books, 1988.

Hakim, Joy. *A History of US: Age of Extremes, 1880–1917*, 3rd ed. New York: Oxford University Press, 2005.

Hakim, Joy. *A History of US: Terrible War, 1855–1865*, 3rd ed. New York: Oxford University Press, 2005.

Hakim, Joy. *A History of US: All the People, since 1945*, 4th ed. New York: Oxford University Press, 2010.

Hamilton, Nigel. *JFK: Reckless Youth*. New York: Random House, 1991.

Hellman, John. *The Kennedy Obsession: The American Myth of JFK*. New York: Columbia University Press, 1997.

Henggeler, Paul. *In His Steps: Lyndon Johnson and the Kennedy Mystique*. Chicago: Ivan R. Dee, 1991.

Hess, Robert D. and Judith V. Torney. *The Development of Political Attitudes in Children*. Garden City, NY: Anchor Books, 1967.

Hilty, James W. *Robert Kennedy Brother Protector*. Philadelphia: Temple University Press, 1997.

Holland, Max. *The Kennedy Assassination Tapes*. New York: Alfred A. Knopf, 2004.

House Select Committee on Assassinations. *Report of the Select Committee on Assassinations of the U.S. House of Representatives*. Ipswich, MA: Mary Ferrell Foundation Press, 2007.

Isserman, Maurice and Michael Kazin. *America Divided*. New York: Oxford University Press, 2000.

Jennings, Peter, ed. *ABC News Presents the Kennedy Assassination: Beyond Conspiracy*. DVD. Port Washington, NY: Koch Vision, 2004.

Jennings, Tom, exec. prod. and dir. *The Lost JFK Tapes: The Assassination*. DVD. Washington: National Geographic Channel, 2009.

Johnson, Lyndon Baines. *The Vantage Point: Perspectives of the Presidency 1963–1969*. New York: Holt, Rinehart and Winston, 1971.

Kearns Goodwin, Doris. *Lyndon Johnson and the American Dream*. New York: St. Martin's Griffin, 1976.

Kennedy, Jacqueline. *Jacqueline Kennedy: Historic Conversations on Life with John F. Kennedy*. New York: Hyperion, 2011.

Lévi-Strauss, Claude. *The Savage Mind*. Chicago: University of Chicago Press, 1966.

Lubin, David. *Shooting Kennedy: JFK and the Culture of Images*. Berkeley: University of California Press, 2003.

Mailer, Norman. *Oswald's Tale*. New York: Random House, 2007.

Manchester, William. *The Death of a President*. New York: Galahad Books, 1996.

Martin, Ralph G. *JFK: A Hero for Our Time*. New York: MacMillan, 1983.

Masutani, Koji, exec. prod. and dir. *Virtual JFK: Vietnam if Kennedy Had Lived*. DVD. New York: Docurama Films, 2009.

McNamara, Robert S. *In Retrospect: The Tragedy and Lessons of Vietnam*. New York: Vintage Books, 1995.

McPherson, Harry. *A Political Education*. Austin: University of Texas Press, 1995.

Miller, Merle. *Lyndon: An Oral Biography*. New York: G.P. Putnam's Sons, 1980.

Mulvaney, Jay and Paul De Angelis. *Dear Mrs. Kennedy*. New York: St. Martin's Press, 2010.

NBC News. *John F. Kennedy: The Week We Lost,* vol. 3. VHS. Norwalk, CT: Easton Press Video, 1988.

Neal, Arthur G. *National Trauma and Collective Memory: Major Events in the American Experience*. Armonk, NY: M.E. Sharpe, 1996.

Neal, Arthur G. *National Trauma and Collective Memory*, 2nd ed. Armonk, NY: M.E. Sharpe, 2005.

Neisser, Ulrich, ed. *Memory Observed: Remember in Natural Contexts*. San Francisco: W.H. Freeman and Co., 1982.

Newseum with Cathy Trost and Susan Bennett. *President Kennedy Has Been Shot*. Naperville, IL: Sourcebooks Mediafusion, 2003.

Nye, Joseph S., Philip D. Zelikow, and David C. King. *Why People Don't Trust Government*. Cambridge: Harvard University Press, 1997.

Olick, Jeffrey K., Vered Vinitzky-Seroussi, and Daniel Levy, eds. *The Collective Memory Reader*. New York: Oxford University Press, 2011.

Parmet, Herbert S. *The Presidency of John F. Kennedy*. New York: Dial Press, 1983.

Pellini, Chuck, dir. *Image of an Assassination: A New Look at the Zapruder Film*. DVD. Orland Park, IL: MPI Media Group, 1998.

Pennebacker, James W., Dario Paez, and Bernard Rim, eds. *Collective Memory of Political Events*. Hove, East Sussex: Psychology Press, 2008.

Posner, Gerald. *Case Closed: Lee Harvey Oswald and the Assassination of JFK*. New York: Anchor Books, 1993.

Public Papers of the Presidents of the United States 1961. Washington: United States Government Printing Office, 1962.

Public Papers of the Presidents of the United States 1962. Washington: United States Government Printing Office, 1963.

Public Papers of the Presidents of the United States 1963. Washington: United States Government Printing Office, 1964.

Reedy, George. *Lyndon Johnson: A Memoir*. New York: Andrews and McMeel Inc., 1971.

Reeves, Richard. *President Kennedy: Profile of Power*. New York: Simon and Schuster, 1993.

Sayers, Sohnya et al., eds. *The '60s Without Apology*. Minneapolis: University of Minnesota Press, 1985.

Schlesinger, Arthur M. Jr. *A Thousand Days*. Boston: Houghton Mifflin Co., 1965.

Schlesinger, Arthur M. Jr. *Robert Kennedy and his Times*. Boston: Houghton Mifflin Co., 1978.

Semple, Robert B. and Tom Wicker, eds. *Four Days in November: The Original Coverage of the John F. Kennedy Assassination by the Staff of the New York Times*. New York: St. Martin's Press, 2003.

Senate Select Committee to Study Governmental Operations with Respect to Intelligence Activities, *The Investigation of the Assassination of President John F. Kennedy: Performance of the Intelligence Agencies, Book V*. Washington: Government Printing Office, 1976.

Shesol, Jeff. *Mutual Contempt: Lyndon Johnson, Robert Kennedy, and the Feud that Defined a Decade.* New York: W.W. Norton & Co., 1997.

Simon, Art. *Dangerous Knowledge: The JFK Assassination in Art and Film.* Philadelphia: Temple University Press, 1996.

Slotkin, Richard. *Gunfighter Nation.* Norman, OK: University of Oklahoma Press, 1998.

Sorensen, Ted. *Counselor: A Life at the Edge of History.* New York: HarperCollins Publishers, 2008.

Sorensen, Theodore C. *Kennedy.* New York: Harper & Row, 1965.

Steel, Ronald. *In Love with the Night.* New York: Touchstone, 2000.

Stewart, Charles J. and Bruce Kendall, eds. *A Man Called John F. Kennedy: Sermons on his Assassination.* Glen Rock, NJ: Paulist Press, 1964.

Strober, Gerald S. and Deborah H. Strober, eds. *"Let Us Begin Anew:" An Oral History of the Kennedy Presidency.* New York: HarperCollins, 1993.

Thucydides. *The History of the Peloponnesian War,* Book II. Trans. Benjamin Jowett, 2nd ed. Oxford: Clarendon Press, 1900.

Walsh, William B., ed. *Children Write about John F. Kennedy.* Brownsville, TX: Springman-King Publishing Co., 1964.

Warren Commission. *The Warren Commission Report.* New York: St. Martin's Press, 1964.

White, Theodore H. *The Making of the President 1960.* New York: Signet, 1961.

White, Theodore H. *The Making of the President 1964.* New York: Signet, 1966.

Wicker, Tom. *JFK and LBJ: The Influence of Personality upon Politics.* Chicago: Ivan R. Dee Publishers, 1968.

Wolfenstein, Martha and Gilbert Kliman Greenstein, eds. *Children and the Death of a President.* Garden City, NY: Doubleday & Co., 1965.

Woods, Randall B. *LBJ: Architect of American Ambition.* New York: Free Press, 2006.

Zelizer, Barbie. *Covering the Body: The Kennedy Assassination, the Media, and the Shaping of Collective Memory.* Chicago: University of Chicago Press, 1992.

Index

Air Force One xi, 33, 35, 51; after
    assassination 2, 43–6, 109–10, 113,
    116
Alsop, Joseph 77–8, 114
Alsop, Stewart 116–17, 129
American Broadcasting Company (ABC)
    151, 167; live assassination coverage
    20, 23, 25, 27, 65, 68
American memory and JFK 2–8, 12,
    14–17, 20, 22, 46, 91; children 98;
    effects on Johnson 104–5, 127–35;
    efforts to protect reputation 13, 34,
    101, 141; flashbulb memories 18–19;
    Robert and Edward Kennedy as heirs
    apparent 125, 128; popular culture
    157–9, 161–6
Arlington National Cemetery xii, 3, 47,
    51, 74
Associated Press 76, 92, 120, 130, 140,
    193
Auchincloss, Janet 48

Ball, George 109, 123
Boggs, Hale 91, 139, 185
Bradlee, Ben 48, 113
Brinkley, David 4, 25, 27, 123
Broder, David S. 41–2
Brokaw, Tom 5
Bugliosi, Vincent 156–7
Bundy, McGeorge xii, 41, 77, 109, 114,
    122, 185
Burkley, George 40, 44

Carpenter, Liz 117
Castro, Fidel 146, 153, 155, 165, 197;
    U.S. plots to topple xiii, 13, 144,
    150–1, 161
Central Intelligence Agency (CIA) 21, 66,
    139, 149–50, 152, 164–5; assassination
    investigation 16, 141, 145–8, 151,
    153–5, 167, 196–7; plots against Castro
    xiii, 13, 15, 155
Children and JFK assassination 16, 69,
    73–4, 80, 96–100
Church Committee xiii, 150–1, 187–8
Civil rights movement 15–17. 85, 152;
    Johnson's role xii, 29–30, 113, 115,
    117, 170; Kennedy's role 6, 9–10,
    21–2, 29–30, 36, 78, 113, 134–5,
    163
Clark, William Kemp 40, 44, 58
Clifford, Clark 117, 133, 171
Clinton, Bill 6, 14
Columbia Broadcasting System (CBS) 20,
    22, 59, 82, 87, 123, 151; Johnson
    interviews 32, 146; live assassination
    coverage 23, 26, 65, 68
Congress 28–9, 31, 111, 128, 145, 179,
    185, 195; assassination investigations
    13; Johnson's legislative record xii, 107,
    113, 115, 118, 122, 130, 134;
    Kennedy's legislative record 1, 6, 78,
    134; (See Church Committee and
    House Select Committee on
    Assassinations)

Connally, John xi, 37–40, 42, 63, 140, 154, 183; Yarborough feud 33; single-bullet theory 48, 142–3, 162

Connally, Nellie 37–8

Crain, Keith 69–70

Cronkite, Walter 1, 7, 23, 27, 68, 123; Johnson interviews 32, 131, 146; Vietnam stand 125

Cuba: Bay of Pigs 9, 21; Cuban Missile Crisis 6, 21–2, 29, 36, 47, 133; Oswald ties 55, 58; possible role in JFK assassination 144–6, 149–50, 152–3, 155, 165, 197

Curry, Jesse 36–8, 43, 62–4, 140

Dallas Morning News 33–4, 87–8, 169

Dallas assassination reaction 24, 65, 69, 81, 85–9, 92

Dallas Times Herald 52, 62, 88, 140

DeLillo, Don 165

Dominican Republic xii, 118, 132, 151

Eisenhower Dwight D. 13, 51, 97, 185, 193, 203n44; Bay of Pigs 21; meeting with Johnson 111–12

Exner, Judith Campbell 13, 151

Federal Bureau of Investigation 39, 145, 151–2, 164; assassination investigation 16, 48, 62, 64, 111, 139, 141, 149, 153, 156, 196–7; ties to Oswald 55, 57; ties to Ruby 66

Ferrie, David 149

Ford, Gerald: presidency xiii, 72, 151; Warren Commission 139, 145, 165, 182

Frazier, Buell Wesley 55, 64

Freeman, Orville 106

Fritz, John William 56–9, 62, 64

Garfield, James 1, 15–17, 70–1, 99

Garrison, Jim 136, 148–50, 155, 163

Goldberg, Arthur 110, 186

Goldwater, Barry xii, 79, 117, 170

Goodwin, Doris Kearns 32, 113, 125

Greenberg, Bradley S. 70

Guthman, Ed 132

Hamill, Pete 6, 131

Hill, Clint 38–9, 49, 51, 180–3

Hilty, James W. 82, 134, 160–1, 167

Hoover, J. Edgar 39, 111, 151, 153–4, 156, 196

House Select Committee on Assassinations xiii, 152–3, 156, 199

Huber, Oscar xiii, 40–2

Hughes, Sarah xi, 44, 46, 51

Humes, Dr. James J. 48

Humphrey, Hubert xiii, 32, 47, 114, 116, 185; as 1968 presidential candidate 126–8; as vice president 123

Huntley, Chet 24–5, 27, 47, 89, 123

Ireland 6, 36, 96

Jackson, Andrew 71

Johnson, Lady Bird xi, 36–7, 40, 43, 50, **107**, 109, 120

Johnson, Luci Baines 110

Johnson, Lyndon B.: 1964 presidential campaign 116–17; 1968 presidential campaign 125; aboard Air Force One 43–6, **45**; ; assassination allegations 150, 163; assumption of presidency xi–xii, 5, 17, 20, 43–7, 67, **107**, 108–14, 185–6; conspiracy beliefs 2, 66, 146; civil rights and African Americans 29–30; 115–16, 118–19, 125; compared to JFK 6, 8, 13, 105–8, 119, 127–35, 170–1, 203n44; *The Death of the President* 120–1, 194–5; Dominican Republic 118; Freedom of Information Act xii, 118, 147; JFK's assassination 34–9, 41–3; JFK funeral events 50–1, 70, 187–8; JFK's legacy 103–5, 113–15, 123, 127 legislative record 115–16, 117–18; presidency xii–xiii, 82, 114; press 129–30, 193; rivalry with Robert Kennedy 28, 32, 34, 105, 110–11, 113–14, 116–17, 124, 126, 128–29, 179; vice presidency 27–33, 119, 121–2, 175, 179, 199; Vietnam, 119, 121–5, 137; view of presidency 30–1; Warren Commission 139, 141–2, 146

Kellerman, Roy, 38–9, 182
Kennedy, Caroline 11, 22, 41, 48–51, 67, 76, 88
Kennedy, Edward "Ted" or "Teddy" xii, 39, 49–51, 124, 126, 128–9, 195
Kennedy family xi, 3, 10–11, 24, 44, 49–50, 153; *Death of a President* 120, 194–5; relationship with Johnson 117; Warren Commission 141, 145
Kennedy, Jacqueline "Jackie": aboard Air Force One 44–47, **45**, 109; at Bethesda 47–8, 150; Camelot 101, 131; *Death of a President,* 120–1, 194–5; image 2, 25, 35, 47–8, 79, 137, 165–6; JFK's assassination 38–42, 166, 168, 170, 181–3; JFK's funeral events xii, 49–52, 189–90; marriage 11, 33–4; morning in Dallas 34, 36–7; planned Oswald trial 63, 66; relationship with Johnson 31–2, 44–**5**, 47, 109–11, 113, 117, 129, relationship with Robert Kennedy 47, 50, 52, 109; sympathy letters 3, 99, 102
Kennedy, John F.: 1960 presidential election 10–11, 97; American children's mourning 97–100; assassination xii, 1, 39–43, 180–3; autopsy 47–8; compared to Johnson 6, 8, 13, 105–8, 119, 127–35, 170–1, 203n44; conspiracy theories xiii, 146–50, 154–6, 167–8; catalyst for hatred 10, 33, 80, 87–9; extramarital affairs 7, 13, 150–1; funeral events xxi–xii, 49–52, **73**, 187–92; image and American memory 2, 5–8, 10, 12, 14–20; inaugural address **9**, 12, 175–8; inquest 200; legacy assumed by Johnson 104–5, 108–9, 112, 115–6; life 11–12; malleability after death 132–5; morning in Dallas 33–8; popular culture 158–60, 165–6; popularity in life 9–10; presidency 21–2, 117, 171; press 20–22, 130; public opinion on assassination 157–8; reactions, trauma caused by death 4–5, 7, 14, 16–20, 68–70, 72–6, 80, 100, 102–3, 160; relationship with Johnson 27–33, 179;

shame over assassination 80–6, 89–91; speech planned for day of assassination 184; televised assassination coverage xi, 3, 12, 20, 23–7, 41, 55, 59, 68–70, 72–3, 92, 94, 99, 140–1; television president 22–3; Vietnam 109, 119, 121, 123, 133; worldwide mourning 94–6
Kennedy, John F. Jr. 11, 22, 25, 76, 137, 164; father's death, 19, 48–9, 51, 67, 91
Kennedy, Robert F.: 1968 presidential campaign 125–6; 1968 assassination xii, 4, 84, 89,91, 126–7; attorney general 10, 12, 30, 151; Castro 146, 150; conspiracy theories 155; day of JFK's assassination 39, 41, 43, 47–9, 109, 183; *The Death of a President* 120–1, 194; JFK's funeral events 50–2; as JFK's heir apparent 105, 199, 128–29; rivalry with Johnson 28, 32, 34, 110–11, 113–14, 116–17, 124, 129, 179; senator xiii, 119, 132; Vietnam 124, 132; Warren Commission 146, 153
KGB 145, 147–156
Khrushchev, Nikita S. 21, 94, 146
Kilduff, Malcolm xi, 37, 42–3, 185–6
King, Martin Luther Jr. 22, 51, 78, 126; 1968 assassination xiii, 4, 19, 89, 91, 152
Klein's Sporting Goods 55, 62–3
Krim, Arthur 130, 146

Ladies Home Journal 5
Lane, Mark xi, 146, 154–55
Life 52, 49, 79, 101, 141, 147; Zapruder film 62, 151, 158, 166
Lincoln, Abraham: assassination 15–17, 19, 25, 49, 70–1, 75, 128; presidency 6, 12, 78
Lincoln, Evelyn 111
Look 120
Luce, Henry 79

Mafia (See organized crime)
Mansfield, Mike 47, 50, 185, 189–90
Marshall, Thurgood 118
McCarthy, Eugene xiii, 125–6

McCarthy, Joseph 149
McCormack, John 41, 50, 181
McHugh, Godfrey 44–6, 49
McKinley, William 1–2, 15–17, 70–1
McNamara, Robert S. xi, 41, 48, 77, 109, 111, 114; Vietnam 122, 132, 171
McPherson, Harry 70, 123, 125, 130, 133
Mob (See Organized crime)
Moyers, Bill 110, 121, 185
Myth of Camelot 7–8, 108, 131, 133, 165, 168, 170–1; origins 101

National Lampoon 166
National Opinion Research Center 75, 77, 80, 92
National Review 78–9
Neal, Arthur G. 4, 76
Newsweek 10, 13–14, 26, 48, 100, 109, 113
New York Times 23, 122, 145, 154, 167; assassination coverage 43, 74–5, 80, 82, 87, 90, 93–4, 140
Nixon, Richard 32, 34, 75, 175; 1960 presidential debates 11, 22; 1960 presidential election 10, 97; 1968 presidential campaign 126–7; presidency xiii, 22, 81–2, 137
Nosenko, Yuri 147–8

Obama, Barack 9, 76, 138
O'Brien, Lawrence 31, 123, 129, 132
O'Donnell, Kenneth 33, 37–8, 42, 44, 46, 117, 132
Operation Mongoose 146
Organized crime 160; Castro assassination attempt 150; Exner 13, 151; JFK assassination 153, 155–6, 165–6; Jack Ruby 60, 145, 169
Oswald, Lee Harvey: arrest and investigation, xi, 52, 55, 56–7, 59, 61–5, 197; life before assassination, 53–5, **148**, 149, 153; Garrison conspiracy theory 148–50; guilt 2, 3, 15–16, 58, 86–7, 91, 99, 137, 139, 142–4,146–7, 151–7, 167–70; murdered by Jack Ruby xii, 3, 12, 24, 26–7, 61–5, 66–7, 88, 90, 140–2, 144–5, 169; popular culture 159–66;

ties to Soviet Union, Cuba 2, 54, 58, 144, 147, 149;
Oswald, Marguerite 53, 58–9, 63
Oswald, Marina 54–5, 57, 59, 63, 152, 208n58
Oswald, Robert 53, 55, 66

Paine, Ruth 55, 57, 63
Peace Corps 22, 29, 96, 102
Peace movement 85, 91, 103, 122–3, 126–7, 134
Perry, Malcolm O. 40, 58
Pettit, Tom 65
Pew Research Center 80
Pierpoint, Robert 26, 87
Polls and studies: children 97–8; spread of assassination news 24, 69; JFK's place in history 6, 10–11, 13–14; during JFK's presidency 6, 33, 76; memories of JFK's assassination 17, 19; memory and history 17–18; reactions to JFK's assassination 75–78, 80, 92, 99, 102; JFK 164; trust in government, 80; truth about assassination xiii, 2, 16–7, 76, 141, 157–8, 163
Posner, Gerald xiii, 143, 154, 156–7
Powers, Dave 37–9

Race riots 4, 85, 118–19, 134, 152, 170; Martin Luther King Jr.'s assassination xiii, 126
Reagan, Ronald 6, 10, 12, 17, 72, 126, 166
Rivera, Geraldo 151
Robb, Lynda Bird Johnson 31–2
Roche, John P., 121, 185–87
Rockefeller Commission xiii, 151
Roosevelt, Franklin D. 6, 9, 60, 71, 76, 78, 138; death 5, 30, 33, 69; and Johnson 30, 115
Roosevelt, Theodore 71
Ruby, Jack: conspiracy theories 141–2, 144–5, 152–3, 155–6, 169–70; FBI connection 66; life before killing Oswald 60–61; Oswald murder xii, 3–4, 15, 55, 61–3, 65–6, 90, 140; popular culture 160, 165; ties to Dallas's violent culture 87–8

Rusk, Dean 31, 41, 105, 110–12, 114; Vietnam 122, 133
Russo, Perry 149

Salinger, Pierre 26
Saturday Evening Post 78
Schlesinger, Arthur M. Jr. 83, 101, 112, 114, 120, 146, 194
Secret Service: in conspiracy theories 152–3, 155; on day of assassination 36–9, 41–6, 109–10; during post-assassination weekend 49, 51–2; assassination probe 52, 57–8, 62–3, 66, 139, 149; performance under investigation 141, 145, 180–3; in press reports 140
September 11, 2001 2, 19, 84, 138
Shaw, Clay 148–50, 163
Shaw, Maude 48, 52
Shriver, Eunice Kennedy 49
Shriver, Sargent 115, 185
Sidey, Hugh 26, 32
Smith, Howard K. 25, 27
Smith, Merriman 39
Sorensen, Theodore 31, 79, 106, 114, 133, 185; memoir 101; *Profiles in Courage* 11
Sorrels, Forrest 57–8
Specter, Arlen 180–3
Stevenson, Adlai 11, 33, 73
Stone, Oliver xiii, 2, 20, 133, 136–7, 154–5, 161–5
Stoughton, Cecil 40, 46
Studies following assassination;
Swindal, James 44–6

Taylor, Maxwell 94
Television 2, 4, 7, 13, 19, 35, 52, 57, 66, 95, 128, 131, 136, 151, 163, 165, 193; changes during JFK era 7, 11, 20, 22–3, 76, 85, 93–4, 97, 105; creating national community 15, 23, 72, 74, 93; culture of violence 81, 89–90, 97, 159–60; live assassination coverage xi, 3, 12, 20, 23–7, 41, 55, 59, 68–70, 72–3, 92, 94, 99, 140–1; Oswald slaying 64–5, 140; Vietnam 122, 125

Texas School Book Depository 42–3, 55, 140–2, 157, 162, 180; police investigation 52, 56–7, 59, 64
Tippit, J.D. xi, 56, 59, 61, 63, 66; in conspiracy theories 142–4, 155
Tippit, Marie 208n58
Truly, Roy 52, 56
Truman, Harry S. 51, 71, 111, 118, 175, 185; relationship with FDR 30, 33

Vanocur, Sander 25
Vietnam war 17, 127, 129, 152; in conspiracy theories 155, 163; Johnson policy xii, 29, 32, 109, 112, 119, 121–6, 133–4, 137, 170; Kennedy policy 8, 21, 132–3, 135, 171; mistrust toward government 7, 13, 85, 136
Violence in America 4, 80–7, 90, 98, 170–1, 192; 1968 124, 127; in Dallas, 25, 46, 61, 64–5, 75, 87–9, 108, 120; police 22, 127; popular culture 136, 139, 151, 159–61, 166; television 81, 89–90, 159–60

Wade, Henry 44, 58, 61–3, 140
Walker, Edwin 55, 144
Warhol, Andy 26, 165–6
Warren Commission: findings 2, 136, 140, 145, 156, 164; shortcomings, criticism 16, 121, 139, 146–7, 150–3, 168, 195–197; testimony 61, 143, 154, 180–3;
Warren, Earl 47, 50, 89, 91, 139, 144–5, 191–2
Watergate xiii, 4, 7, 13, 136, 150–2
West Berlin 6, 21, 29, 36, 95, 133
White, Theodore H. x, 3, 101
Wicker, Tom 5, 43, 127, 137
World War II 11, 17, 20, 29, 60, 69, 85; JFK's service 147, 75

Youngblood, Rufus 38

Zapruder, Abraham 18, 38, 57, 142, 147, 157; *Life* 62, 151, 158–9, 166

You may be interested in these other titles in the Critical Moments in American History series:

The Battle of the Greasy Grass/Little Bighorn: Custer's Last Stand in Memory, History, and Popular Culture
By Debra Buchholtz
ISBN 13: 978-0-415-89559-0 (pbk)
ISBN 13: 978-0-203-11678-1 (ebk)

Freedom to Serve: Truman, Civil Rights, and Executive Order 9981
By Jon E. Taylor
ISBN 13: 978-0-415-89448-7 (pbk)
ISBN 13: 978-0-203-08152-5 (ebk)

The Battles of Kings Mountain and Cowpens: The American Revolution in the Southern Backcountry
By Melissa Walker
ISBN 13: 978-0-415-89561-3 (pbk)
ISBN 13: 978-0-203-08186-0 (ebk)